essential

BIBLE

essential

BIBLE

Everything You Need to Understand
the Old and New Testaments

Rev. John Trigilio Jr., Ph.D., Th.D., and
Rev. Kenneth Brighenti, Ph.D.

Adams Media
Avon, Massachusetts

Contents

Acknowledgments

Special thanks to our dear families, Elizabeth Trigilio (mother), Mark Trigilio (brother), Norma and Percy Brighenti (mother and father), and Priscilla Brighenti Colin (sister) whose love and faith made us cherish the written Word of God all the more. We are also grateful for the academic and spiritual assistance of our colleagues and friends at EWTN (Eternal Word Television Network); Mother Angelica and the Poor Clare Nuns; the priests, deacons, and seminarians of the Confraternity of Catholic Clergy; and the prayers of all our parishioners. Finally, we thank our bishops, the Most Rev. Nicholas C. Dattilo, DD (Bishop of Harrisburg, PA) and the Most Rev. Paul Gregory Bootkoski, DD (Bishop of Metuchen, NJ), for their support in our ordained ministry.

Top Ten Little-Known Facts
about the Bible

1. The word "bible" is not anywhere *in* the Bible.

2. The Bible never identified the forbidden fruit eaten by Adam and Eve as being an *apple*.

3. The Ten Commandments are not numbered in the Bible.

4. The names of the Kings or "Wise Men" are never mentioned in the Bible.

5. The Bible never said that Saint Paul fell "off a horse."

6. The Bible was originally written with no chapter or verse.

7. The Bible does not contain a list of which books belong in it.

8. The King James Version was not the first English translation of the Bible.

9. The Bible was originally written as separate books by different authors spanning many centuries.

10. The Bible is the oldest and most consistent bestselling book of all time with more than 20 million copies sold annually.

Introduction

▶ FOR CHRISTIANS, the Bible is considered the written Word of God. It is thought to be inspired by God, but written by human beings with divine assistance. Since there is no one human author, and it took centuries to write and then collect all the parts to form the one volume book we call the *Holy Bible*, it is important for any reader to appreciate the different type of literature contained inside; discern what the text actually says as originally written by the sacred (inspired) author; discover what the intended meaning and intended audience is for each book of the Bible; and hopefully make spiritual applications in one's daily life.

Don't let the size and age of the Bible intimidate you. It may be very old, but it was written for you, the average person. It may take a little time, effort, study, and prayer, but when you think of how long the Bible has been around, it is worth it to unravel its mysteries and beauties. You will find some parts more enjoyable to read than others, some easier or more difficult to understand, some very helpful, and others somewhat esoteric.

Just as there are several branches of Christianity—from Protestant to Catholic to Eastern Orthodox, and all their subdivisions—there is no one version, translation, or edition of the Bible that suits everybody's needs. There are also differences of theology among the various denominations and churches, which affect how the Bible is interpreted and applied. The goal of *The Everything® Bible Book* is not to exhaust or even examine every possible avenue, but to expose you—the reader—to a broad overview and offer some helpful hints on how to digest and appreciate the vast source of wisdom found in this book. For the purposes of consistency, however, all biblical references in *The Everything® Bible Book* are from the New International Version.

Even though you may have already read the Bible from cover to cover, each time you read it you will get something new from it. Despite the fact that you may already know how many of the stories end either by reading it beforehand or from seeing adaptations of it on television or in the movies, even the most familiar story has the potential of giving more insight, teaching, advice, and guidance. The Bible is a book that you can never know too well or too much.

Christians themselves do not agree on what every passage of Scripture means and neither do all their respective churches. The Bible is for individuals and for faith communities as a whole. It has something for everyone, the one and the many, the young and the old, the believer and even the unbeliever. Even if someone does not share all the religious teachings associated with the Bible, they can still better appreciate where Christians are possibly coming from since they allow the Bible to influence them so much.

Like an onion with many layers or a diamond with many facets, the Bible is more than just one book; it is a collection of different books, with different messages, by different authors, written at different times and places. There is so much the Bible has to say that you can never exhaust its meaning nor run out of material. Hopefully, this epic work of faith will give you a little more appreciation and desire to read either for the first time or for the hundredth time. Ⓔ

Chapter 1

What Is the Bible?

Since the printing press made its appearance in A.D. 1450, more than 6½ billion Bibles have been printed in 371 languages. It has been the most read, translated, and bestselling book of all time, and it is for billions of people today a source of faith, truth, and guidance. This chapter will look at the book called the Bible, the various books of the Bible, and the very word *Bible* itself.

What's in a Name?

Aside from being a book that U.S. presidents use on inauguration day, the Bible has been called by many as "*the* Book of Books." Other names include "the Written Word of God" and "Sacred Scripture." Actually, rather than being just one big book with many chapters, the Bible is a collection of books, from Genesis to Revelation. The difference between the Bible and other types of collections is that the Bible claims to have one source of inspiration.

FACT

The Bible is called the *Word* of God. Hebrew uses *dabar,* Greek uses *logos,* and Latin uses *verbum* for what English translates as *word*. A spoken or written "word" is a symbol that human beings use to communicate ideas to one another.

The Bible remains one of the most mysterious, misunderstood, and misquoted books of all time. Many people regard the Bible as the inspired, infallible, inerrant Word of God, yet you'd be surprised how many of them inaccurately quote, refer to, and use quotations (or alleged ones) to make a point. For instance, the very word "bible" is not even in the Bible. Thanks to computers, we can now do word searches in a millisecond. If you run one on any version of the Bible, you will not find the word "bible" anywhere. So, if the word "bible" isn't in the Bible, where did it come from and why do we use it to name this special book?

Origin of the Word "Bible"

Gubla (present-day Jbail in Lebanon) is a Phoenician town noted for its plentiful papyrus. Before paper was derived from trees, the ancients used fiber from the stem of the papyrus plant upon which to write messages and documents. They rolled them up into scrolls for safekeeping and handled these delicately due to their tendency to become brittle over time. Unlike wood and stone, which the ancients used for inscriptions, papyrus was lighter, easier to transport, and certainly easier to use and keep.

In 1200 B.C., the Greeks renamed the city *Byblos* from their word for "book," which by this time was made of papyrus. Since books were made from pages of papyrus and Gubla was the known world's center of papyrus, they called the town Byblos. Later, Romans translated the Greek word for book (byblos) into the Latin *Biblia*, and it is this word from which the English word "bible" was derived.

ESSENTIAL

Jerome's Latin translation of the Bible is called the "Vulgate" from the Latin word *vulgus*, meaning "common people." The common folk of the Roman Empire, who were literate, could only speak, read, and write in Latin, whereas only the elite could understand Greek and even fewer could read Hebrew.

Saint Jerome was the first to use the term "bible" (actually he used the Latin: *biblia*) as well as the first to assemble a complete version of it around A.D. 396–400. Pope Damasus, the Bishop of Rome, commissioned him in the fourth century to translate the existing scrolls of Hebrew, Aramaic, and Greek scriptures into the Latin language. Since only scholars could read and write Greek and Hebrew at that time, the general public needed a translation in their common tongue, which was Latin for the Roman Empire. This would be the first time the entire Bible would appear in one language as well as the first time all the books would be together in one volume.

Origin of the Word "Scripture"

The English word "scripture" comes from the Latin *scriptura*, meaning the act of writing. (The Greeks used the word *graphe*, and the Hebrews used *kathab*.) The early Christian church, which was heavily influenced by Greek philosophy and language, coined the phrase *hagios graphe* (i.e., Holy or Sacred Scripture) to exclusively refer to the writing we now call the Bible. Originally, every book of the Bible was written on scrolls of parchment. These sacred writings became known by the word "scripture," since the Christian believers regarded it as the holiest of all written documents. The Bible, or Scripture, is typically divided into two parts: the Old Testament and the New Testament.

Origin of the Word "Testament"

The English word "testament" comes from the Latin *testamentum*, meaning written testimony or witness. The early church used it to translate the Greek word *diatheke* and the Hebrew word *berith*, both of which mean "covenant." Hence, the Old Testament is the written testimony of the covenant between God and the "Chosen People," whereas the New Testament is the written testimony of the covenant between Christ and his church. The concepts of testament and covenant are synonymous and are central themes in the Bible.

Sacred Literature

The Bible is considered literature; in other words, a collection or body of written works. Though many believers maintain that the writing of the Bible was inspired by God—it was actually humans who wrote the text. Human beings use different types of literature or ways of speaking to convey various messages and meanings. The same is true for the Bible as it employs a variety of literary techniques.

Literary Forms and Figures of Speech

When two people speak with each other, they're engaging in a dialogue. When one person speaks, he or she is giving a monologue, or narrative. These are examples of literary forms, just like poetry and prose. The Bible has plenty of dialogue, monologue, narrative, and prose, and some poetry as well. It even contains figures of speech since they, too, are considered literary forms and are valid ways of making a point.

The most obvious "sense," or meaning of a text, is called the "literal sense." Basically, it is nothing more than having words mean exactly what they say. When you read in the Bible, "And God said 'Let there be light'" (Genesis 1:3), it is presumed the reader understands what every word in that phrase means.

> When reading and interpreting the Bible, it is essential to know what type of literature and literary forms are being used so as to ascertain the intended meaning of the author.

At one level, every word in the Scripture has a literal meaning—if it did not, then it could not be translated into other languages. This is not to say that everything must be interpreted literally, but every word has a literal or precise meaning in the language it is written. English uses the word "God," but the Hebrew language uses the word *Elohim* just as the Greek language uses *Theos*, and Latin, the word *Deus*. The "literal sense" is nothing more than individual words being translated and understood correctly. A "literal interpretation" is when groups of words (phrases or sentences) in a particular context have only one meaning.

Even though every word has a literal sense and literal meaning, sometimes words are used symbolically to represent another idea. There is both an internal and an external allegory in the Bible. Internally, a figure of speech is used, such as a metaphor like "You are the salt of the earth" (Matthew 5:13), or an analogy like "I am the vine; you are the branches" (John 15:5). The reader is not asked to interpret literally that he or she is actually sodium chloride (table salt) any more than he or she is expected to consider himself or herself a plant branch rather than a human being. The allegory within the text is a figure of speech meant to make a point. Externally, this happens when a connection is made between a text in the Old Testament and one in the New Testament—for example, the crossing of the Red Sea by Moses in Exodus 16, and Saint Paul's reference to it in his Epistle to the Corinthians in 1 Corinthians (10:2) when he says, "They were all baptized into Moses in the cloud and in the sea."

The moral meaning of the biblical text is intended to influence how the reader is to behave. The famous phrase "But I tell you, Do not resist an evil person. If someone strikes you on the right cheek, turn to him the other also" (Matthew 5:39), is to be given a moral interpretation; in other words, to forgive one's enemies and not simply to move your face away. Similarly, when Jesus says in the Bible, "Why do you look at the speck of sawdust in your brother's eye and pay no attention to the plank in your own eye?" (Luke 6:41), that is meant to be a moral message of keeping things in perspective and with humility.

An ancient Bible study aid from the Middle Ages goes: *"Letter* (literal sense) speaks of deeds; *Allegory* to faith; *Moral* how to act; *Anagogy* points to our destiny."

The anagogical sense is the most sublime of them all. It points the listener/reader to a future reality not yet happening, but which is no less real than the present moment since God allegedly foretold it. When Revelation 21 speaks of the new, heavenly city of Jerusalem, many scholars believe this is a foreshadowing of the Church at the end of time.

Faith and Reason

The Bible is a book of faith, in that it is meant to foster faith, explain it, and nourish it. Reason does not conflict nor contradict faith, which is believing something that cannot be proved or disproved. Faith means to believe the word of another since there is no empirical evidence. But reason is needed and used when reading the Bible—otherwise it will make no sense.

Creationism Versus Evolution

There has been an ongoing debate among some Christians over the issue of evolution. Two extreme positions are:

1. *The Genesis story is pure myth.* Life evolved on its own merely out of consequences from natural forces acting upon various species—those being able to adapt survived, while those that did not disappeared; there is no intelligent plan or creator—simply chance, change, and survival.

2. *Genesis literally teaches that God created the world.* He created the plants, the animals, and ultimately human life, and he did it in a short period of time—some maintain an actual six calendar days, others claiming a symbolic six periods or intervals of time.

A middle position is also present among many believers, considered a modified theory of evolution. Rather than maintaining an absence of any intelligence, this view is that the Creator God is the one who made the laws of physics and chemistry, as well as biology. Using laws and material already created by the same Creator, this perspective claims that God could have allowed organisms to grow and develop, but at some juncture intervened in the process to endow human beings with the ability to reason, thus separating them from the animals. While human bodies could theoretically evolve according to the same laws of science that apply to everything on the planet—like the law of gravity—some believe the human soul is something directly created by God and does not come from the material world.

Biochemists have shown that every man and woman on earth—past, present, and future—can be traced genetically to one human woman via mitochondrial DNA. To that one woman they gave the name "Eve," which means "mother of all the living."

That's Reasonable

The key to better understanding the Bible is knowing what the author is trying to say. Even though some believers steadfastly hold to the divine authorship and inspiration of Scripture, nevertheless, they admit God used many human authors or as they are frequently called, "sacred writers," to help compose the Bible as we know it. Saying that Matthew wrote his Gospel does not deny that he was inspired by God to write it. Having numerous human agents, but being inspired by one intelligent and divine source, is plausible to one who believes in this sacred text.

Secondly, the type of literature—the literary forms, genres, and so forth—tells us what kind of message the author is trying to communicate. When you pick up a chemistry textbook, you expect to read what elements compose the known world. There is no motivation, no rationale, just simple answers to basic questions, like, what is this made of? When you pick up the Bible, it is not a textbook; it is a book of faith. In other words, science books seek to answer the questions of *what* and *how*, while the Bible—being a book of faith and theology—seeks to answer *why* and *who/whom?*

The chemistry book will tell you that water is composed of two parts hydrogen to one part oxygen. The Bible will tell you that God created water so as to sustain and maintain life. The former explained what and how; the latter answered the questions of who is responsible and why.

Logic and Grammar

Just because the Bible is a book of faith does not mean that logic or the rules of grammar do not apply. Nouns have adjectives, verbs have adverbs, sentences have phrases, and so forth, and the same grammar rules apply in the Bible as well. So, plural subjects go with plural objects and pronouns must also match. The problem in the English language is that it is not always that clear. "You" can be singular or plural, and the verb "are" is the same for either case.

ESSENTIAL

Logic still holds in any tongue and the laws that govern reason help us interpret the biblical text. If the sentence makes no sense to the reader, then he or she needs to either look up the unknown words in a dictionary, or find a translation that is more comprehensible. Not many have the knowledge and ability to read the original Hebrew or Greek in which the Bible was written, and so getting an accurate and readable translation is important.

Fact or Fiction?

Are the stories in the Bible just stories, fables, and myths, or are they true? Most fairy tales begin with "Once upon a time . . ." whereas the Bible opens in Genesis with "In the beginning . . ." Instead of reading the Bible as one would read the newspaper or a textbook, the Scripture is meant to be read with the intent and desire to absorb the message that sometimes is hidden among the facts. When reading the Bible, don't let the details overwhelm you; in other words, don't let the ancient names and archaic places keep you from gaining the central theme. Instead, focus on the substance of the message.

It is believed that the Bible tells the stories of real people. Without photos and fingerprints, DNA, and Social Security Numbers, it is difficult to verify every identity in the Sacred Scripture, but the persons described seem very real even if their names are often enigmatic.

While not a history book, the Bible is historical. The cultures and places mentioned did indeed exist. Egypt, Persia (present-day Iran), Babylon (present-day Iraq), and Assyria (also present-day Iraq) were real places then as today, and Ramses the Pharaoh and Caesar Augustus did reign in their respective times and regions. However, the Bible seeks to explain the history of salvation and not the intricate details historians often investigate in their discipline of study.

Custom permeates the Bible in the sense that traditions of both human and divine origin can be found. Resting on the Sabbath, celebrating Passover, attending temple or synagogue in addition to rules for social behavior, and so forth are evident in the sacred text. Traditions, such as procedures to obtain an inheritance, marriage rituals, and dietary laws, are all in there. Oral tradition is the precursor to the actual writing of the Sacred Scripture since it was first told by word of mouth and handed on down (*traditio* in Latin) from one generation to the next.

Author, Author

Normally, the author writes his or her own book. However, we know that the Bible is not one book, but a collection of books, and thus a collection of human authors—more accurately a compilation of human writers, who believers maintain were inspired to write what God wanted. One can speak of the "divine author" being God, and the human author or writer as one who physically put the ink onto parchment paper. Biblical theology attempts to study how much and to what extent human freedom is given to the sacred writer in his choice of words and concepts, while maintaining the delicate balance of remaining loyal to the inspiration of the Holy Spirit.

It is believed that the divine component of the sacred text is that it was produced by the inspiration and instigation of God. It was God's idea, his message, and his truth. As such, some believe there is a universality to the message, which transcends human boundaries of race, culture, language, and gender. The Bible has been called the "Word of God" written by man because human perceptions, influences, likes and dislikes, education, and so forth affect how the divine message is told.

Stages of Development

The Bible, as we know it today in its final form, did not drop out of heaven as a written book. Before any ink was ever inscribed by a sacred writer to any piece of parchment, there were stages of development. The Old Testament stories were passed on by word of mouth from one generation to the next. Then, after a period of time, a writer finally put the oral tradition on paper. Later, several writings were joined to form a collection. Finally, the collections were combined into one complete volume, or book, which we now know as the Bible.

The Bible was not originally written with chapter and verse numbering as we read it today; it didn't even have a table of contents telling you what books were inside. In 1227, Stephen Langton, the Archbishop of Canterbury, divided the books of the Bible into chapters, and in 1551, Robert Stephanus subdivided the chapters into verses with his edition of the Latin Vulgate.

In ancient times, the idea of the story was not limited to bedtime stories and fairy tales. The story was how an individual person told others about the origins of the world, as well as of personal and family origins. Many of us remember grandma and grandpa telling their story of how they survived World War II, or mom and dad explaining how they first met and fell in love. Storytelling of this type is called "oral tradition." It is the way human beings explain things using ideas, concepts, symbols, and words that listeners can identify with personally. From one generation to the next, this word of mouth communication is more than just telling the facts, it is also expressing and evoking emotions and feelings, or teaching and promoting values and principles.

Some scholars speak of various authors or writers—such as the *Priestly*, the *Jahwist*, the *Elohist*, and the *Deuteronomic* sources—who individually and corporately helped compose the texts of the early and first part of the Bible. Others ascribe authorship directly to the prophets Isaiah, Amos, Jeremiah, Matthew, Mark, Luke, and John. It is then very important to remember that within the Bible are individual books written by different and distinct authors. For example, the epistle of James is believed to have been written by the apostle James, and the letter to the Corinthians was written by Paul. Two distinct and different documents, two distinct and different authors, yet both found in the one New Testament of the Bible.

Often in ancient times the name of the redactor (editor) would be ascribed to a book or manuscript especially when the original author(s) was unknown and/or when the collection of books involved several sources. Even today, books are classified by the name of the editor if they are collections from various authors.

Biblical scholars use a technical term for the person who in essence put together the various separate sources, elements, and books into a single entity. That person is a *redactor*, or editor. This editor is someone who is not the author, but who collects the works of several authors and connects them to one another. For instance, ancient and pious tradition claimed that Moses wrote some and gathered other fragments of the scrolls to form the Pentateuch, or Torah, the first five books of the Bible (Genesis, Exodus, Leviticus, Numbers, and Deuteronomy).

The Greek word *kanon* means a reed used for measuring. Bible scholars used that same term to denote the authoritative list of authentic books of Scripture—in a sense, a measure of what is acceptable and what is not. Once the individual books of the Bible were written by either one or more authors, and after the redactor gathered them into groups and collections of writings, the last phase was to determine which books and collections would comprise the Canon of Scripture. No official list exists within the Bible; in other words, there is no index or table of contents in the inspired text, but some measure (*kanon*) or criteria needed to be established.

Bible Timeline

The Bible is a historical book in two ways. One, it is part of human history and it has a history in its development. There are stages when it was put together, translated, and promoted. The following dates relate to the writing of the book as a book. The Bible also describes and covers human events from the creation of the first man and woman all the way to the end of the world. It spans periods of history from antiquity to the classical era. Here are some significant dates for the development of the Bible as a whole:

Bible Development

1250 B.C.: Possible earliest date for writings from the Torah or Pentateuch.

250–150 B.C.: Translation of all Hebrew manuscripts into *Greek* Septuagint (LXX); Alexandrian (Greek) Canon established; 46 books in Old Testament.

A.D. 100 (COUNCIL OF JAMNIA): *Hebrew* (Palestinian Canon) established: 39 books in O.T.

A.D. 394: Saint Jerome translates and compiles first complete Bible in *Latin* with 72 books total, based on Septuagint Version.

A.D. 995: First Anglo-Saxon translation of New Testament.

A.D. 1384: Wycliffe Bible written in English.

A.D. 1450: Gutenberg invents printing press with movable type; Mazarin Bible is the earliest book printed from movable type (1455).

A.D. 1522: Martin Luther translates Bible from Latin into German and adopts the shorter and younger (Hebrew) Canon of the Old Testament (39 Books).

A.D. 1525: Tyndale's English translation of New Testament.

A.D. 1535: Coverdale's English translation of entire Bible.

A.D. 1609: Douay-Rheims—first complete English translation of Catholic Bible.

A.D. 1611: King James Version (KJV) with Apocrypha.

A.D. 1885: KJV officially removes Apocrypha.

A.D. 1973: New International Version is written.

Old and New Testament Dates

The Old Testament covers the antediluvian era (pre-flood of Noah time) to the patriarchal eras, to the Babylonian Captivity, but the New Testament covers a smaller amount of time. Note how the list of Old Testament dates spans nearly 2,000 years, whereas the New Testament list spans only 100 years. The reason for this? More was written in the New Testament times than in Old Testament period when written documents were extremely rare.

Relevant Old Testament Dates

1800–1600 B.C.	Patriarchs
1600 B.C.	Hebrews (Jews) in Egypt
1250 B.C.	Exodus
1210–1020 B.C.	Judges
1020–1000 B.C.	King Saul
1000–961 B.C.	King David
961–922 B.C.	King Solomon
922 B.C.	Division of Kingdom into North (Israel) and South (Judah)
721 B.C.	Conquest of Israel by Assyrians
587–538 B.C.	Conquest of Judah by Babylonians; Destruction of Temple

Important New Testament Dates

A.D. 51–100	New Testament (Gospels, Epistles, and Revelation) written in Greek
A.D. 50	Aramaic version of Matthew's Gospel possibly written
A.D. 51–52	Paul's Epistles, 1 and 2 Thessalonians possibly written
A.D. 57–66	Paul's Epistles, Galatians, 1 and 2 Corinthians, Romans, Philippians, Colossians, Ephesians, Philemon, 1 and 2 Timothy, and Titus
A.D. 60	Mark's Gospel possibly written
A.D. 62	Luke's Gospel possibly written
A.D. 69–70	Greek (canonical) version of Matthew's Gospel possibly written
A.D. 70	Destruction of Temple of Jerusalem
A.D. 98–100	Book of Revelation (Apocalypse) written by John

Antiquity

While reading the Bible, it is helpful to be acquainted with a little world history to keep things in context and perspective. Present-day Iraq is where the former Babylonian and Assyrian empires once hailed, just as current Iran used to be the seat of the Persian empire, and Lebanon the former Phoenicia. The Greeks and Romans came much later and are not even mentioned until the end of the Old Testament, while the Egyptians were around since 3400 B.C., some sixteen centuries before Abraham.

Modern Times

The land of the Bible is not just for history. Even today, world events, wars, treaties, peace initiatives, terrorism, economics, politics, and faith permeate the region where the ancient kingdoms of Israel, Palestine, Babylon, Assyria, Persia, Mesopotamia (land between the Tigris and Euphrates rivers in modern day Iraq), and so on once ruled vast armies, lands, and peoples. Global communities and international commerce, trade, and diplomacy connect the so-called New and Old Worlds, the East and West. Judaism, Christianity, and Islam remain active elements in the life and future of the descendants of Abraham, whether it be through Isaac, Ishmael, or Jesus.

Reading the Bible will help you appreciate the modern region and its complex problems, and knowing the current turmoil will help you understand what also happened in the past.

How to Read the Bible

Some insist that the best and only way to read the Bible is from cover to cover, starting with Genesis and going chapter by chapter, verse by verse, until you reach the end of Revelation. There is benefit in that since that is how the Bible is arranged, and a consistent and thorough reading from cover to cover is a good approach, even if done only once in your life.

For most newcomers to the Bible, however, that might be a bit intimidating. If you belong to a church or religious group that uses a Lectionary (a book of Bible passages used for public worship), one alternative is to follow along in your personal Bible by reading the daily or weekly selections from Scripture assigned for that date. Over a period of three years on this plan, you will cover most of the Bible, whereas a day-by-day reading can be accomplished in one calendar year.

Choosing a Version of the Bible

When it comes to which version of the Bible to use, the length is not the issue, but rather how much you will get out of it. Finding a user-friendly but accurate translation and version may take a little time, but it is well worth it. Your faith tradition may influence your selection to some extent. Most Protestants feel very much at home with the King James, the New International, or the American Standard versions of the Bible; whereas Catholics prefer the Douay-Rheims, New American, the Jerusalem, or RSV-CE versions since they contain the Deuterocanonical books (seven books considered the Apocrypha in non-Catholic Bibles) for a total of forty-six for the Old Testament.

FACT

Commentaries try to bridge the gap between how the ancient Hebrew or Greek text read, and how contemporary language interprets these texts today. They also give you the benefit of many scholars' thoughts over the centuries.

Using a good commentary and Bible dictionary is also helpful since there are many places, names, and terms that are difficult to understand, and even the best version can leave a reader with plenty of questions. Over the past two millennia, thousands of people have written on what the Scriptures mean to them and what the original text actually says.

Bible Study Groups

One is encouraged to read the Bible on his or her own for the sake of study, to read it again for the sake of prayer, and to tackle it a third time for the benefit of others. Bible study, be it three to five people in a home or a small group of ten to twenty in a congregation, can be of invaluable assistance to those who like and need the input of others. Discussing and even debating biblical teachings with others helps one appreciate his or her own faith all the more. When in a group or church setting, knowing the ground rules is important, however. Some Christians regard the Bible as the sole source of doctrinal and moral authority (called *sola scriptura*—meaning, "scripture alone"), while others regard it as the inspired, inerrant, and infallible Word of God, which, working alongside and in harmony with Sacred Tradition, composes the entirety of Divine Revelation. This view does not place the authority of the church over or above the Bible, but sees the Scripture as being entrusted to the guardianship of the church for all authentic interpretation.

Source of Worship

Many Christian churches use the Bible as the source for their public and weekly worship—often called the Sacred Liturgy. In some denominations, the preacher or pastor reads sections from the Bible and asks the congregation to follow along with their own Bibles. The minister has complete control over what passages are read and explained in the sermon.

Other churches have a modified Lectionary, with preselected sections for every Sunday of the year. In this way, the congregation reads most of the Bible over a period of a few years, and more importantly, consistently examines the same passages covered across the board in all churches who share that same Lectionary. Catholics, Lutherans, and Episcopalians, for example, share common passages from the Old and New Testaments, including the Gospels, and read them every week.

First-Time Reader?

One modest suggestion for first-time readers is to read the Bible fifteen to thirty minutes a day, at the same time every day of the week. How much material you cover will depend on how fast you read and comprehend. Another method is to read at least one chapter a day. After several weeks, you can easily progress and increase either the amount of time or the amount of text being read. It is not a contest, so reading to understand is the key here. At the back of this book, in Appendix B, are two suggested daily reading plans to cover the entire Bible in one year.

It is not recommended that you watch movie versions (e.g., *The Ten Commandments*) before you read the actual biblical text, since you are being given an interpretation of the text based on how some director or producer interpets the story, rather than on what the actual words say as written in the Bible.

If you have children or grandchildren nearby, reading to them from a children's version of the Bible or a kiddie Bible storybook will help them and you, for when you sit down to read the "grown-up" version, you will at least be familiar with some of the names and places.

Bible in a Movie?

The Ten Commandments, with Charleton Heston and Yul Brynner, is a favorite classic often viewed around a religious holiday, but many have never read the entire text of what Moses said and did and simply rely on what the movie depicts for them. Read Exodus first and *then* see the movie. You will appreciate it more and you will get something out of the text the next time you read it. You may even use your imagination differently than director Cecil B. De Mille did with the film version.

While entertaining and easy, watching a movie version of a biblical story gives you one person's interpretation of what the text means. The writer, producer, director, and actors all contribute their part, but it is their own personal spin, as you might say.

The Book of Books

The Bible is a book of books and that should always be remembered. It is considered by many as God's Word written by human beings. For believers, it contains revealed truths, as well as religious and moral values. It contains history, poetry, narrative, imagery, metaphor, parables, sermons, dialogues, genealogies, and many other types of genres and writing methods. There is no more diverse a book than the Bible.

The overall theme among many teachings, doctrines, and principles is one of *covenant*. The sacred pact God entered into with His Chosen People (the Hebrew nation) and the continuation and perfection of it in a second covenant between His Son and the church (the People of God) are the two main hinges of the Bible. It is divided into Old and New Testaments, and the word "testament" is just another term for covenant: "I will be your God and you will be my people" (Jeremiah 7:23). As you will see from the Bible, God, from Genesis to Revelation, has been, is, and shall be ever faithful to His covenant even if human beings continue to violate, break, or ignore their end of the bargain.

Chapter 2
Divine Revelation

The last book of the Bible is called Revelation (or the Apocalypse in some versions), and believers consider the Bible itself to be a part of Divine Revelation. This chapter will look at Revelation, what it is and how it's experienced. Since the Bible and Revelation are intimately connected, it is important to know what the two main religious positions are on the means God uses to reveal His divine truths.

The Origin of the Word

The English word "revelation" comes from the Latin *revelare*, which means "to unveil." The Greek word is *apokalupto*, or apocalypse, which is sometimes used to refer to the last book of the Bible, more commonly known as the Book of Revelation. In Hebrew, the word *galah* also means "to uncover" or "to unveil." This physical image of pulling back a veil to reveal what's behind it is key to understanding biblical revelation. The Temple in Jerusalem had a veil, which covered the entrance into the Holy of Holies—the place where the Ark of the Covenant resided, containing the Ten Commandments.

Only the High Priest could pull back the veil and enter the Holy of Holies, and only on the Day of Atonement (the Jewish day of observance, Yom Kippur). It was on this day that the High Priest could speak the sacred name of God—*Yahweh.*

What Is Revealed?

To answer the question of why there is revelation at all, it is important to know what is being revealed. Revelation is basically the unveiling or the disclosure of truth. Human beings have a rational intellect and a free will, which separates us from the animals and other living creatures on earth. The intellect (or mind) seeks to know the truth. Rather than a subjective judgment or opinion, truth is a correspondence between what one thinks and what actually exists.

Kinds of Truth

There are three basic kinds of truth that are knowable to the human intellect (mind). They are scientific (empirical) truth, philosophical (logical) truth, and theological (religious) truth. Scientific truth is known by using the senses and observing reality. Philosophical truth is known by thinking and using reason. Theological truth is known by faith and believing what God reveals.

Purpose of Revelation

Some things or facts are immediately or easily known by everyone (or are at least knowable to anyone who possesses the use of reason). Some things take more time and effort to figure out, and a few things are so complicated that only a few very intelligent people can know and understand them. Anyone who has reached the age of reason (about seven years old) is presumed to know the difference between lying and telling the truth. A more mature mind is needed to know that ethically speaking, one is not morally obligated to tell everyone everything and yet there is a way to withhold the truth under certain circumstances without telling a lie.

FACT

An example of a scientific truth is that fire is hot, which anyone can know by sticking his hand in a flame. A philosophical truth is that nothing can contradict itself; in other words, something can be either real or imaginary, alive or dead, true or false, but it can't be both since either one excludes the other. A theological truth is that the Bible is the inspired written Word of God.

Equality of Revelation

Believers claim that revelation merely evens the playing field since there are some truths (theological) that human beings could never know—either scientifically or philosophically—if God did not reveal them himself. There are other truths that are possible for human beings to know, but—due to differences in levels of education, temperament, environment, culture, etc.—not everyone knows these truths at the same time and in the same way. By revealing both what could not be known by human reason alone and that which is not universally and simultaneously known puts everyone on the same page.

Divine Revelation does not depend on your IQ for you to know and accept it. Faith is all that is needed. Anyone can accept that God exists by believing the revealed Word of God, which says that very thing.

Natural Versus Supernatural Revelation

There are two kinds of revelation: natural and supernatural. Believers claim natural revelation is that which God reveals or communicates to human beings through nature and the physical universe, whereas supernatural revelation is the disclosure of specific truths by God directly to man. Both kinds are found in the Bible.

The natural moral law, which tells us what are basic moral and ethical standards of human behavior, is one example of natural revelation. The Ten Commandments, which explicitly define what is sinful activity, forbid idolatry and blasphemy, and mandate weekly observance of the Sabbath, are an example of supernatural revelation.

Spreading the Word

Natural revelation is more subtle than supernatural and requires the use of the reasoning process. Supernatural revelation begins with God disclosing the truths he wants to communicate to humankind. The next step involves a human agent who hears the Word of God and then transmits it to others. The transmission occurs by word of mouth—oral communication—or through the printed word, by writing it down on paper.

Oral and Written Traditions

At first, the stories appearing in the Bible were passed down from one generation to the next through word of mouth, long before anyone even knew how to read and write. It was only after a written language had emerged (and by the inspiration of the Holy Spirit) that the sacred authors put into writing the actual text of Scripture. Even the Gospels of the New Testament were written some years after Jesus' death. However, before Matthew, Mark, Luke, and John wrote the Gospels, the apostles and disciples had already preached Jesus' message to thousands. This is also known as Sacred Tradition—the unwritten or spoken Word of God—as opposed to Sacred Scripture (the Bible), meaning the *written* Word.

Just because the word "story" is used doesn't mean that the stories of the Bible are not considered to be true, nor does it imply that the characters within them are fictional. A religious story is a narrative of past events but told with feeling, passion, emotion—and perhaps a little imagination.

Paul's Tradition

The passage found in 2 Thessalonians 2:15 says "So then, brothers, stand firm and hold to the teachings we passed on to you, whether by word of mouth or by letter." The original Greek text uses the word *paradosis*, which is rendered as "traditions" instead of "teachings" in several translations. The word "tradition" comes from the Latin word *tradition*, meaning "to hand down." Saint Paul spoke and preached more than he wrote, yet his Epistles (letters), which are in the Bible, are all that remain. The only time he discounts tradition is when it is purely human or man-made but as he himself says in 2 Thessalonians, the message (revelation) comes "by word of mouth or by letter" as handed down from him.

Written Tradition

At some moment in time, under the inspiration of the Holy Spirit, each sacred author made a decision to put into writing what had been up to that time spread only verbally. When you read any book of the Bible, at no time in any place does the human author say, "And then God told me to write this down." Scholars believe that most, if not all of the sacred authors were unaware that they were inspired to write; yet, it wasn't necessary for them to be aware of the inspiration in order to write what God wanted. Since human authors are used by God, then some of their personal tastes, perspectives, nuances, and so forth do enter into the equation.

Extinct Originals

The actual written scrolls and manuscripts, which the original authors penned, no longer exist, and only copies of copies remain. Because people considered them to be inspired writings, painstaking efforts were made to accurately and precisely translate and copy them. Some scholars claim that more care was given to these writings than to the copies of Plato, Aristotle, Socrates, Caesar, and Cicero, to name a few, since these were the God-inspired words.

Roman Catholicism and Eastern Orthodoxy give equal importance, reverence, and respect to Sacred Tradition and Sacred Scripture, whereas many mainline and evangelical Protestants give priority and pre-eminence to the written word (Bible). At the time of the Reformation in the sixteenth century, Dr. Martin Luther coined the phrase *sola scriptura* (Latin for "scripture alone") and that has been a hallmark for Protestant Christians ever since.

The Unwritten Tradition

Catholics and Orthodox Christians maintain that the Bible shows evidence that tradition is an equal and valid mode of revelation. John's Gospel (21:25) ends with "Jesus did many other things as well. If every one of them were written down, I suppose that even the whole world would not have room for the books that would be written." Those unwritten things were considered part of tradition—the fact that Jesus never married and never had children is never stated, but all Christian religions believe it nevertheless.

Response to the Word

When city officials install a stop sign on a corner of a street, they presume and expect that drivers will read, understand, and comply with the word "Stop" painted on the sign. Likewise, believers claim that when God revealed his Word, he presumed and expected that human beings would hear it, understand it, and then live by it. The biggest hurdle, however, is understanding it, and that is why intelligent and accurate translations and versions of the Bible are important.

The Outcome

Since Saint Paul first preached on one of his many missions, believers have followed in his footsteps and have verbally communicated the Word of God. Today, there are still evangelists and preachers spreading God's Word, claiming that even the most well-read and the best educated individuals sometimes need a little reinforcement, encouragement, and explanation to accompany what they have already learned on their own.

ALERT!

Some people think the Latin translation of the Bible was done to keep it away from the common people. However, it wasn't just the clergy who could understand Latin. Anyone who could read and write also understood Latin fluently since it was the official language of the empire for commerce, as well as in schools and universities.

Newcomers

First-time Bible readers may be intimidated by archaic names and extinct places. They may get overwhelmed by the magnitude of time covered in the Bible and the infinite amount of knowledge and wisdom contained inside the text. What they need to remember is that finding a version, edition, or translation that is both accurate and comprehensible is very important.

Bible Reading Effects

Listening to the preached Word and reading the written Word are essential components to understanding the sacred text. The words contained within the Bible can possibly change one's view of the world, of life, of death, and make the reader see things in a different perspective. Besides giving doctrinal truths, the inspired Word of God also gives moral teaching to live by so as to attain eternal happiness in the next life. Ⓔ

Chapter 3

(E) Inspiration and Inerrancy

Millions of believers know the Bible as the inspired and inerrant Word of God, yet there are no definitions of these terms in the sacred text, and, in fact, these words never appear throughout the book. Various denominations of Christians disagree on the issue of these ideas, but some consensus exists among the major affiliations. This chapter looks at both ideas—inspiration and inerrancy—since they are essential elements of the Scriptures.

What Is Inspiration?

People often talk about an inspiring speech or an inspiring speaker, and when they do the text or the person is usually able to motivate, arouse, or stimulate particular feelings or emotions in the audience. A famous example is the inspiring speech of Patrick Henry, which he concluded with "Give me liberty or give me death!" While this is indeed one valid way of understanding inspiration—in other words, the ability to persuade and motivate—in biblical terms it is necessary to go back to the basics.

The word "inspiration" comes from the Latin word *inspirare*, which means "to breathe upon." It is a translation of the Greek *theopneustos*, which is rendered "God-breathed" and is very close to the Hebrew *neshamah* and *ruwach*, which are often used interchangeably. The idea here is that "breath" represents "spirit," which signifies life. Genesis 1 speaks of the Spirit of God hovering over the waters of the earth and in Genesis 2, God creates Adam from the dust of the earth by breathing into him the breath of life.

After His Resurrection, Jesus appeared to His apostles and "breathed" (*emphusao* in the original Greek) on them and said, "Receive the Holy Spirit" (John 20:22). The connection with breath and spirit are obvious. The Septuagint (Greek Old Testament) uses the word *emphusao* only once, in Genesis 2:7, when God "breathed" into Adam's nostrils, giving him life.

Biblical inspiration, therefore, is an action of, by, and from God upon human beings. Two good definitions of inspiration might prove to be helpful in understanding what biblical scholars mean when they say the Bible is inspired.

According to Dr. Charles C. Ryrie . . .

"My own definition of biblical inspiration is that it is God's superintendence of the human authors so that, using their own individual personalities, they composed and recorded without error His revelation to man in the words of the original autographs" (*A Survey of Bible Doctrine*, Chicago: Moody Press, 1972).

This excerpt is from a Protestant Christian Bible Scholar, former president of Philadelphia School of the Bible and current Dean of the Graduate School and Professor of Systematic Theology at Dallas Theological Seminary. His definition entails an action of God and the cooperation of human beings in a manner free from error.

According to Pope Leo XIII . . .

"Inspiration consists in that supernatural influence by which God so arouses and directs the sacred authors to write, [and] assists them in writing, so that all and only what He Himself wills do they correctly formulate in their minds, determine to write faithfully, and express aptly in an infallibly truthful manner" (*Providentissimus Deus*, #20, 1893).

This is an official definition of inspiration from the Catholic Christian community. It claims that God has complete control over the human agents to ensure that "all and only" what God wants gets put into print. In 1992, the Catechism of the Catholic Church (#106) reiterated this definition with the addition of "God . . . made full use of [the sacred authors'] own faculties and powers."

FACT

Inspiration does not mean that the person being inspired must be saintly or holy. While it would be unlikely that an evil sinner would cooperate with God's inspiration, at the same time inspiration in and of itself does not "sanctify" the person. The Gospel writers, for example, are considered saints not because they were inspired evangelists, but because they lived faith-filled lives.

In other words, the Catechism of the Catholic church claims that biblical inspiration is an action of God upon human authors to write only what God wants written, while utilizing the differences of the authors involved to infallibly communicate his message. In terms of the written Bible, no one chose to become an inspired author and it was not an appointed nor elected position. It is believed that God alone chose whom He wanted as his human authors. Also, it was God's message being written, yet the authors retained their humanity—their imagination, intelligence, personalities, and so forth influenced not *what* is written, but *how*.

Who Is Inspired?

One of the greatest mysteries of faith deals with the question of why God chose someone to be an inspired sacred author? In fact, many of the sacred authors are not even known since they did not leave their names on the manuscripts. The New Testament books are known by their reputed authors like Matthew, Mark, Luke, John, Paul, Peter, James, and Jude, but the Old Testament is more problematic since many believe that Moses either wrote all five books of the Pentateuch, or at least collected and edited what he himself did not write.

Since it is not always possible to identify the inspired author, it is easier and more accurate to speak of the inspired text. This way some personalities do not dominate more than others. For instance, Saint Paul is not more inspired than Saint Mark, or the prophet Isaiah.

Only the authors of the canonical books of the Bible are considered inspired. Even if Saint Thomas did write a gospel and it could be irrefutably proven to be in his own handwriting, it would not be considered inspired and it would not be inserted into the current Bible. The twenty-seven books of the New Testament are the only ones considered inspired, and it is not just based on the identity of the author. The early Christian Church, acting in the name of Christ, decided which books were inspired and which were not.

Inspiration does not guarantee the authenticity of the source, but guarantees that whomever the author is, God inspired him to write "all and only" what God wanted. It is not the identity of the author that makes or establishes its inspiration. It is the recognition by the Christian Church that these and only these books are inspired.

How Inspiration Takes Place

There are numerous theories on how the mysterious process of Divine Inspiration occurs, but not one of them answers all the questions. In the tradition of the great scholastic theologians of the Middle Ages, such as Aquinas and Bonaventure, it is better to examine the *via negative* (i.e., to see what inspiration is *not*) to better appreciate what it is. This concept is similar to the Sherlock Holmes' bit of wisdom: "When you have eliminated all which is impossible, then whatever remains, however improbable, must be the truth."

Verbal Dictation

There is no part of the Bible where the sacred author says, "And God told me to sit down and write this as I tell it to you." Had God wanted to dictate sacred Scripture, He could have easily used angels instead of man or any other creature or just wrote it Himself. Instead, He chose to use human beings, who have a free will and an imagination. These elements which make us human were used by the sacred authors as they wrote the sacred text. The author freely chose what to say and what not to say, how to say it, and when to say it as he or she wrote the text. However, despite this freedom on man's part, it does not destroy nor diminish the power of Divine Inspiration.

FACT

An artistic rendering of a dove—representing the Holy Spirit whispering into the ear of Matthew as he wrote his Gospel—may be a masterpiece, but it is probably not an accurate portrait of what happened. Many believe that Matthew just sat down and decided to write his account of the Gospel. Nowhere in it does he claim that God "told" him to write.

Subsequent Approbation

Another concept of inspiration is subsequent approbation. This is a theory that the sacred author came up with the idea to write, and the only action of God was that of final editor—in other words, to approve or reject the text. Many believe, however, that inspiration occurs at the moment and throughout the process the author writes every word, phrase, and sentence.

Negative Assistance

This peculiar notion is more akin to how Catholics understand papal infallibility. Negative assistance merely means that the only time and reason for divine intervention is to prevent a moral or doctrinal error from being written and communicated. This portrays God as a policeman or intervener who waits for mistakes before stepping in, whereas Divine Inspiration operates from the first instant and continues to the last letter.

Ideological Inspiration

According to this theory, only ideas and concepts are inspired but not any of the details of the text. A parallel notion is one that says only those books, chapters, and verses that concern faith and morals are considered inspired, nothing else. Both show a limited or restricted idea of inspiration. However, if this was the case, then all the superfluous text would be removed and the Bible would contain just moral and doctrinal texts—and it does not.

ESSENTIAL

Inspiration is not the same as infallibility. The former is a positive action, the latter a negative one. Inspiration is the direct action of God to influence the sacred author to write all and only what God wants. Infallibility means the text is free from error. A phone book can be technically free from error, but it can never be considered inspired.

The Concept of Inerrancy

When it is said that the Bible is inerrant, it means it is free from all errors. Since most believers claim that God is the ultimate author who inspired the sacred authors to write all and only what he wanted, it then follows that there can be no mistakes in the biblical text.

Inerrancy, therefore, is the logical conclusion of inspiration. If it is God's Word that he, himself, is communicating, then how can a perfect supreme being transmit mistakes? Free from error, however, applies only to the original text—the Bible today is a translation of translation, or a copy of a copy.

FACT

Saint Augustine (A.D. 354–430), Bishop of Hippo, said that if you run across an apparent error in the Bible, you must not conclude that the sacred author made a mistake. Rather, you should consider first if the manuscript is faulty; secondly, if the version is inaccurate; and finally, that perhaps you just don't understand the matter in question.

Mysteries of the Bible

Since the authors of the Bible, by virtue of inspiration, were able to write an inerrant book, what about the human beings who copied the manuscripts and/or translated them from the original languages? So-called mysteries of the Bible or apparent errors can often be explained through faulty translation or a mistake in the copying process. But what about apparent mistakes or unexplained mysteries of the Bible? Do they not negate the concept of inerrancy?

Galileo Incident

When we consider inerrancy, the famous case of Galileo comes to mind. In 1616, the church admonished Galileo's sun-centered theory of the solar system (the heliocentric system) as contrary to the Scripture. The church asked Galileo to abandon his theory, and when he refused, the church officials convicted and sentenced him to house arrest, where he remained for the last ten years of his life.

However, the concept of the heliocentric system was not a new one. Even a century before Galileo, Polish astronomer Copernicus had already discredited the church accepted geocentric notion—which claimed that the moon, sun, planets, and stars rotate around the earth—with his idea that the earth actually revolves around the sun.

During his lifetime, Galileo also insisted that the Bible was wrong in several respects. He claimed the heliocentric system disproved Ecclesiastes 1:5: "The sun rises and the sun sets, and hurries back to where it rises." However, figures of speech and common idioms cannot be given the same scrutiny as factual data. The terms "sunrise" or "sunset" are still used today, and are just a way of expressing time.

In 1992, Pope John Paul II lifted Galileo's admonition after a thorough examination of the case showed that the scientist who was right about the solar system also later admitted his theological errors about the veracity of Scripture.

Conflicting Creations

Conflicting accounts of Creation exist between the Genesis 1 and Genesis 2 books of the Bible. The first story of Creation in Genesis 1 teaches the hierarchy of Creation—that humankind was the crowning jewel from inanimate matter to plant life to animal and finally to human life. The second Creation story in Genesis 2 teaches the interdependence of human beings on one another.

Genesis 1 describes the sequence of Creation in this order:

- **Verse 3:** God creates light.
- **Verse 11:** He makes the plants.
- **Verses 20–25:** He creates animals.
- **Verses 26–27:** God creates a man and woman.

Genesis 2, however, has a different chronology:

- **Verse 7:** God creates Adam.
- **Verse 9:** God creates trees and vegetation.
- **Verse 19:** God creates animals.
- **Verse 22:** God creates Eve as Adam's companion.

If only looked at from a linear point of view, one could say that one story had to be true and the other false since they apparently contradict one another. However, many believe the intent was to communicate a theological reality in each story by showing two different religious truths concerning Creation.

Fail safe Measure

Why even make an issue of inerrancy? If mistakes can be found in the sacred text, which are not explainable by faulty translations, human or mechanical copying errors, or misunderstanding on the part of the reader, then all the truths of the Bible can be discredited or at least placed in jeopardy of doubt. Why would the miracles of Jesus be true if the Old Testament miracles of Noah and the Ark, the Ten Plagues of Egypt, and Jonah and the Whale were creations of fiction? If inerrancy is not a component, then neither is inspiration and then the Bible becomes just another book written by human beings and nothing more.

ALERT!

Every word of Scripture has a literal sense that must be understood—in other words, the intent of the author is first found in the words themselves. The context of those words will affect the determination of the intended meaning.

Rudolph Bultmann

Rudolph Bultmann (1884–1976) was a liberal theologian and Bible scholar who proposed the "demythologization" of Scripture. According to him, miracles were impossible; hence, any mention of them in the Bible was not intended to be fact. He had great influence in modern biblical research as many abandoned the notion of inerrancy and began to use the historical critical method of interpreting the Bible. While many scholars before and after him used literary and form criticism to interpret Scripture, this radical break with the adherence to inerrancy caused great divisions among Christians and their view of the Bible.

Literalism

In order to preserve the inerrancy of Scripture, some Christians interpret the entire Bible literally. If that method is not part of your faith tradition, however, does that mean you must choose to follow the ideas of Bultmann, discarding any supernatural or miraculous event as being pure myth?

Not necessarily. A middle ground is possible and it is one that sees the Bible as a mosaic of different types of literary styles or genres. Metaphors, allegories, idioms, hyperboles, and parables are all present throughout the Bible, in both Old and New Testaments, and are not meant to be taken literally. Ⓔ

Chapter 4
Salvation History

The Bible is a collection of stories, especially in the Old Testament, of how God made a covenant with His people, and despite their frequent infidelity, He kept forgiving them. This chapter looks at the perspective of the Bible as a testimony to "salvation history": one big story of faith from Creation in Genesis to the end of the world in Revelation. It covers the past and the future with our present in between.

What Is Salvation History?

History is primarily a narrative of past events. Salvation is the deliverance from the consequences of sin. Salvation history is the story of humankind—from Creation to the Fall, to the Promise and Covenant, and ending in the fulfillment achieved by Christ's redemptive death and Resurrection. Where secular history lists facts, dates, and other details, salvation history focuses not so much on the minute details as on the substance—the salvation of the human race by the Savior. There is obvious overlap between profane or secular history and salvation history since there is only one timeline the human race follows.

Many Christian religions are open to a modified form of evolution, which tries to balance scientific discovery and theological truth. Rather than blindly accepting the premise that human beings evolved from apes, this adapted theory maintains that God allowed natural processes to work and once a human body was present, he infused it with an immortal soul.

Prehistoric and Primeval Time

"Prehistoric" means anything that occurred before recorded (written) history. The problem with that is that since no one documented it, much is speculation based on archeological artifacts and fossil remains. Strict Creationists dismiss the idea of prehumans (Neanderthals) living in caves and gradually evolving into human beings (homo sapiens). They maintain that based on the Genesis account of Creation, God created human beings separate from animals. Strict Evolutionists, however, claim that all humans developed from prehuman, ape ancestry. A possible middle ground is the theory that Neanderthals coexisted with human beings (homo sapiens) and while similar to the human race, they were a distinct and separate species that became extinct.

The Antediluvian Period

It is possible humans developed alongside other species with similar characteristics, but retained their unique DNA. Similarity, however, does not prove common ancestry. Also, the existence of cavemen does not contradict the Bible since no specific time is mentioned in Genesis as to when Adam was created or when the Flood of Noah occurred. What happened in between, often called the antediluvian period, may never be fully discovered or known.

FACT

The Bible is not a science, biology, history, or cosmology book. It is a book of faith. The religious answers it contains are to religious questions that humankind has had from time immemorial. Comparing religious truths to anthropology, paleontology, and other sciences is like comparing apples and oranges.

The Fall

The book of Genesis begins with the Creation of the world and the first human beings, Adam and Eve. Chapter 3 describes the sin of disobedience that Adam and Eve committed against God, which resulted in their expulsion (the Fall) from the Garden of Eden. This is also known as the Original Sin since it was the first transgression ever committed by human beings—which ultimately affected human nature itself, and is, therefore, inherited by all men and women. Spiritually speaking, many Christians believe that the sin of Adam and Eve wounded human nature and while not destroying or corrupting it, the wound was so deep that only a Savior or Messiah could remedy it.

Three's Company

According to the Bible, after God expelled Adam and Eve from the Garden of Eden, he first cursed Eve, saying: "I will greatly increase your pains in childbearing; with pain you will give birth to children. Your desire will be for your husband, and he will rule over you" (Genesis

3:16). To Adam, God said: "Cursed is the ground because of you; through painful toil you will eat of it all the days of your life. It will produce thorns and thistles for you, and you will eat the plants of the field. By the sweat of your brow you will eat your food until you return to the ground, since from it you were taken; for dust you are and to dust you will return" (Genesis 3:17–19).

ESSENTIAL

Adam and Eve had two sons, Cain and Abel. Cain eventually murdered his brother and became an outcast. Eve later gave birth to Seth, who carried on the lineage. Seth had a son named Enosh, who had Kenan; who had Mahalalel, the father of Jared; who had Enoch, who was the father of Methusela; who had Lamech, who had Noah.

Noah's Ark

The Book of Genesis then continues with the story of Noah's Ark. Once human beings populated the earth, they became evil and sinful in the eyes of God. To punish them, God sent a forty-day deluge, but decided to save one righteous man—Noah. He ordered Noah to build an ark, where he was to house two of every kind of animal, as well as his entire family. As the monstrous rains covered the lands, all the evil people drowned, but Noah was saved. God then made a covenant with Noah never to destroy all living creatures again. Noah and the animals began a new life for the world.

Tower of Babel

Soon after the covenant was made, human beings decided to build the Tower of Babel. According to the Bible, this was a monument to human pride, power, and arrogance rather than an attempt to invade heaven, as some maintain. Up to this time, everyone spoke the same language, but to punish the people for their misdeeds, God scattered the human race all over the world and confused their language (hence the word "babel").

Just as human genetic science has shown that the entire human race can trace itself genetically to one human woman via mitochondrial DNA, linguistic experts now believe every spoken language has common roots in an original proto-language, which was known and used by everyone at one time.

The Age of the Patriarchs

Abraham is the first person of the Bible who can be given some chronological dating. The problem is that there is no exact or hard evidence for a specific year, so scholars continue to debate whether he was born in 2000 B.C. or 1800 B.C., with most endorsing the latter date. Abraham, his son Isaac, grandson Jacob (later known as Israel), and great-grandson Joseph are known as the "biblical patriarchs." The twelve sons of Jacob later became the patriarchs or heads of the twelve tribes of Israel.

Father Abraham

The first of the principal patriarchs, Abram, was from Ur (modern-day Southern Iraq), and God chose him to establish a covenant (*berith* in Hebrew; *testamentum* in Latin, the basis for the English word "testament") with him and his descendants forever. Abram later became known as Abraham and his fidelity to God was tested and rewarded. It is believed his wife Sarai also had her name changed to Sarah.

Though more is written and known about Moses the Lawgiver, Abraham, as the Father of Many Nations, retains the place of being the first patriarch and the one with whom God sealed the covenant. The three major monotheistic religions of Judaism, Christianity, and Islam trace their roots back to Abraham in some way.

Isaac's half-brother Ishmael was the son of Abraham and his maidservant Hagar. Islam claims its connection to Abraham through Ishmael, whereas Judaism flows from the line of Abraham and Isaac.

Isaac

Isaac, Abraham's son, continued the legacy as the second of the patriarchs. Isaac's wife Rebecca came from Mesopotamia and gave them two sons, Esau and Jacob. According to the Bible, Isaac is considered to be Abraham's beloved son, but his father was still willing to sacrifice him as a sign of his loyalty to God. Fortunately, an angel stopped Abraham from killing Isaac, who then helped fulfill the covenant by continuing the line of Abraham as God intended:

"When they reached the place God had told him about, Abraham built an altar there and arranged the wood on it. He bound his son Isaac and laid him on the altar, on top of the wood. Then he reached out his hand and took the knife to slay his son. But the angel of the Lord called out to him from heaven, 'Abraham! Abraham!' 'Here I am,' he replied. 'Do not lay a hand on the boy,' he said. 'Do not do anything to him. Now I know that you fear God, because you have not withheld from me your son, your only son.' Abraham looked up and there in a thicket he saw a ram caught by its horns. He went over and took the ram and sacrificed it as a burnt offering instead of his son. So Abraham called that place The Lord Will Provide. And to this day it is said, 'On the mountain of the Lord it will be provided.' The angel of the Lord called to Abraham from heaven a second time and said, 'I swear by myself, declares the Lord, that because you have done this and have not withheld your son, your only son, I will surely bless you and make your descendants as numerous as the stars in the sky and as the sand on the seashore. Your descendants will take possession of the cities of their enemies, and through your offspring all nations on earth will be blessed, because you have obeyed me.'"

(Genesis 22:9–18)

The Hebrew concept of "only son" or "firstborn son" has to do with legal birthright, that is, who inherits the clan and all the family wealth. Ishmael was the first biological son of Abraham from his mother Hagar, but Isaac was the first and only son born from Abraham's wife Sarah.

Hagar was a servant, Sarah the wife. Offspring of the wife have precedence and priority in terms of birthright. Children born not of the wife only have legal claim if there are no children born of the wife.

Jacob

It is believed Esau's younger brother, Jacob, used his wits to accomplish his ambitions. Whereas Esau married two Hittite women against the desires of his parents, Jacob married a girl within his clan. He fell in love with Rachel, but in order to get her hand in marriage, Jacob agreed to work seven years for her father Laban. After the seven years had passed and the wedding day arrived, Jacob discovered that Laban had switched daughters on him. Instead of marrying Rachel, he married the eldest daughter Leah.

After another seven years of work, however, Jacob finally got his true love. He had two sons with Rachel, named Joseph and Benjamin, whereas Leah gave him six: Reuben, Simeon, Levi, Judah, Isaachar, and Zebulun. Two other wives gave Dan, Naphtali, Gad, and Asher. Then after wrestling an angel, Jacob received a new name, Israel. His twelve sons became the twelve tribes of Israel, and God's chosen people.

Joseph

According to the Bible, Joseph was Jacob's favorite son. His brothers, however, were jealous of the father's favoritism as well as of Joseph's light workload, and so they decided to get rid of him. After Jacob gave Joseph a beautiful cloak as a gift, his brothers sold him into slavery in Egypt. Joseph, however, did not resent his brothers, and later as Pharoah's governor even saved them from the famine ravaging the Egyptian lands.

The Exodus

The history of the Exodus, or the escape from the persecution in Egypt, is the history of the Hebrew people. Abraham was the first patriarch, but until Moses led God's people from Egypt into the desert, there was no hope for a nation. Freedom from slavery was first on the agenda, and so God chose Moses to lead His people.

FACT

It took forty years in the desert to reach the land of Canaan (modern-day Israel), or the Promised Land, due to the disobedience of God's people.

Exile and Captivity

After the Exodus from Egypt in 1250 B.C., the nation of Israel was not fully solidified until their first monarch, King Saul (1020–1000 B.C.). He was then followed by King David (1000–961 B.C.) and then by his son, King Solomon (961–922 B.C.). Under Solomon's son's rule, the kingdom was divided into two parts: the country of Israel to the north, and Judah to the south.

In 721 B.C., the Assyrians conquered the northern kingdom of Israel, and the Babylonians captured the south in about 586 B.C. This period of time was the Exile, the great scattering of the Israelites (Jews), and later became known as the Babylonian Captivity.

Greece, Rome, and Christianity

Alexander the Great's conquest of the Persians, in 333 B.C., marked the beginning of the Hellenization (process by which Greek culture and language influenced other cultures) of the region, incorporating what is known as the Holy Land (Israel and Palestine). General Pompey's conquest of Jerusalem, in 63 B.C., marked the period of Roman domination of the area. When Constantine issued the Edict of Milan in A.D. 313, thus legalizing Christianity, the Roman Empire quickly converted and ushered in a Christian era of dominance.

Chapter 5

Canon of Scripture

One of the controversial questions of the Bible is how to determine what books belong in it. Modern publishers print a table of contents in every Bible, listing the books of the Old and New Testaments. The inspired text begins with Genesis 1:1 and ends with Revelation 22:21. This chapter will examine the criteria for accepting or rejecting books of the Bible, and why there is a discrepancy between the Protestant and Catholic versions.

What's in the Bible?

The Bible was not written by one human author nor was it done all at one time. It took hundreds and hundreds of years to write individual books, which were later arranged in collections and finally combined to form the one single book now called the Bible. No list ever existed within the text of any inspired book as to which books belong in the Bible. The Christian Bible has two parts, the Old Testament and the New Testament.

ALERT!

The Hebrew Scriptures do not use the term Old Testament since that would imply there exists a New Testament and only the Christian Bible has both of these. When discussing relevant passages from the Christian Bible with a person of the Jewish faith, it's best to use terms like "Hebrew Scriptures" or just the specific name of the book—Genesis, Exodus, and so forth.

Hebrew Scriptures

The oldest grouping of books comes from the Old Testament, or otherwise called the Hebrew Scriptures. The *Torah* is the collection of the first five books, consisting of Genesis, Exodus, Leviticus, Numbers, and Deuteronomy. According to an old tradition, Moses himself wrote or edited and put together these books as the Jews wandered in the desert for forty years before reaching the Promised Land. Christians often refer to these books as the *Pentateuch* from the Greek words *penta + teukhos,* meaning "five scrolls."

TaNaK

The Jews, however, typically refer to these five books as the Torah, meaning "the law," since the law of Moses predominates the five books. The Torah is then combined with the *Nevi'im* (Prophets) and finally with *Ke'tuvim* (Writings). The acronym TaNaK is formed from these three groupings of books.

Bible Decisions

If the Bible itself doesn't say which books belong in it, then how did some books get chosen? It is an easy answer for faith traditions such as Eastern Orthodoxy and Roman Catholicism, which regard the teaching authority of the church as competent to decide on these matters. While not superior to the Word of God, these Christian religions also believe that one of the church's missions is to protect and interpret the Scriptures, as well as to obey and implement them.

Vincentian Canon

Most Protestant Christian churches depend on the Scriptures alone (*sola scriptura*) for authority, yet still question which books belong in the Bible. They use a principle invoked by Saint Vincent of Lerins in A.D. 434, "that which has been believed everywhere, always and by all" (*quod ubique, simper et ab omnibus*). This simple formula is used by religions that do not have a doctrine of church authority to guard and interpret Scripture. Basically, it depends on what has been established universally (or in most places), most of the time, and by mostly everyone. It is also called the "Vincentian canon."

FACT

Saint Vincent, an ecclesiastical writer in Southern Gaul (modern-day France) in the fifth century, wrote his famous canon in chapter 2 of the Commonitory. He used the pseudonym Peregrinus. He believed that the ultimate source of Christian truth was Holy Scripture and that the authority of the church was to be invoked to guarantee the correct interpretation of Scripture.

Church Fathers

The Doctors of the Church, Saint Athanasius (A.D. 296–373) and Saint Gregory Nazianzus (A.D. 325–389), recognized only the Palestinian (Hebrew) canon for the Old Testament and rejected the Alexandrian (Greek) canon. In A.D. 170, Melito of Sardis declared the collections of Hebrew Scriptures found in the Jerusalem church as the official Old

Testament canon for Asia Minor. Saint Jerome had some personal reservations about including the deuterocanonical books of the Old Testament, but did so anyway when he translated the Greek, Hebrew, and Aramaic texts into the Latin Vulgate. Saint Augustine, however, fully endorsed the older Greek canon in A.D. 397, as did the Third Council of Carthage that same year, and Pope Innocent I in A.D. 405.

It is crucial to ascertain the complete list of the authentic books of the Bible to ensure that no part of revelation is omitted or ignored, as well as to prevent distortion and corruption of the authentic Word by allowing false or artificial documents to take equal prominence.

Old Testament Canon

King Ptolemy II Philadelphus of Egypt (309–246 B.C.) established a magnificent library at Alexandria (Egypt) and wanted to enrich it with a copy of the sacred books of the Jews. Since the time of the Babylonian Captivity (586–538 B.C.) and subsequent Diaspora—when two-thirds of the Jews were exiled and dispersed away from the Holy Land—the majority of Jewish people could no longer read, write, or speak Hebrew. Most of them were fluent in Greek, however, which was the *lingua franca* (common tongue among peoples of various languages) at the time. It, therefore, became necessary to translate all the Hebrew texts into Greek, not just for the library, but for the Jews of the Diaspora, who could not read the Hebrew version.

Septuagint

According to legend, in 250 B.C., approximately seventy Jewish scholars took seventy to seventy-two days around the clock to translate all the sacred texts of the *Torah* (Law), *Nevi'im* (Prophets), and *Ke'tuvim* (Writings) into Greek. This became known as the Septuagint from the Latin *septuaginta*, meaning the number seventy.

Alexandrian Jews welcomed the Greek Septuagint with open arms, but the Palestinian Jews rejected it as being a hybrid or impure—they only recognized Hebrew versions and only books originally written in Hebrew. The Greek version had collected forty-six books total, seven of which were originally written in Greek. Those seven books would be a source of controversy for centuries to come.

FACT

The Septuagint is often abbreviated with the Roman numerals LXX, which equals seventy. Legend says seventy to seventy-two scholars took seventy or more days to translate the Hebrew Scriptures into Greek, so the LXX became a shorthand means of writing the name Septuagint. Actually, the development of the Septuagint spans 100 years from 250–150 B.C., so, the name is, therefore, a misnomer.

Palestinian Canon

The Jews in the Holy Land, who had survived the Babylonian Captivity, clung tightly to their Hebrew identity. At that time, the Holy Land was known as Palestine and so the term "Palestinian canon" referred only to the books of Hebrew Scripture, which the Jews recognized in about A.D. 100 at the Council of Jamnia. By the first century B.C., however, the Alexandrian (Greek) canon was well known and used even by Jews of the Holy Land. By the time of Jesus, it was an unwritten and unspoken presumption that the complete list of forty-six books was allowable for study and worship.

Alexandrian Canon

The Jews of the Diaspora, who did not live in the Holy Land and who were not fluent in the Hebrew language, widely accepted the Septuagint. Combined with the thirty-nine books originally written in Hebrew, the Septuagint (containing forty-six books) established the first written canon of Scripture.

Old Testament Books

The canonical books of the Old Testament consisted of:

- Genesis
- Exodus
- Leviticus
- Numbers
- Deuteronomy
- Joshua
- Judges
- Ruth
- 1 and 2 Samuel
- 1 and 2 Kings
- 1 and 2 Chronicles
- Ezra
- Nehemiah
- Esther
- Job
- Psalms
- Proverbs
- Ecclesiastes
- Song of Solomon
- Isaiah
- Jeremiah
- Lamentations
- Ezekiel
- Daniel
- Hosea
- Joel
- Amos
- Obadiah
- Jonah
- Micah
- Nahum
- Habakkuk

Zephaniah

Haggai

Zechariah

Malachi

Second or Deuterocanon: Tobit, Judith, Wisdom, Sirach, Baruch, 1 & 2 Maccabees

New Testament Canon

The Council of Laodicea (A.D. 363) and the Third Council of Carthage (A.D. 397) declared the number of books for the New Testament to be twenty-seven. These were composed of the four Gospels, the Epistles and Acts, and the Book of Revelation. They were originally written in Greek, but in A.D. 394, Saint Jerome translated them into Latin and compiled the first complete Bible containing both the Old and New Testaments. At the request of the pope in Rome, he also included the seven deuterocanonical books in the Christian Bible.

FACT

In A.D. 100, Jerusalem (Israel) officially rejected both the Greek language of the text and the addition of the seven extra books: Tobit, Judith, Wisdom, Sirach (Ecclesiasticus), Baruch, 1 and 2 Maccabees, as well as additions to Daniel and Esther.

Books of the New Testament

The New Testament consists of:

Matthew

Mark

Luke

John

Acts

Romans

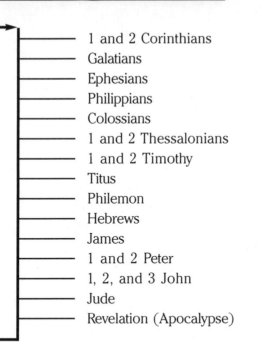

- 1 and 2 Corinthians
- Galatians
- Ephesians
- Philippians
- Colossians
- 1 and 2 Thessalonians
- 1 and 2 Timothy
- Titus
- Philemon
- Hebrews
- James
- 1 and 2 Peter
- 1, 2, and 3 John
- Jude
- Revelation (Apocalypse)

Catholic and Orthodox Perspective

Both the Eastern Orthodox and the Roman Catholic churches recognize and accept the authenticity of the deuterocanonical books as first listed in the Septuagint Bible and later translated into the Latin Vulgate. The fact that these seven books were not originally written in Hebrew is not a problem for them since all the New Testament books were written in Greek.

Even though Protestants regard the second canon of the Old Testament as not inspired, often you will find them listed as Apocrypha and inserted at the end of the canonical books, before the New Testament. This is an attempt to recognize that even though considered noninspired, they may be of some benefit.

The other point is that the Jewish scholars did not officially denounce and reject these books until A.D. 100. Until the destruction of the Temple in Jerusalem in A.D. 70, Christianity was tolerated to a degree as a fringe element of Judaism. After the Romans plundered the Holy City, the Jewish leaders regrouped and eliminated all accretions, additions, and infiltrations of anything not Jewish or Hebrew.

Protestant Perspective

Since the time of Martin Luther, John Calvin, John Knox, and John Wesley, Protestants have embraced the Palestinian (Jewish) canon of the Old Testament. The Catholic and Orthodox churches, on the other hand, retained the Alexandrian (Greek) canon. Relying on Scripture alone, the Protestants often invoke the previously mentioned Vincentian Canon to determine what belongs to the Christian faith: "that which has been believed everywhere, always and by all." Melito, Bishop of Sardis (A.D. 170), was the first Christian to list books of the Old Testament, but only used the Hebrew canon (thirty-nine books), which omitted the (seven) deuterocanonical/apocryphal books. Ⓔ

Chapter 6
The Abandoned Books

Go into any local bookstore and often near the religious books section you will see some "lost books of the Bible." However, these books were never lost— they were abandoned. Written between 100 B.C. and A.D. 100, they never made it into the Christian or Hebrew Bibles—they are not considered inspired and therefore have no guarantee of inerrancy. This chapter will look at what these books are and why they were left out.

Apocrypha or Pseudepigrapha?

The term *Apocrypha* means "hidden" and is often used to describe the seven books of the deuterocanon (from the Greek *deutero* meaning "second canon") of the Septuagint. Protestants use the word in that way as well, but Catholics and Orthodox Christians use Apocrypha exclusively for books they do not consider inspired nor found in any Bible. Protestants refer to Apocrypha as *Pseudepigrapha*, meaning falsely ascribed. Therefore, it matters whether the source using the term is Protestant, Catholic, or Orthodox since there are two ways in which the word Apocrypha is used today.

FACT

Even though some Christian churches classify the deuterocanonical books as Apocrypha, they do not use the same term for the books never regarded as inspired. Books that they call Pseudepigrapha are never found in any Bible, yet deuterocanonical/apocryphal books can often be found at the end of the Old Testament.

Catholic Deuterocanonical Books

The Roman Catholic Old Testament has seven deuterocanonical books: Baruch, 1 and 2 Maccabees, Tobit, Judith, Ecclesiasticus (Sirach), and Wisdom, which are from the Greek Septuagint (250–150 B.C.) and the Latin Vulgate (A.D. 400). In A.D. 1546, the Council of Trent solemnly defined their status as equal to the thirty-nine canonical books of the Old Testament.

Orthodox Deuterocanonical Books

The Greek Orthodox Old Testament has the seven deuterocanonical books, as well as 1 Esdras, Psalm 151, Prayer of Manasseh, and 3 Maccabees (with 4 Maccabees in the appendix). The Russian Orthodox Old Testament has the same seven books, plus 1 and 2 Esdras (listed as 2 and 3 Esdras), Psalm 151, and 3 Maccabees.

The Syrian Orthodox Church and all connected Eastern Churches regard the *Peshitta* with the same authority as the Septuagint or Vulgate. In Aramaic, the name Peshitta means "straight," as in straight from the original common Aramaic language spoken by Jesus and all Jews of his time. In 1642, the Council of Jassy (Romania) declared the deutero-canonical/apocryphal books as genuine Scripture.

Whether they are called pseudepigrapha or apocryphal, there are several books that never appeared in any Bible. Unlike the allegedly dubious seven deuterocanonical books first found in the Septuagint, the others are not listed in any canon—be it Hebrew, Greek, or Latin.

Historical Origins

Many of the apocryphal/pseudepigraphical writings from both the Old and New Testaments came from various sources. Often one anonymous person wrote them, having something to say about the local government or local religious leaders of his time. Fabricating stories was a way to promote ideas, stir up dissent, and antagonize the enemy. Jews living inside and outside the Holy Land, Christians, as well as many other hybrids of Judaism, Christianity, and Paganism, created their own writings to proliferate doctrines much different than those espoused by Jews or Christians.

ALERT!

The author, date, and place of the manuscript are not the primary criteria upon which one judged books as inspired or not. Even if an archeologist found an original parchment from the Virgin Mary, or from John the Baptist, while historically invaluable, they would not automatically be declared and accepted as divinely inspired.

Flavius Josephus

Authenticity is not the only component of Divine Inspiration. Neither is veracity alone. In A.D. 93, Flavius Josephus published a history of the Jews, and even mentioned the name of Jesus, referring to Him as the

Messiah. While Christians regard the statement as true—and verified that Josephus was the author of the text and indeed wrote it in the first century A.D.—none of his writings was ever considered inspired. His history of the Jews—before, during, and after Jesus—are accurate accounts, yet they were never included in the Bible since the church never considered them divinely inspired.

Endorsements

Ancient writings were often ascribed to famous authors. It was not so much that the original author actually hoped to impersonate someone else, but affixing a well-known name to a writing ensured it would be read and copied. Students and disciples of great masters used their mentor's name and writing style to convey an important message. Apocryphal writings are more of this genre than the New Testament Gospels and Epistles, which have been identified with their reputed authors as listed in the Bible.

QUESTION?

Isn't attaching one's name to someone else's work plagiarism? Today, plagiarism is considered illegal and immoral. Long ago, attaching famous names to someone else's work was a marketing technique that most readers expected anyway as long as the document was faithful to the same ideals and came from the same region and/or time frame.

Religious Overtones

The Gnostics were best known for spreading apocryphal literature. They blended and borrowed from Asian, Babylonian, Egyptian, Greek, and Syrian pagan religions, astrology, the occult, as well as Judaism and Christianity to formulate a system of beliefs meant to be kept secret. *Gnosis* means "knowledge," and the Gnostics prided themselves on knowing the "secret" to salvation. Making a mysterious and eclectic system of doctrines and rituals attracted people who were fascinated by the bizarre.

ESSENTIAL

The original King James Version (KJV), the most famous and most popular of all the Protestant Bibles, had the deutero-canonical /apocryphal books printed after the canonical Old Testament books, just before the New Testament. Later editions of the KJV completely removed these.

Strange Tales

Although various miracles are told of in the Bible, both in the Old and New Testaments, the noninspired apocryphal/pseudepigraphical books are preoccupied and obsessed with supernatural phenomena. This is one indicator of a Gnostic influence. "Bizarre" and "incredible" are better adjectives for the stories these writings contain, whereas the canonical and deuterocanonical have plenty of genuine miraculous events within them.

Here is a selection from the Arabic Infancy gospel, one of the many noninspired apocryphal texts:

"... The eighth day, being at hand, the child was to be circumcised according to the law. Wherefore they circumcised Him in the cave. And the old Hebrew woman took the piece of skin; but some say that she took the navel-string, and laid it past in a jar of old oil of nard. And she had a son, a dealer in unguents, and she gave it to him, saying: See that thou do not sell this jar of unguent of nard, even although 300 denarii should be offered thee for it. And this is that jar which Mary the sinner bought and poured upon the head and feet of our Lord Jesus Christ, which there-after she wiped with the hair of her head."

Incongruities

Historical inaccuracies, logical gaps of chronology, and people and places that never existed except in myth and folklore are also part of the so-called "missing books." Therefore, it might be better to consider these fanciful fables as historical-biblical fiction. Because they're not believed to have been divinely inspired, the apocryphal/pseudepigraphical books have no gift of inerrancy either. There are many substantial inconsistencies and contradictions between the biblical books (canonical and deuterocanonical/apocryphal) and the esoteric apocryphal/pseudegraphical, so when Christians are in doubt, they generally rely on the inspired text.

FACT

The names of Jesus' maternal grandparents, Joachim and Ann, are only mentioned in the apocryphal Protevangelium of James (distinct from his canonical Epistle). Nevertheless, Sacred Tradition and Christian custom have embraced these identities. "Noninspired" does not mean the contents are false or untrue, just that they are not divinely inspired.

Chapter 1 of the Gnostic Pistis Sophia, for example, says, "It happened that after Jesus had risen from the dead he spent eleven years speaking with his disciples. And he taught them only as far as the places of the first ordinance and as far as the places of the First Mystery."

Christians consider this statement untrue, since they firmly believe that Jesus ascended into Heaven forty days after His Resurrection, not eleven years. Secondly, the statement contains an implication of hidden secrets that Jesus did not teach His disciples everything they needed to know.

The reference to untold, unrevealed, and secret information is the essence of Gnosticism. It also contradicts the Judaeo-Christian notion of complete revelation—that God revealed all that was needed. What was not revealed—such as the exact day, time, and year of the end of the world—remains a secret, and not one person knows the answer to this "because you do not know the day or the hour" (Matthew 25:13).

ESSENTIAL

Using Egyptian prayers from the Book of the Dead and other pagan sources, the Gnostics cut and pasted a diverse collection of mythologies and folklore, which promoted the secretive idea that the spiritual life was too complicated for mere mortals to comprehend. Manichaeanism or Dualism also heavily influenced the Gnostics, claiming that good and evil are equal forces and that God and the devil are rivals.

Abandoned for a Reason

The abandoned or "lost" books of the Old and New Testament canons are not missing in the sense that they were once in the Bible and someone took them out intentionally or inadvertently. Rather, they are missing because they are not considered inspired.

Bizarre tales—such as the alleged boyhood of Jesus where He supposedly turns clay birds into real ones—might be good comic book material but have no effect on the spiritual life of an individual. They have been "missing" from the Bible from the time of Jerome's Vulgate (390–405 A.D.), all the way through Martin Luther in the sixteenth century, and continuing to today. However, New Age and other movements have "rediscovered" some of these writings.

Old Testament Apocrypha

The most significant apocryphal books of the Old Testament are: the Books of Adam and Eve, Apocalypse of Moses, Book of Enoch, Apocalypse of Adam, Apocalypse of Abraham, Martyrdom of Isaiah, Testaments of the Twelve Patriarchs, and the Book of Jubilees. These books were never regarded as inspired by any church or religion, and even genuine works of their alleged author do not change their status. They can, however, be categorized into three types: apocalyptic, historical, and didactic.

Apocalyptic Apocrypha

The books of Enoch, Assumption of Moses, 4 Esdras, Apocalypse of Baruch, Apocalypse of Abraham, Apocalypse of Elijah, Testament of Abraham, Apocalypse of Zephaniah, and the Sibylline Oracles fit into the apocalyptic apocrypha. These texts use colorful imagery, prolific metaphors, and cryptic symbolism, and offer encouragement to those being persecuted or discouraged that there is a hopeful future.

Historical Apocrypha

The books of Jubilees, 3 Esdras, 3 Maccabees, Apocalypse of Moses, Ascension of Isaiah, Testament of Job, and Testament of Solomon are considered historical apocrypha. This style blends biblical narrative from the inspired books with legend and folklore to tell a more colorful story of past events.

Didactic Apocrypha

The Testaments of the Twelve Patriarchs, Psalm 151, Psalms of Solomon, Prayer of Manassah, and 4 Maccabees are called didactic apocrypha because they tend to focus on giving a moral or ethical message. Of the three Old Testament Apocrypha types, this one more closely resembles the inspired canonical text, which is why a few of these books have been found along with the biblical books merely for their teaching value.

Angels and demons play a major part in Old Testament Apocrypha. Fallen angels, as told in these books, allegedly married human women and had children with them. These hybrid angel-human beings were giants known as Nephilim who ate human flesh.

The Angel Stories

The apocryphal Book of Enoch lists the three angels mentioned in the canonical text—Michael, Raphael, and Gabriel—but also includes angelic identities, such as Uriel and Phanuel. The Book of Adam tells how the devil was first an angel who fell the day Adam was created. According to the story, Michael took Adam as soon as God created him and asked the other angels to bow down before the image and likeness of God. The devil refused and his act of defiance cost him an eternity in hell.

The Psalms of Solomon

The Psalms of Solomon are an apocryphal work. They parallel the themes contained in the inspired canonical Psalms of David in the Bible and are suspected to have been written around 63 B.C., when the Roman general Pompey captured Jerusalem. There are eighteen apocryphal Psalms in this noncanonical book.

FACT

The gospel (Protevangelium) of James and the Assumption of Mary, while never considered inspired, have nonetheless been considered helpful insofar as being a possible source of incidental and peripheral information on the early life of the Virgin Mary and her final days on earth.

New Testament Apocrypha

The apocryphal books of the New Testament are just as numerous as those of the Old Testament. The significant ones are: Gospel of Thomas, Gospel of James, Gospel of Nicodemus, Gospel of Peter, Death of Pilate, Acts of Andrew, Acts of Barnabas, Passing of Mary, History of Joseph the Carpenter, Apocalypse of Peter, and the Revelation of Paul. Like their counterparts in the apocryphal Old Testament, these books were never considered inspired.

Chapter 7

Versions and Translations

Bibles come in all kinds of varieties and flavors, so to speak. They come in different languages and are classified by how close or accurate they are to the original Greek and Hebrew text. This chapter will examine the differences between various Bible translations with the hope of helping the reader find the one most useful for him or her.

Languages of the Bible

Hebrew is the first language of the Bible and most of the Old Testament was written in it. Aramaic is the second language and it is derived from Hebrew. Whereas Hebrew was the official liturgical language for temple and synagogue worship, as well as for writing and proclaiming the sacred texts, Aramaic is what the common folk spoke at home and at work. Jesus and His apostles spoke Aramaic as well as Hebrew. Greek is the third language of the Bible. It was the best language at the time for spreading the gospel because even the Latin-speaking Roman Empire used Greek for commerce and diplomacy. The New Testament was written in Greek as were the seven deuterocanonical/apocryphal books of the Old Testament.

You do not need to know these three languages to read the Bible since it is now available in the vernacular (everyday language). Even the English translations, however, retain several key Hebrew, Aramaic, and Greek words. *Selah* is a Hebrew word that appears seventy-five times in numerous Psalms of the English Bible and is never translated. *Maranatha* is an Aramaic word ("Our Lord has come"), which appears transliterated in the Bible (1 Corinthians 16). Jesus says, "I am the *Alpha* and the *Omega*" in the Book of Revelation (22:13). These are the first and the last letters of the Greek alphabet.

FACT

After the Edict of Milan (A.D. 313) when Emperor Constantine legalized Christianity, but especially from Charlemagne (A.D. 800) until the time of the Renaissance (fourteenth century A.D.), anyone who could read and write in Western Europe could also read, write, and speak Latin, the language of the University and Law as well as the church.

Latin

No book of the Bible was originally written in Latin, yet by the end of the fourth century A.D., Christians in the Roman Empire needed a Latin translation of the sacred texts since it was the official language in the West. In A.D. 394, Pope Damasus commissioned Saint Jerome to translate the extant Hebrew, Aramaic, and Greek texts into one common language (Latin) and in one complete volume (Bible). After six years, in A.D. 400, the task was completed and the first complete, one volume Bible, containing the Old and New Testaments, was published.

English

An English scholar, Venerable Bede, wrote the Anglo-Saxon versions of the Bible, and it first appeared in fragments as far back as the eighth century A.D. By A.D. 600, Saint Augustine of Canterbury had converted the Britons. After the Norman Conquest (A.D. 1066), work was under way to render an Anglo-Norman translation. In A.D. 1384, John Wycliffe produced an English version of the Bible, but the church did not approve it since his teachings had been condemned as heretical. Thus, there was fear that his translation was tainted.

Vernacular translations were not forbidden nor undesired. The hesitancy in *approving* translations was based on the fact that church Bible scholars wanted to ensure accurate translations. Latin had been around quite a long time, whereas modern European languages were still establishing formal rules of grammar, syntax, and vocabulary.

In A.D. 1525, William Tyndale, a Protestant, was next to translate an English Bible. He was followed by the Coverdale Bible in A.D. 1535, then by the Great Bible in A.D. 1541, the Geneva Bible in A.D. 1560, and finally by the Bishops' Bible in A.D. 1568.

The Douay-Rheims Bible (A.D. 1582–1609) was the first Catholic Bible translated in English since the Reformation and predated the King James Version by two years.

Autographs and Copies

When biblical scholars speak of autographs, they don't mean the kind you get at the baseball or football game from your favorite player. An autograph in this case means the original document written in the hand of the sacred author himself. Unfortunately, none exists anymore. They have all been lost or destroyed over time. What are available are copies of the autographs and copies of the copies. These were copied by hand, often by religious monks who painstakingly and scrupulously copied manuscript after manuscript until the invention of the printing press, of course.

Copying Mistakes

While the original autograph is considered to be the inspired and inerrant text, copies and translations, on the other hand, do not carry the same absolute guarantee. One can be reasonably confident that accurate translations protect the integrity of the original text but only the autograph has the complete assurance of inerrancy. Human beings can make mistakes when copying manuscripts and yet the substance can still remain intact.

Here is a list of some types of errors:

- **"Dittography"** is the accident whereby a copier writes something twice instead of once (e.g., "latter" instead of "later").
- **"Fission"** is improperly dividing a word (e.g., "nowhere" into "now here").
- **"Fusion"** is combining the last letter of one word with the first letter of the next (e.g., "there in" becomes "therein").
- **"Haplography"** is writing once what should have been written twice (e.g., "later" instead of "latter").
- **"Homophony"** is confusing a word with the same pronunciation but different meaning (e.g., "their" instead of "there").
- **"Metathesis"** is mixing up the order of letters in a word (e.g., "cast" instead of "cats").

Bible Translation Styles

There is an old Italian proverb which says *"traduttorre traditore,"* the translator is a traitor. This just means that often whenever anyone translates any document—be it Scripture or not—from the native language of the author and the original audience to another language, choices will have to be made and some meaning may be inadvertently changed or modified. Someone seeking an idiomatic translation, for example, does not care about the word for word equivalence of the original language into the translated one. He or she merely wants to convey and communicate the same or pretty identical idioms (ideas). Even literal translations have to make changes or choices as words have double meanings in different languages.

Many people make these same mistakes today and your computer will not discover them since there is no misspelling involved, per se. Only the *context* determines how the word should be spelled. Imagine monks copying by hand with quill and ink late at night by dim candlelight. Errors would be inevitable.

Formal Correspondence Translation

Formal correspondence translation is an attempt to make a literal translation with a word for word correspondence, when possible. It also seeks to retain the same word order from the original into the translated language. The problem is that grammar rules are different for each language. Latin, for instance, likes to leave the verb at the end of the sentence, whereas in English it likes to be as close as possible to the noun associated with it. Examples of this style of translation are: King James Version, New King James Version, Douay-Rheims, Revised Standard Version, New Revised Standard Version, New American Bible, and the New International Version.

Dynamic Equivalence Translation

This style of translation does not enslave itself to exact same word for word equivalence, but seeks to provide a faithful equivalent, which is more comprehensible to the reader or listener in the translated tongue. Dynamic equivalence translation tries to say what the author meant, whereas the formal correspondence relies on remaining faithful to the original text and leaving the reader or listener the task of determining what the author wanted to convey. Examples of this type of translation are: New English Bible, Revised English Bible, Jerusalem Bible, New Jerusalem Bible, Today's English Version, and the Contemporary English Version.

QUESTION?

How did the churches prevent people from stealing early Bibles? Until the printing press, hand copied Bibles were expensive and valuable, hence objects of desire by thieves. Therefore, like pens in today's banks, the Bibles were chained to the church's pews to keep them from being stolen.

Biblical Paraphrase

The paraphrased translation is not so much a translation as modified, revised, condensed, abridged, or reworded renderings of accurate translations but phrased with words and idioms common to the current times. John 1:14 is written in Greek as "*kai o logos sarx egeneto kai eskenosen*," which the literal (formal correspondence) translation renders as "the Word became flesh and made his dwelling among us" (New International Version, NIV); the loose (dynamic equivalence) translation says "the Word became a human being and lived here with us" (Contemporary English Version, CEV); the paraphrased translation reads "the Word became flesh and blood, and moved into the neighborhood" (The *Message* Version by Eugene Peterson); or "the Word became a human being and lived here on earth among us" (Living Bible Translation).

From Pen to Print

The sacred authors hand wrote the original manuscripts of the Bible. Religious scholars scrupulously made copies until the advent of the printing press. One of the quirks of modern biblical study is that since no original documents still exist, experts depend on copies of copies of the originals. The inerrancy resides in the original and there is no absolute guarantee for the copy, especially when it was done by hand. Furthermore, one or more persons wrote each book of the Bible as an individual book. Written on scrolls, no one back then came up with the idea or intention of collecting all the sacred books into one volume. When reading the Bible, then, do not presume the author knows what you know, nor what you have already read.

Only the sacred author who wrote the original autograph was divinely inspired and only that text is inerrant. The copier was never considered inspired nor inerrant. That means that there is no inspired nor inerrant version or edition of the Bible, either. No perfect version or edition exists today.

Bible Editions

Just as there are numerous translations into different languages and types of translations, there are also many versions of the Bible. Historical development, theological background, and other elements shape the type or version of the Bible that is in print. Many choose the King James or Douay-Rheims versions of the Bible, which use formal English ("Thee" and "Thou," for example). Others find the archaisms too difficult and prefer a simpler but still accurate version, such as the Revised Standard or New International.

Protestant Versions

Protestant versions of the Bible, such as the King James Version, Revised Standard Version, and New International Version, basically omit the deuterocanonical seven books in the Old Testament or retain them as Apocrypha. Commentary in the footnotes corresponds with Reformation Theology (e.g., the role of Peter and the church as found in

Matthew 16:18, the doctrine of the Eucharist as found in John 6, or the brethren of Jesus in Mark 6:3 are all treated differently in Catholic and in Protestant circles). Other than the deuterocanonical/apocryphal books, there is very little difference between Protestant and Catholic Bibles.

FACT

The Jerusalem Bible is actually an English translation (A.D. 1966) of the French Catholic Bible *La Sainte Bible* (A.D. 1954), so it is considered a translation of a translation, rather than a brand new interpretation. Nonetheless, it has excellent introductions and footnotes throughout the text.

King James Version (KJV)

The King James Version is the most popular and well-known English version of the Bible. In 1611, King James I commissioned it as the official or authorized version of the Bible in the English language. In 1607, fifty scholars worked at Oxford and Cambridge to produce this famous edition. The King James Version greatly influenced subsequent English literature based on its use of words and grammar.

FACT

The KJV was a vast improvement on the Wycliffe, Tyndale, Coverdale, and Bishops' Bibles, which preceded it. While an icon of the Protestant Bible, the King James did use and benefit from the Catholic English translation of Rheims in A.D. 1582, just as the Douay-Rheims benefited from the Coverdale, Bishops', and Geneva Bibles before it.

Revised Standard Version (RSV)

In 1937, the National Council of Churches invited forty denominations to revise the KJV, based on contemporary biblical scholarship, which had discovered several Greek manuscripts of Bible books older than anything previously available. Finished in 1946, the RSV did not replace the King James everywhere. However, it did give it good competition in that many found a benefit in the reduction of old English words—*thee* and *thou*. In addition, the New Revised Standard Version (NRSV) appeared in 1989.

Catholic Versions

Catholic versions, such as the Douay-Rheims, Knox, New American, Jerusalem, and RSV Catholic Edition, all have the deuterocanonical books in their proper places in the Old Testament. That is the biggest and most obvious difference. Rather than omitting them or relegating them to a position at the end of the Old Testament, these seven books are coordinated in the same location as they are in the Septuagint Greek version.

Douay-Rheims (DR)

This Catholic version of the Bible was written as an English translation for Catholics in exile from Elizabethan England, and was completed before the KJV. The New Testament was finished in Rheims (1582) and the Old Testament in Douay (1610). It relied heavily on the Latin Vulgate of Jerome rather than the translation from the Greek that other English Bibles depended on.

Monsignor Ronald Knox (Anglican convert to Catholicism) did a revision of the English translation (A.D. 1945) of the Latin Vulgate, trying to improve upon the Douay-Rheims by employing a more literary style. He tried to balance accuracy with good grammar and elegance.

New American Bible (NAB)

The Catholic Bishops of America had commissioned a revision of the 1941 Confraternity of Christian Doctrine (CCD) Version of the Bible, and in 1970—only five years after the close of the Second Vatican Council (1962–1965)—the New American Bible (NAB) was published. As a completely new translation from the Greek, Hebrew, and Aramaic sources—instead of an English translation of the Latin Vulgate—the NAB greatly influenced Catholics in the United States. The NAB became widely read and heard after the Second Vatican Council approved the Catholic Mass to be celebrated in the vernacular. Previously, the Mass—and all the Scripture readings—was said in Latin. Ⓔ

Chapter 8

Interpreting the Bible

This chapter will investigate universal methods anyone can use to take the biblical text from any version and make some basic and fundamental interpretations. The methods are not infallible nor foolproof, but work well for many who want to study and delve deeper into the meaning of God's Word. Hermeneutics and literary criticism will be explained so that anyone can try these tools out to see if they work.

Science of Interpretation

Bible scholars use the term "Hermeneutics" to describe the science of interpreting the Scriptures. It is a form of exegesis (critical analysis), which simply means to interpret the text of a document. Hermeneutics seeks to discover the intended meaning of the author by first closely examining the text and then its context. Words have different meanings when used in different contexts. A dictionary alone is not enough, since grammar, logic, and literary devices can all influence what the author intended to say and what he actually did say.

The Bible as literature (just like any other book) has three parts: the author, the message, and the audience. Hermeneutics involves the process of discerning what the message is, who sent it, and to whom it is addressed. When you see a stop sign, for example, you know the sender (the local civil authorities) intends for motor vehicle drivers (the receiver) to stop their cars at that intersection.

FACT

The word "Hermeneutics" is derived from the name Hermes, the Greek messenger god. The Romans also used the name Mercury for this same divine messenger. Hermes often brought messages from Zeus (Jupiter for the Romans) and so in Acts 14:12, the crowd at Lystra referred to Barnabas and Paul as Zeus and Hermes (Jupiter and Mercury).

Sender/Author

The name of the person who painted the stop sign or who put it up is irrelevant. The source is what counts. For believers, the ultimate author and source of the Bible is God, since it is His Word that is written down in the biblical text. The human author is not equally important but is not insignificant either. Also, unlike the sign painter, the sacred author did not just write what he was told—he retained his personality, opinions, preferences, tastes, background, education, intelligence, experience, and so forth before, during, and after he wrote the inspired text.

For example, knowing that Matthew or John were not only evangelists (Gospel writers) but also two of the original twelve apostles makes their accounts firsthand. Mark and Luke were never apostles, only disciples, and so their accounts are considered secondhand, corroborated by firsthand assistance—Peter for Mark and Virgin Mary for Luke.

In most cases, the messenger is distinct from the message and from the sender. The Bible is unique in that God is the ultimate sender, yet the sacred authors are both messengers and senders using their own free will, preferences, gifts, talents, and so on. The biblical text is the message.

Audience/Reader

The biblical texts were written by the sacred writers (proximate authors) and inspired by God (ultimate author). The readers are the ultimate intended audience. Back in the first century Ephesus (Turkey), a group of Christians was the proximate audience of Saint Paul's Epistle to the Ephesians. When reading the Bible, it is crucial to know the intended audience of God's Word. It, therefore, helps to understand when you read the letter to the Corinthians, for example, that Paul was writing to a Christian community, which had deteriorated and turned away from God.

Message

Since the ultimate source of the message is God, then the message is also of extreme importance. The content of the "Word" depends on what each individual word, phrase, sentence, paragraph, chapter, and book has to say. Accurately translating the original words is the first task, which scholars have been trying to do for centuries. The reader must also consider the definition of the words (content) as well as their arrangement (context). The literal, allegorical, moral, and anagogical senses need to be determined to interpret the true meaning.

Making Sense of the Bible

When somebody says, "That doesn't make sense," it means they are unable to figure out the meaning of the spoken or written words. Sense is the meaning words have by themselves and when placed in context with other words to form phrases and sentences. It is presumed that every word someone writes is intended to make sense—to convey an idea or message. Having accurate translations from original languages is, therefore, indispensable.

ALERT!

The Hebrew language uses hyperbole to express the superlative. Jesus uses a figure of speech in Matthew 5:29 when He says, "If your right eye causes you to sin, gouge it out and throw it away." The obvious exaggeration of physically removing your own eyeball is meant to make a point, and not promote an act of self-mutilation.

Literal Sense

This is the most necessary step to correctly interpret the Bible. The literal sense is namely the meaning of the word(s). When Jesus says, "I am the good shepherd. The good shepherd lays down his life for the sheep" (John 10:11), no one interprets that *literally* to mean Jesus is actually a shepherd tending to his flock of sheep on green pastures. Yet, the *literal sense* of the words "shepherd" and "sheep" is still necessary to understand what is meant by the author. Jesus still wants the literal sense of "shepherd" and "sheep" to be understood, so that in turn, the figurative meaning of the word or phrase becomes clear.

Figures of Speech

Literal sense can be further divided into figurative and proper speech. Again, the literal meaning of the word is essential to understand a figure of speech, such as, "I am the vine; you are the branches" (John 15:5). You need to know what is a "vine" and what is a "branch" just to know it is a figure of speech.

The various figures of speech are: metaphors, ironies, idioms, hyperboles, euphemisms, allegory, analogy, metonymy, synecdoche, and so on. When someone says, "He's pulling my leg," you would most likely infer that he means someone is playing a joke on him unless you never heard that expression (idiom). If that's the case, you would logically presume he means someone is physically tugging on his limb. Proper speech is always meant to be understood literally, as in the case of, "My name is John."

Literal Versus Figurative

A figure of speech is often quite obvious to recognize, such as in the case of "It is easier for a camel to go through the eye of a needle than for a rich man to enter the kingdom of God" (Mark 10:25). When Jesus says that His followers must "hate his [their] father and mother, his [their] wife and children, his [their] brothers and sisters" in Luke 14:26, this figure of speech means that a believer must love God more than even his own family. The literal interpretation, on the other hand, would be to despise and hate family, which would make no sense since one of the Ten Commandments is to love and honor one's parents.

FACT

Some biblical passages are difficult to interpret. For example, Catholics and Orthodox Christians literally interpret the passage "unless you eat the flesh of the Son of Man and drink his blood, you have no life in you" (John 6:53), whereas Protestants consider it figuratively.

Typical Sense

This is the deeper meaning that words and phrases have in the Bible because they are the inspired Word of God. Genesis 14 speaks of Melchizedek, a king and a priest who offers up bread and wine. This is used in the typical sense (also called typology) when connecting that same passage with Jesus Christ in Hebrews 7, describing Him as a king and priest who also offered up bread and wine.

Literary Forms

Again, the Bible is composed of different types of literature, inluding poetry, drama, epic, narrative, and even fiction (e.g., the parables). There are also prayers, hymns, poems, genealogies, dialogue, sermons, and epistles. Whether or not the text is to be understood literally or figuratively may be determined by the type of literary form used. Just picking up the Bible and reading it like a textbook or a newspaper will not always be possible. Knowing that a section uses metaphor or hyperbole or that you are reading a poem or hymn instead of a narrative or dialogue will help you accurately interpret the text.

When Jesus gives interpretations to the Commandments, Bible scholars say He is giving a fuller meaning to the original literal text. Hence, the Old Testament commandments forbidding murder and adultery are now given a deeper and fuller interpretation to also mean the desire and the willingness to do these deeds.

Parables

It is important to know accurately what words Jesus used when telling a parable, otherwise both the proximate and remote meanings will be lost. For instance, in the parable about the weeds and the wheat Jesus says:

"The kingdom of heaven is like a man who sowed good seed in his field. But while everyone was sleeping, his enemies came and sowed weeds among the wheat, and went away. When the wheat sprouted and formed heads, then the weeds also appeared.

The owner's servants came to him and said, 'Sir, didn't you sow good seed in your field? Where then did the weeds come from?'

'An enemy did this,' he replied.

The servants asked him, 'Do you want us to go and pull them up?'

'No,' he answered, 'because while you are pulling the weeds, you may root up the wheat with them. Let both grow together until they harvest.

At that time I will tell the harvesters: First collect the weeds and tie them in bundles to be burned; then gather the wheat and bring it into my barn.'"

(Matthew 13:24–30)

In this passage, the reader needs to look at the literal sense in order to understand the words "weed" and "wheat." Knowing the difference between them helps to interpret the passage as well as to understand the meaning of the parable—and thus the message Jesus is trying to convey through it. Parable means words are used symbolically and metaphorically. One interpretation of the above passage might be that weeds represent resistance to the Word of God as represented in the wheat.

Apocalyptic Writing

Apocalyptic literature is not as common as other forms, such as poetry, history, and genealogy. The author's intended audience is of his own time period and often one of persecution, so he writes to encourage and to affirm while also using symbolism, metaphor, and figurative language. Usually, apocalyptic writings place events in terms of a cosmic battle between good and evil. Even though the story is told as if it were to happen in the distant future or distant past, there is also an underlying theme of the present.

The Book of Daniel in the Old Testament and the Book of Revelation (Apocalypse) are examples of apocalyptic literature. The Book of Daniel wanted to encourage the Jews, who were being tormented by the Seleucid King Antiochus IV Epiphanes, by placing the scene in the past at the Babylonian court of Nebuchadnezzar. The Book of Revelation wanted to encourage the Christians being attacked by Emperor Domitian by placing the time and place into the far future. Since both books are considered inspired, the key here is not the details since they are symbolic, but the overall big picture and message.

Also, numbers are used throughout apocalyptic writings, again, not for details but for their symbolic meaning. "Three" is considered a divine number representing God (good, better, best), hence the threefold "Holy, holy, holy." "Four" symbolizes the earthly world as in the "four corners of the earth" due to the four elements of earth, wind, water, and fire. "Six" represents man as he was created on the sixth day. The number "Seven" signifies the seven days of the creation, and seven days of the week. "Twelve" is the number of religion, as in the twelve tribes of Israel and the twelve apostles.

ALERT!

The use of allegory and metaphor do not mean that the prophecies contained in apocalyptic books (e.g., Daniel or Revelation) are not real. Apocalyptic writing contains messages for both the then present as well as for the later future.

Text and Context

It is important to know the text and the context in which the text is found. Jesus says in Matthew 7:6, "Do not give dogs what is sacred; do not throw your pearls to pigs." First, look at the text and think about what "dogs," "sacred," "pearls," and "pigs" mean—the literal sense. Then look at the context. No one in his right mind would give something expensive, valuable, or sacred to a wild animal. However, besides the obvious, many Christians also see this passage as a reminder that all too often humans squander the truly invaluable and precious gifts God has given them, such as life, faith, family, in place of materialistic things the world offers.

Integrity and Diversity

It is believed that each and every book of the Bible is inspired and inerrant. One can read Genesis and understand it all by itself, but the fuller meaning only comes when placed in the context with the whole Bible. Similarly, the Gospels, which tell of Jesus' words and deeds, have more impact when you see the fulfillment of Old Testament prophecies. This is why no one Gospel gives a complete portrait of Christ. Each one is like a different facet of a diamond and all of them together show the beauty of the whole. When reading one verse, one chapter, or one book, try to see its connection with the others that come before or after it.

Braving the Ambiguous

There are various ambiguous or difficult passages in the Bible and you will run across them from time to time. If your faith tradition has an ecclesiastical (church) teaching authority, then consult the appropriate creeds or catechisms since they often address some of these Bible verses. If your faith tradition, on the other hand, regards the Bible as the sole rule and ultimate authority, you may want to get a general consensus of fellow believers, your pastor, and respected scholars to see what the collective wisdom might show.

Getting Help

When it comes to difficult and problematic biblical sayings (as opposed to apparent contradictions and mistakes), the reader is challenged to do more study, research, prayer, and meditation. Another biblical text or perhaps a scholarly commentary might aid in overcoming a particularly difficult passage. Also, words of advice from a local pastor and/or the input from fellow colleagues in a Bible study group may give some needed illumination.

ESSENTIAL

Many believe that apparent contradictions or alleged errors in the Bible can only be resolved by employing the wisdom of Saint Augustine; otherwise, inerrancy goes out the window. He said that one of three things is at work: the translation is faulty, the copied manuscript (not the original autograph) has mistakes, or the reader is misinterpreting or misunderstanding the text.

Personal Interpretation

Once you understand a particular text—figured out its literary style and genre, the figures of speech, and the intended meaning of the author— the next step is to incorporate it into your life. Many believe that personal application of the Scripture is one reason God revealed His Word in the first place. Hearing, reading, and even understanding it are all preliminary steps, but the mission is to accept and implement the Word (message). When a certain passage or verse affects you personally, this leads to a private interpretation.

For example, after coming across, "And if your eye causes you to sin, pluck it out" (Mark 9:47), some may think this verse is asking them to be more prudent as to what Internet sites they visit or what kind of movies they watch. Others could erroneously interpret this to be taken literally as in the case of verse 43 in Mark 9—"If your hand causes you to sin, cut it off,"—which is done to thieves in some parts of the world. Only after determining the literal sense, the figurative sense, the context, the genre, and the intended audience will a reasonable person interpret this passage accurately. Ⓔ

Chapter 9
The Pentateuch

The first five books of the Bible are called the Pentateuch, which in Greek means "five books" or scrolls. The Pentateuch consists of Genesis, Exodus, Leviticus, Numbers, and Deuteronomy, all of which are found in the Old Testament. This chapter will offer a synopsis for each of these books as a tool in helping you understand and appreciate these sacred passages.

The Torah

The Jewish people do not use the Greek term *Pentateuch* when referring to the first five books of the Old Testament. Instead, they use the Hebrew word *Torah*, or "law," since the law of God given to Moses is contained in this collection of books. Law is the theme throughout these five books, but it is not the same as modern day civil law. For the Jews, obeying the law is the best and the most complete way to show their love for God. Keeping the law means keeping the covenant. If you kept the covenant, you would live and be happy—disobey it, and risk death and misery.

Keeping the Law

Long before the Temple of Jerusalem was built and long after it had been destroyed, the Jews had one sure way to worship and show their love of God and that was by keeping the law and thus fulfilling the covenant between them and the Lord. The faithfulness in keeping the law and the covenant is the one thing that can never be taken away from them.

ALERT!

The theme of service is prominent in the Bible. Obeying God's law was the best way of serving Him. The Bible also tells of what happens when people rebel, disobey, and break His law.

The Hebrew notion of obedience to the law as fulfillment of the covenant is rooted in the sense of fidelity to the will of God. The things of the world—from the mountains to the rivers, to the rocks and the plains—must comply with the same laws of nature, be it gravity or other laws of physics and chemistry. When human beings follow the law of God, they do so, however, not out of instinct (as with animals), nor out of design (as with inanimate matter), but out of free, deliberate, and conscious choice. The Hebrew notion of law is to be faithful to the most Faithful One: to obey the will of the One who deserves our obedience.

Genesis

The word *Genesis* is Greek for "beginning" or "origin." Jews call this book *Bereshith* for "in the beginning" since that is how the book opens. Since the time of the Septuagint, Christians used the Greek name Genesis to identify this inspired book. Composed of fifty chapters, Genesis can be divided into two parts: the first being chapters 1 through 11, the second, chapters 12 through 50.

FACT

Some scholars ascribe Moses as the author of Genesis and the rest of The Pentateuch, while others propose two separate groups: the Priestly source (fifth century B.C.) and the Yahwist source (tenth century B.C.).

Two Creation Stories

Chapters 1 through 11 of the Book of Genesis tell of the origins of things, from the creation of the world, the creation of man, the first human sin, the first murder, to the first and last global flood, and so on. Genesis 1 describes the hierarchy of Creation. It teaches that humankind is the crowning of Creation: from inanimate matter, to plants, to animals, and finally to rational beings (men and women). There is a hierarchy or progression of life.

"And God said, 'Let there be light,' and there was light . . .—the first day. And God said, 'Let there be an expanse between the waters to separate water from water . . .' God called the expanse 'sky.' . . .—the second day. . . . And God said, 'Let the water under the sky be gathered to one place, and let dry ground appear.' . . . God called the dry ground 'land,' and the gathered waters he called 'seas.' . . .—the third day . . . God made two great lights—the greater light to govern the day and the lesser light to govern the night. He also made the stars . . .—the fourth day . . . And God said, 'Let the water teem with living creatures, and let birds fly above the earth across the expanse of the sky.' . . .—the fifth day. . . . And God said, 'Let the land produce living creatures according to their kinds: livestock, creatures that move along the ground, and wild animals, each according to its kind.' . . . Then God said, 'Let us make man in our image, in our likeness . . .' So God created man in his own image, in the image of God he created him; male and female he created them . . . God saw all that he had made, and it was very good. And there was evening, and there was morning—the sixth day."

(Genesis 1:3–31)

Genesis 2 takes a different perspective and shows that humans were created differently from the rest. Verse 7 says God "breathed into his nostrils the breath of life." That breath was the immortal soul, something which separates men and women from all the other animals.

"The Lord God formed the man from the dust of the ground and breathed into his nostrils the breath of life, and the man became a living being . . . The Lord God said, 'It is not good for the man to be alone. I will make a helper suitable for him.' Now the Lord God had formed out of the ground all the beasts of the field and all the birds of the air. He brought them to the man to see what he would name them; and whatever the man called each living creature, that was its name. So the man gave names to all the livestock, the birds of the air and all the beasts of the field. But for Adam no suitable helper was found. So the Lord God caused the man to fall into a deep sleep; and while he was sleeping, he took one of the man's ribs and closed up the place with flesh. Then the Lord God made a woman from the rib he had taken out of the man, and he brought her to the man."

(Genesis 2:7, 18–22)

Possible Contradiction?

The first Creation story (Genesis 1) has men and women as being created on the sixth day after God made the plants and animals on previous days. The second Creation story (Genesis 2) has God creating man (Adam), then the animals—to see what he would name them—and then woman (Eve), Adam's partner. However, both Creation stories (just like any story in the Bible) are not written or intended to be taken as historical or scientific explanations.

> Genesis and the entire Bible for that matter are not textbooks for science or history. They are religious and theological explanations and since God exists outside time and space, He is not limited to human constraints of linear time.

Original Sin

The bliss of Paradise (Garden of Eden) was shattered when the first man and woman—Adam and Eve—disobeyed God by eating the forbidden fruit from the Tree of the Knowledge of Good and Evil. As a punishment for their first sin (known as the Original Sin), God threw Adam and Eve out of the Garden. Genesis 2:15–17 says: "The Lord God took the man and put him in the Garden of Eden to work it and take care of it. And the Lord God commanded the man, 'You are free to eat from any tree in the garden; but you must not eat from the tree of the knowledge of good and evil, for when you eat of it you will surely die.'"

Then the serpent tempted the woman Eve to eat of the forbidden fruit. She did so and gave some to Adam. Thus the first sin—that of disobedience—entered into human experience and Adam and Eve were expelled from the Garden of Eden. God punished the serpent (the devil) for his wicked temptation: "And I will put enmity between you and the woman, and between your offspring and hers; he will crush your head, and you will strike his heel" (Genesis 3:15). Some believe this prophecy was fulfilled when Jesus was born. In his Gospel, Luke shows through genealogy that Jesus is a descendent of Adam and Eve.

Noah and the Tower of Babel

Chapters 6 to 10 of Genesis continue with the story of Noah and the Ark, the flood, and the rainbow (as a sign of a new covenant). Chapter

11 tells of the Tower of Babel and people's evil ways. To punish them, God scattered them all over the world and confused their languages.

The Patriarchs

Chapters 12 through 50 of Genesis concern the great Patriarchs: Abraham, Isaac, Jacob (also called Israel), and Joseph. Chapter 12 starts with the tale of Abram and his wife Sarai, who were childless. God then made a covenant with Abram and promised him that he would be the father of many nations. He then changed Abram's name to Abraham and Sarai became Sarah. She became pregnant with Isaac.

FACT

Changing a person's name is important in the Bible since your name told others who you were and where you came from. "Abram" meant "exalted father," whereas "Abraham" meant "father of many nations."

Then there is the tale of Abraham and his nephew Lot and the infamous destruction of Sodom and Gomorrah in chapter 19. Finally, in chapter 22, God tests Abraham to see if he would be willing to sacrifice Isaac for Him. When Abraham showed that he was prepared to do whatever God asked him, God spared Isaac's life. Isaac then married Rebecca, the sister of Laban the Aramean.

Genesis then continues with the story of Isaac, who had two sons, Esau and Jacob. Jacob tricked his father into giving him the birthright and continued Abraham's dynasty instead of Esau. Jacob later wrestled with an angel and was given the name Israel. He had twelve children—Reuben, Simeon, Levi, Judah, Dan, Naphtali, Gad, Asher, Issachar, Zebulun, Benjamin, and Joseph—who grew up to become the heads of the twelve tribes of Israel. Because Joseph was Jacob's favorite son, his brothers were jealous and sold him into slavery. Joseph then joined the Pharaoh's court in Egypt and became a powerful governor. He forgave and was reunited with his brothers. Genesis closes with Joseph's death in Egypt.

Exodus

Called *Shemot* (meaning "names") in Hebrew, the Book of Exodus describes God's deliverance (from which the word "exodus" originates) of His Chosen People from the Egyptian slavery into the freedom of the Promised Land. Raised as an Egyptian prince in the court of Pharaoh, Moses discovered his Hebrew roots and led his people from slavery into freedom. Before leaving town, God commanded Moses to celebrate the first Passover, during which the blood of a lamb was smeared around the doors of Israelites' houses, symbolizing the angel of death "passing over" the homes of the firstborn.

"Tell the whole community of Israel that on the tenth day of this month each man is to take a lamb for his family, one for each household . . . Then they are to take some of the blood and put it on the sides and tops of the doorframes of the houses where they eat the lambs. . . . On that same night I will pass through Egypt and strike down every firstborn—both men and animals—and I will bring judgment on all the gods of Egypt. I am the Lord. The blood will be a sign for you on the houses where you are; and when I see the blood, I will pass over you. No destructive plague will touch you when I strike Egypt."

(Exodus 12:3,7,12–13)

Ten Plagues of Egypt

The famous ten plagues God sent upon Pharaoh and the Egyptians before they released the Jews from slavery were: the river turning into blood, frogs, gnats, flies, livestock disease, boils, hail, locusts, darkness, and death of the firstborn. Moses, along with his brother Aaron, visited Pharaoh several times, asking him to let his people go. But it was only after he lost his own firstborn son that Pharaoh allowed Moses' people to leave—but then sent his army after them.

Forty Years in the Desert

After the Israelites crossed the Red Sea (while fleeing from Egypt), God gave them water from the rock, as well as manna (a bread-like substance) and quail from heaven. However, while Moses was on Mount Sinai receiving the Ten Commandments, the people rebelled against their God. They made a golden calf for public worship, and God punished them by making them wander in the desert for forty years.

FACT

The number "ten" is important in the Bible. The world is created with ten divine words (according to Jewish mysticism); there are ten patriarchs before the Flood, the ten temptations of Abraham, the ten plagues of Egypt, the Ten Commandments, and the one-tenth offering (tithing) for the church.

The Ten Commandments

The Ten Commandments, or in Hebrew *Debarim* (words), are listed both in Exodus and in Deuteronomy. Most Protestants have a different numbering sequence for the Commandments than the one used by Catholics. The reason can be seen below as it only involves where you begin a commandment and where you end it. The Bible does not number the Commandments from one to ten. Actually, there are fourteen statements, which when combined make ten. The following are from the Deuteronomy listing:

I AM THE LORD YOUR GOD, who brought you out of Egypt, out of the land of slavery. **YOU SHALL HAVE NO OTHER GODS BEFORE ME.** (First commandment.)

YOU SHALL NOT MAKE FOR YOURSELF AN IDOL in the form of anything in heaven above or on the earth beneath or in the waters below. (Protestants count this as number two; Catholics and Lutherans consider this a continuation of number one.)

YOU SHALL NOT MISUSE THE NAME OF THE LORD YOUR GOD, for the Lord will not hold anyone guiltless who misuses his name. (Protestants, number three; Catholics and Lutherans, number two.)

OBSERVE THE SABBATH DAY BY KEEPING IT HOLY, as the Lord your God has commanded you. (Protestants, number four; Catholics and Lutherans, number three.)

HONOR YOUR FATHER AND YOUR MOTHER, as the Lord your God has commanded you, **SO THAT YOU MAY LIVE LONG** and that it may go well with you in the land the Lord your God is giving you. (Protestants, number five; Catholics and Lutherans, number four.)

YOU SHALL NOT MURDER. (Protestants, number six; Catholics and Lutherans, number five.)

YOU SHALL NOT COMMIT ADULTERY. (Protestants, number seven; Catholics and Lutherans, number six.)

YOU SHALL NOT STEAL. (Protestants, number eight; Catholics and Lutherans, number seven.)

YOU SHALL NOT GIVE FALSE TESTIMONY AGAINST YOUR NEIGHBOR. (Protestants, number nine; Catholics and Lutherans, number eight.)

YOU SHALL NOT COVET YOUR NEIGHBOR'S WIFE. (Protestants, number ten; Catholics and Lutherans, number nine.)

YOU SHALL NOT SET YOUR DESIRE ON YOUR NEIGHBOR'S HOUSE OR LAND, his manservant or maidservant, his ox or donkey, **OR ANYTHING THAT BELONGS TO YOUR NEIGHBOR.** (Protestants consider this a continuation of number ten; Catholics and Lutherans, number ten.)

Leviticus

Called *Vayikra* (meaning "he called") in Hebrew, the Book of Leviticus—at first glance—seems devoted to the priestly class and duties of the Levites (from which the word Leviticus originates), who were in charge of public worship. The Hebrew title, however, shows the full nature of this book being a "call to holiness" by God to all of His people, and not just the Levites and the priests and rabbis.

It was actually Saint Augustine (A.D. 354–430), the Catholic Bishop of Hippo, who assigned numbers to the Commandments. The Lutheran Church, started by Martin Luther, retains the Catholic numbering, whereas other Protestant denominations follow the Swiss numbering sequence, which came out of Geneva under John Calvin.

The Layout

Chapters 1 through 7 of Leviticus give laws pertaining to cultic sacrifice; chapters 8 through 10 concern the installation of Aaron (Moses' brother) and his sons as priests; chapters 11 through 16 deal with ritual impurity and directions for Yom Kippur (Day of Atonement); chapters 17 through 26 concern more purity laws; and chapter 27 deals with votive offerings.

Numbers

The Hebrew Bible calls the Book of Numbers *Bamidbar* (meaning "in the wilderness"). Since it mentions two censuses in chapters 1 through 4 and in chapter 26, the Greek Septuagint gave it the name "numbers." The book also concerns camp assignments and several rebellions among the rank and file.

Rebellious Brother

One such rebellion involved Aaron. Numbers 12 tells how Aaron and his wife Miriam go against Moses for marrying a "Cushite" woman and are also jealous that he is getting all the accolades (remember, it was Aaron who had to speak for Moses before Pharaoh). As a result, the story claims Miriam was punished with leprosy, which turned her skin snow white. She also was ostracized from the camp for seven days and then allowed to return, presumably healed and repentant.

FACT

Deuteronomy is one of the most theological books of the Old Testament. It speaks of election (being chosen by God) and the response of true and faithful worship. In it, idolatry is seen not only as a sin against religion, but an act of infidelity against the beloved spouse. This image would be further elaborated by the prophets who call the chosen people to come back to the Lord and abandon their pagan idolatry.

Deuteronomy

The Book of Deuteronomy gets its name from the Greek meaning "second law." The Hebrew Bible calls this book *Devarim* ("words") since it contains more words of the Lord, especially the great law of Deuteronomy 6:4, *sh'ma Yisrael: Adonai Eloheynu Adonai Echad* ("Hear, O Israel: The Lord our God, the Lord is one."). These words are said by faithful Jews in the morning and in the evening as well as on one's deathbed. Deuteronomy also reiterates (with small variations) the Ten Commandments first found in Exodus 20:2–17 and contains Moses' four addresses on how to observe the covenant with God. The book closes with the death of Moses in chapter 34. Ⓔ

Chapter 10

Historical Books

The Hebrew Bible is divided into three parts: the Law (*Torah*), the Prophets (*Nevi'im*), and the Writings (*Ke'tuvim*), whereas the Christians later divided their Old Testament into four parts: the Pentateuch, the Historical Books, Poetry and Wisdom, and the Prophetic Writings. This chapter looks at those historical books, which continue the story of salvation history—from the postmortem period after the death of Moses up until the death of Judas Maccabeus in 160 B.C.

Joshua, Judges, and Ruth

The three historical Books of Joshua, Judges, and Ruth describe the history of the Chosen People in the Promised Land of Canaan—from the death of Moses to the brink of the monarchy. Joshua was the leader of the Israelites after Moses died, and it was he who led them across the River Jordan into Canaan. Judges were the rulers of Israel after the death of Joshua. They were tribal leaders, or chieftains. Ruth was the great-grandmother of King David and the book given her name is a story of family loyalty and fidelity to God.

Joshua and the Battle of Jericho

Before the famous battle of Jericho—during which Joshua conquered the city—Joshua enlisted the assistance of two spies, who sought help from a prostitute named Rahab. She gave them sanctuary and hid them while the king unsuccessfully scoured the town, looking for these two spies. During the battle of Jericho, Rahab dangled a red cord down the wall from her window so that the Israelites would know to spare those inside.

FACT

Joshua was memorialized as a great military leader, but his success came mainly because of his obedience to the Lord—unlike many of his own countrymen, who continued to dabble more and more in idolatry, temple prostitution, and all kinds of debauchery.

Jericho was protected by fortified walls, which were almost impregnable. Joshua had no rocket propelled grenades, no Patriot missiles, and not even a decent catapult to help him conquer the city. The Israelites first crossed the Jordan after the priests carried the Ark of the Covenant in front of them, which separated the waters of the mighty river to give them passage. Once on the other side, Joshua's soldiers marched around Jericho once every day for six days in a row while the priests blew their trumpets. On the last and seventh day, they went seven times around the city and the trumpets blasted and the people shouted. Then, miraculously, the walls of Jericho came tumbling down.

Judges

The Judges of Israel were not court judges as people see on television today. They were men and women of Israel whom God appointed to rule and govern the people. If anything, their role was more like a governor of a region who was only consulted in time of dispute. Once deceased, his or her office became vacant and was not inherited by their offspring—as would be the case in aristocracy and monarchy. Deborah the Judge was one of the most astonishing women in the Bible. She was a judge, prophetess, and military leader all in one.

The last judge, Samson, was an incredible hulk, who had enormous strength since he was under a Nazirite vow even while in the womb. The word *Nazirite* (or *Nazarite*) comes from the Hebrew word *nazir* meaning "consecrated" or "dedicated." However, Samson lost his strength when the vixen Delilah tricked him into cutting his hair. When the Philistines captured him, they gouged out his eyes. Samson was made a human beast of burden until his hair grew back. Once that happened, he regained enough strength to push two pillars of a building, which collapsed on more than 3,000 Philistines.

The Philistines were members of the Aegean Sea people, who settled Philistia (ancient region of southwestern Palestine) in the twelfth century B.C. It is now considered a great insult to be called a Philistine, since the name denoted a boorish, vulgar, smug middle-class person who disdained art and culture.

Ruth

According to the Book of Ruth in the Old Testament, Naomi, Naomi's husband, and their two sons were Israelites, who migrated to Moab (located within the Kingdom of Jordan) in time of famine in Palestine. While there, the boys found Moabite wives for themselves. One of them was called Ruth. Within ten years, however, all three men died, leaving their wives childless. Naomi heard that the situation was better back in Palestine and tried to send her daughters-in-law away so they could create new lives for themselves. Ruth refused to go and uttered the famous line, "Where you go I will go, and where you stay I will stay. Your people will be my people and your God my God" (Ruth 1:16). Ruth later married Boaz of Bethlehem and became the mother of Obed, whose son was Jesse, the father of King David.

First Three Kings of Israel

Saul, David, and Solomon are considered the first three kings of Israel, as well as the last kings of a united kingdom. Originally one book (Samuel) in Hebrew, the Greek Septuagint divided it into two books, and then combined them with the two books following it as the "Books of the Kingdom." When writing the Latin Vulgate translation, Saint Jerome shortened it to "Kings."

ALERT!

In older Catholic Bibles and the Latin Vulgate, the books of 3 and 4 Kings refer to what Protestant and contemporary Catholic Bibles now call 1 and 2 Kings.

1 and 2 Samuel

The Book of 1 Samuel tells of the birth, the calling, and the ministry of Samuel the Prophet. It covers his whole life, from the womb to the tomb. Elkanah had a wife named Hannah, who was barren. In ancient times, this was considered a curse from God since children, especially sons, meant prosperity and security for the family and the clan. One day Hannah prayed in the temple and pleaded with God to give her a son. If He did, she would dedicate him to the Lord and no razor would cut his hair (remember the Nazirite vow of Samson?). She then gave birth to Samuel.

In keeping her word, Hannah dedicated her son to the Lord, and then gave him to the priest Eli, who trained him to eventually be his successor. Samuel then replaced Eli as priest and prophet. Once he assumed the office, Samuel contended with the people, who were concerned that they didn't have a king since all their neighboring countries had rulers. Israel was the only nation that had no earthly king since God was in essence and actuality their king.

Expensive Monarchy

God ordered Samuel to inform his people what having an earthly king would be like (see excerpt below), but despite the high price, the people demanded a king so they could be like the other nations. Samuel eventually anointed Saul as the king of Israel, who then conquered the Ammonites (an ancient tribe residing in Jordan), but was driven back by the Philistines.

"He [the king] will take your sons and make them serve with his chariots and horses, and they will run in front of his chariots. Some he will assign to be commanders of thousands and commanders of fifties, and others to plow his ground and reap his harvest, and still others to make weapons of war and equipment for his chariots. He will take your daughters to be perfumers and cooks and bakers. He will take the best of your fields and vineyards and olive groves and give them to his attendants. He will take a tenth of your grain and of your vintage and give it to his officials and attendants. Your menservants and maidservants and the best of your cattle and donkeys he will take for his own use. He will take a tenth of your flocks, and you yourselves will become his slaves. When that day comes, you will cry out for relief from the king you have chosen, and the Lord will not answer you in that day."

(1 Samuel 8:11–18)

Some time later, Saul returned to the battle and faced Goliath, a nine-foot Philistine in more than 100 pounds of armor. When all of his soldiers refused to battle Goliath, a shepherd-boy named David volunteered. With nothing more than a slingshot, David lobbed a bull's-eye on Goliath's forehead and knocked him out cold. He then decapitated the giant with his own huge sword.

God told Samuel to find a replacement for King Saul since he no longer deserved the throne. Told to decimate the Amalekites, Saul killed every man, woman, and child, but kept some livestock for himself. Disobedience did not bode well with God, and later David replaced Saul as King of Israel after a bitter and prolonged feud between them.

FACT

Jonathan was the son of King Saul and David's best friend. Though heir to the throne, Jonathan renounced his right of ascension to the throne in favor of David. He later died in battle with his brothers and father against the Philistines.

King David

The Book of 2 Samuel picks up with King David setting up Jerusalem as his capital (known afterwards as the City of David). Once a king, David restored the Ark of the Covenant, which the Philistines had stolen in battle, and placed it in a secure location. However, later David got into trouble with a woman named Bathsheba, the wife of Uriah. After seducing Bathsheba, she became pregnant, and David arranged for her husband to be killed in battle. As a result, adultery and murder were on King David's conscience.

The prophet Nathan (who succeeded Samuel) confronted the king with his sins, and David repented. However, his atonement did not save the life of his unborn son. Later, David had another son, Absalom, who grew up and rebelled against his father. He died ignominiously when his long hair got caught in a tree branch. However, two of David's other sons, Adonijah and Solomon, survived.

"The Lord sent Nathan to David. When he came to him, he said, 'There were two men in a certain town, one rich and the other poor. The rich man had a very large number of sheep and cattle, but the poor man had nothing except one little ewe lamb he had bought. He raised it, and it grew up with him and his children. It shared his food, drank from his cup and even slept in his arms. It was like a daughter to him. Now a traveler came to the rich man, but the rich man refrained from taking one of his own sheep or cattle to prepare a meal for the traveler who had come to him. Instead, he took the ewe lamb that belonged to the poor man and prepared it for the one who had come to him.' David burned with anger against the man and said to Nathan, 'As surely as the Lord lives, the man who did this deserves to die! He must pay for that lamb four times over, because he did such a thing and had no pity.' Then Nathan said to David, 'You are the man!'"

(2 Samuel 12:1–7)

1 and 2 Kings

David's son Adonijah was the elder of the two brothers and presumed he should be king when his father died. He threw a party in preparation for his ascension to the throne as heir apparent, but did not invite his brother Solomon. Seeing the handwriting on the wall, Bathsheba (Solomon's mother) went to David and informed him about Adonijah's intentions. David, then, hastily anointed Solomon as king.

1 Kings 11:1–3 indicates Solomon had 700 wives and 300 concubines, who lured him into idolatry and worshipping their false gods. To punish the king, after his death, God divided Solomon's kingdom.

Solomon took the throne after David died, and as a coronation gift, God granted him one wish. Rather than wishing for the death of his enemies, wealth, or longevity, Solomon asked for wisdom to rule God's people. Because of his humble request, God made him the wisest man in the world. Solomon then built the Temple of the Lord, which God had prevented David from doing. Under Solomon, the kingdom of Israel became the most powerful and wealthiest.

1 and 2 Chronicles

The Books of 1 and 2 Chronicles are also known by their Greek title *Paraleipomena*, which means things omitted, since the books cover details not mentioned in 1 and 2 Kings. Soon after Solomon's death, his son Rehoboam took the throne but impetuously wanted to show off his authority, which resulted in the kingdom being split in two. In 928 B.C., Jeroboam became the first king of the northern kingdom of Israel (comprised of ten out of the twelve tribes), and Rehoboam became the ruler of the southern kingdom of Judah. Assyria conquered Israel in 722 B.C., while Babylonians dissolved Judah in 586 B.C.

The Book of 1 Chronicles does not pick up where 2 Kings left off, but rather goes backward and provides a genealogy for nine chapters tracing Adam to David. Family tree and lineage information is given to show what happened with the twelve sons of Jacob, who became the heads of the twelve tribes of Israel. I and II Chronicles cover the same time period of Samuel and Kings, but whereas those four books focus on personalities of the monarchs, Chronicles give emphasis to the Ark of the Covenant, the Temple, and the worship performed there.

FACT

1 Chronicles 4:10 has an interesting prayer of Jabez in the midst of genealogies: "Oh, that you would bless me and enlarge my territory! Let your hand be with me, and keep me from harm so that I will be free from pain."

Ezra, Nehemiah, and Esther

In the Latin Vulgate, Ezra and Nehemiah were 1 and 2 Esdras, respectively. Ezra concerns the King Cyrus of Persia helping some of the Israelites return to Jerusalem by ordering a restoration of the Temple in 536 B.C. Nehemiah deals with his own commission to rebuild the walls of Jerusalem. It continues with the reading of the law by Ezra and the confession of sins by the Israelites.

Esther

Esther is the story of a Jewish Queen who saved her entire race from a fiendish and genocidal plot to eliminate them in one day. The King of Persia, Xerxes, married the maiden Esther after the first Queen

Vashti was exiled and forced to abdicate for disobeying the King. Esther's parents had died since the Exile and so she was under the care of her cousin Mordecai, who forbid her to reveal her Jewish indentity.

When Mordecai uncovered a plot to assassinate King Xerxes, he told Queen Esther about it, and she in turn informed her husband. One of the king's officials, Haman, hated Mordecai because he refused to bow before him. He found out Mordecai was Jewish, and plotted to kill him and all of his people by lying to the king that there were traitors in his kingdom. Mordecai learned of his treachery and informed Esther, who then exposed Haman and revealed her Jewish identity to her husband. King Xerxes spared her people and punished Haman instead.

It is rather ironic that Haman was hanged on the same seventy-five foot-high gallows, which he himself built for Mordecai. "The king said, 'Hang him on it!' So they hanged Haman on the gallows he had prepared for Mordecai. Then the king's fury subsided" (Esther 7:9–10).

Tobit and Judith

Tobit and Judith are two of the seven deuterocanonical/apocryphal books found in the Greek Septuagint, Latin Vulgate, and the English translations of the Catholic Bible. Historically, they fit right after Ezra and Nehemiah even though in some Bibles, they are clumped together with other deuterocanonicals, under the listing of Apocrypha.

Tobit

The Book of Tobit is actually a love story and is often used as one of the readings at wedding ceremonies. Tobit was a God-fearing and just man who kept the law of Moses. His son, Tobias, met an unfortunate woman named Sarah—she had been married seven times, and each of her husbands was killed by the demon Asmodeus on their wedding night.

Despite Sarah's track record as a local Black Widow, Tobias fell in love with her. Together they prayed to God, who then sent the archangel Raphael to help them. The archangel expelled the demon and allowed the two to live in peace and love. Before going to bed with his new wife, Tobias said this prayer:

"Blessed art thou, O God of our fathers, and blessed be thy holy and glorious name for ever. Let the heavens and all thy creatures bless thee. Thou madest Adam and gavest him Eve his wife as a helper and support. From them the race of mankind has sprung. Thou didst say, 'It is not good that the man should be alone; let us make a helper for him like himself.' And now, O Lord, I am not taking this sister of mine because of lust, but with sincerity. Grant that I may find mercy and may grow old together with her. And she said with him, 'Amen.'"

(Tobias 8:5, from the RSV Catholic Edition)

Judith

The Book of Judith deals with King Nebuchadnezzar of the Chaldean Empire (also known as Neo-Babylonian) and his general Holofernes, who sought to conquer all peoples and force them to worship Nebuchadnezzar as a god. Although most of the peoples fell under King Nebuchadnezzar's rule, the Israelites continued to oppose and fight him.

According to the book, Holofernes believed that the only way the Israelites could be defeated was if they abandoned and disobeyed God. The Israelites, however, refused to worship Nebuchadnezzar and continued to pray. It took Holofernes a month after cutting off their water supply to see any hope of victory. Pushed to their absolute limits, the

Israelites were almost ready to surrender, but then Judith arrived to rally them to resist and remain faithful.

Under the ruse that she wished to defect and give vital information, Judith then visited Holofernes. Her beauty got her past the guards, and she convinced the general that she was an authentic defector. After Holofernes drank too much wine and passed out, Judith took his sword and with two blows decapitated him. She then headed back to the Israelites' camp. After the Assyrians heard that Holofernes was slain, they fled.

The Pharisees who contended with Jesus in the New Testament were laymen followers of Judas Maccabeus, who believed in the resurrection of the dead. The Sadducees were priest followers of Simon Maccabeus who denied there was a resurrection of the body.

1 and 2 Maccabees

1 and 2 Maccabees also belong to the seven deuterocanonical/ apocryphals of the Greek Septuagint, which finish up the historical books of the Old Testament. The Maccabees tell of the heroism of the Israelites who fought for independence from foreign control. Judas Maccabeus emerged as a hero for defeating the Syrians. The eight-day Jewish holiday of Hanukkah (Feast of Lights) commemorates his victory over Antiochus Epiphanes in 165 B.C. The Book of 2 Maccabees contains themes such as the resurrection of the dead (2 Maccabees 7:9,11,14,23; 12:43, 14:46), intercession of the saints in heaven for the living on earth (2 Maccabees 15:11–16), and the efficacy of offering prayers for the dead (2 Maccabees 12:39–46).

Chapter 11
Poetry and Wisdom

The Bible, as an inspired work of literature, has many forms of literature within it. This chapter will look at the books of the Scripture that can be classified as poetry and wisdom. These books are poetic not because they rhyme, but because they have a rhythm in the chosen words (primarily in the original language) as a means to emphasize and express emotion. They are also considered wisdom literature because they contain insights, values, and morals.

Patient Job

The Book of Job is poignant poetry and wisdom in that it uses eloquent dialogue (which speaks volumes to the reader) and addresses an issue which conventional wisdom (the accepted or standard knowledge) is unable to answer adequately. Rabbi Harold Kushner wrote his famous book *When Bad Things Happen to Good People*, which incorporates the story of Job as told in the Bible. His premise, like that of Father Benedict Groeschel, CFR, author of *Arise From Darkness: What to Do When Life Doesn't Make Sense*, is that we should take our cue from Job.

When Bad Things Happen to Good People

It seems illogical and certainly unfair for bad things to happen to good people. Job believed, as do many today, that if he lived a life of being and doing good, then God would bless and reward him. This is why he was greatly puzzled when a string of tragedies befell him and yet he could not recall what sin or evil he could have done to merit this punishment.

ALERT!

Many believe that bad things happen as a punishment for bad things done and vice versa, but the Bible never says that exactly. It does teach, however, that God rewards good and punishes evil, either in this life or the next.

Test of the Mettle

In chapter 1, Job is presented as a man who "was blameless and upright; he feared God and shunned evil." He had 7 sons, 3 daughters, 7,000 sheep, 3,000 camels, 500 oxen, 500 donkeys, and plenty of servants. In other words, Job was well off and had a comfortable life.

However, unknown to Job, Satan (the name means "adversary") had a conversation with God about him. The Lord was pleased with Job since he was a just and upright man, but Satan retorted that his good behavior was only a result of the many blessings God had showered upon him. "But stretch out your hand and strike everything he has," Satan insisted, "and he will surely curse you to your face" (Job 1:11). Because God had complete faith in Job, He allowed Satan to test Job.

FACT

Satan is not portrayed as the horned, cloven-hoofed, sulfur-smelling demon who controls the bowels of hell. The name "Satan" merely means God's adversary and the image of the devil as a cold-hearted, calculating, and scheming spiritual opponent (albeit still a fallen angel) is what is being shown here. Later writings, especially from the first century B.C. to the late Middle Ages, depicted the Prince of Darkness as a terrifying demon.

Talk about Having a Bad Day

One day Job was with his family when he received all sorts of bad news. He was told that his oxen and donkeys were stolen, that his sheep and servants were destroyed by fire, that his camels were also taken away, and finally, the worst of all, that his children were killed in a tragic accident. For many, Job's response to this news is, to this day, a model of courage, strength, and faith: "Naked I came from my mother's womb, and naked I will depart. The Lord gave and the Lord has taken away; may the name of the Lord be praised" (Job 1:21).

Satan, however, was still not satisfied that Job was good for the right reasons, and so he plagued Job with painful sores all over his body. Seeing how much he suffered, Job's wife tempted him to curse God. But just as in the first instance, Job once again showed patience and restraint.

ESSENTIAL

During his suffering, three of Job's friends visited him, urging him to ask God for forgiveness of his sin. They pleaded with him to reveal what sin he had committed that brought upon him such anguish and pain. Job, however, maintained he was a righteous man.

Enough Is Enough, Already

Whereas patience was his hallmark in the first two chapters, in chapter 3 Job showed humanity and vulnerability when he cursed, not God (as his wife suggested), but the day of his own birth: "May the day of my birth perish, and the night it was said, 'A boy is born!' That day— may it turn to darkness; may God above not care about it; may no light shine upon it. May darkness and deep shadow claim it once more; may a cloud settle over it; may blackness overwhelm its light. That night— may thick darkness seize it; may it not be included among the days of the year nor be entered in any of the months" (Job 3:3–6).

Finally in chapter 10, Job became frustrated, and even angry, at what had happened to him. And so, he then pleaded with God to tell him why He was causing him such great suffering.

God's Reply

In chapter 38, God finally responded to Job, but His long response did not answer any of Job's questions. God never told Job why these bad things happened to him, but instead asked Job why he dared to question Him. God then answered Job's question with a question.

"Who is this that darkens my counsel with words without knowledge? Brace yourself like a man; I will question you, and you shall answer me. Where were you when I laid the earth's foundation? Tell me, if you understand. Who marked off its dimensions? Surely you know! Who stretched a measuring line across it? On what were its footings set, or who laid its cornerstone—while the morning stars sang together and all the angels shouted for joy? Who shut up the sea behind doors when it burst forth from the womb, when I made the clouds its garment and wrapped it in thick darkness, when I fixed limits for it and set its doors and bars in place, when I said, 'This far you may come and no farther; here is where your proud waves halt'? Have you ever given orders to the morning, or shown the dawn its place, that it might take the earth by the edges and shake the wicked out of it? The earth takes shape like clay under a seal; its features stand out like those of a garment. The wicked are denied their light, and their upraised arm is broken. Have you journeyed to the springs of the sea or walked in the recesses of the deep? Have the gates of death been shown to you? Have you seen the gates of the shadow of death? Have you comprehended the vast expanses of the earth? Tell me, if you know all this . . . ."

(Job 38:2–18)

For many, the bottom line of the Book of Job is that human life must accept the reality of unanswered questions, such as why there is evil in the world and why innocent people must suffer. Being able to accept that there may just be no answers after all and being able to live with these unanswerable questions is what Job learned at the end of this tale.

Psalms

The Psalms—by far—are the most poetic of all the wisdom books in the Bible. They contain imagery, parallelism, internal rhythm, and were written to be sung as hymns and/or to be prayed individually or in a group setting. Just as there is a slight discrepancy in the Protestant and Catholic/Lutheran numbering of the Commandments or in the classification of the seven deuterocanonical or apocryphal books, older versions of the Catholic Bible had different numbering of some of the Psalms.

FACT

Song of Songs is another book of the Old Testament, also known as the Song of Solomon, or Canticle of Canticles. It describes lovers, true love, and the wedding. The image of two loving spouses is the allegory that the early Christian church adopted from Saint Paul when he said Christ loves the Church as a groom his bride. The image of God as a faithful husband and Israel his beloved is another valid application.

Crunching the Numbers

The Greek Septuagint and the Latin Vulgate coincide exactly with the Hebrew and Protestant Bible numbering of Psalms 1 through 8. The change occurs in Psalm 9. The Greek and Latin versions have thirty-nine verses in Psalm 9, whereas the Hebrew version has only twenty-one and counts verses 22 through 39 as Psalm 10. That results in the Septuagint and Vulgate having Psalm 10 be equivalent to the Hebrew Psalm 11 and so on, until Psalm 147 in the Hebrew equals to Psalms 146 to 147 in the Greek and Latin. By this point, Psalms 148 to 150 catch up in all three. To reduce confusion, modern Catholic Bibles, however, have adopted the Hebrew numbering of the Psalms.

Psalm Types

Psalms, like contemporary prayers and hymns, can be classified in several ways. Traditionally, there are four types: liturgical, lament, thanksgiving, and imprecatory (curse Psalms). Liturgical Psalms were used in the Temple for worship services, on high holy days, or for royal events, such as the coronation of the king. Laments were expressions of sorrow and contrition for sins, or pleas for deliverance from suffering. Thanksgiving Psalms were songs that showed gratitude and appreciation for God's blessings. Imprecatory or curse Psalms were cries for justice (not revenge). Some have also used classifications like Messianic and didactic and so on, but these four have been the most common labels.

When the Bible speaks of "curse" or imprecatory Psalms, it is not in the sense of placing a curse on someone, which is done in magic, sorcery, and witchcraft. These cries for justice are not to be equated with revenge or the *vendetta*.

Psalm Themes

One can also categorize the 150 Psalms according to the Torah or Pentateuch—the first five books of the Bible. Genesis, which has the theme of Creation, can also be seen in Psalms 1 to 41. Exodus, which has the theme of deliverance and redemption, can be associated with Psalms 42 to 72. Leviticus, which focuses on worship, can be linked with Psalms 73 to 89. Numbers, which describes the period of wandering in the desert, is reflected in Psalms 90 to 106. Finally, Deuteronomy, which highlights the Word given by God, can be identified with Psalms 107 to 150.

Familiar Psalms

Psalm 23 is often recited/read at funerals and in times of calamity, chaos, persecution, danger, trial, or tribulation. It is one of the best known and most memorized Psalms Christians of all denominations learn by heart. You will see it on many sympathy cards and tombstones.

"The Lord is my shepherd, I shall not be in want. He makes me lie down in green pastures, he leads me beside quiet waters, he restores my soul. He guides me in paths of righteousness for his name's sake. Even though I walk through the valley of the shadow of death, I will fear no evil, for you are with me; your rod and your staff, they comfort me. You prepare a table before me in the presence of my enemies. You anoint my head with oil; my cup overflows. Surely goodness and love will follow me all the days of my life, and I will dwell in the house of the Lord forever."

Another favorite is Psalm 51, also called the *Miserere* (first word in Latin, meaning "have mercy"). This Psalm is a favorite with Lutheran, Episcopalian, and Catholic Christians, especially during the season of Lent (forty days between Ash Wednesday and Easter), a penitential time of introspection, repentance, and conversion of the heart. This Psalm is a source of profound meditation.

There are a total of seven penitential Psalms: 6, 32, 38, 51, 102, 130, and 143. Pious tradition is that King David wrote Psalm 51 (following) after repenting from his sin of adultery with Bathsheba.

"Have mercy on me, O God, according to your unfailing love; according to your great compassion blot out my transgressions. Wash away all my iniquity and cleanse me from my sin.

For I know my transgressions, and my sin is always before me. Against you, you only, have I sinned and done what is evil in your sight, so that you are proved right when you speak and justified when you judge. Surely I was sinful at birth, sinful from the time my mother conceived me. Surely you desire truth in the inner parts, you teach me wisdom in the inmost place. Cleanse me with hyssop, and I will be clean; wash me, and I will be whiter than snow. Let me hear joy and gladness; let the bones you have crushed rejoice. Hide your face from my sins and blot out all my iniquity. Create in me a pure heart, O God, and renew a steadfast spirit within me. Do not cast me from your presence or take your Holy Spirit from me. Restore to me the joy of your salvation and grant me a willing spirit, to sustain me. Then I will teach transgressors your ways, and sinners will turn back to you. Save me from bloodguilt, O God, the God who saves me, and my tongue will sing of your righteousness. O Lord, open my lips, and my mouth will declare your praise. You do not delight in sacrifice, or I would bring it; you do not take pleasure in burnt offerings. The sacrifices of God are a broken spirit; a broken and contrite heart, O God, you will not despise. In your good pleasure make Zion prosper; build up the walls of Jerusalem. Then there will be righteous sacrifices, whole burnt offerings to delight you; then bulls will be offered on your altar."

FACT

Wisdom, as opposed to intellectual knowledge, is the ability to make good and prudent decisions—it is not having all the answers but rather having the courage and knowledge to look for them.

Proverbs

It is believed that King David wrote the Psalms and played and sang them before the Ark of the Covenant. Solomon, on the other hand, is traditionally given the credit for the Book of Proverbs as they denote words of wisdom, which he was known for more than anyone else. Wisdom, as described in the Bible, is not necessarily synonymous with intelligence. One does not have to be smart to be wise.

Americans are familiar with proverbs from Benjamin Franklin, like "early to bed, early to rise, makes a man healthy, wealthy and wise." These and other tidbits of human wisdom are often considered trite and mundane, but they should not be confused with the divinely inspired proverbs found in the Bible.

Proverbs 1:2–4 tell us that these writings from this book are good "for attaining wisdom and discipline; for understanding words of insight; for acquiring a disciplined and prudent life, doing what is right and just and fair; for giving prudence to the simple, knowledge and discretion to the young."

Considered an anthology of didactic poetry, the Book of Proverbs gives more than just pithy statements insofar as it finds its origin in Divine Wisdom and its audience in the whole human race, regardless of geography or chronology. Jesus and His Disciples quoted Proverbs as evidenced by John 7:38; Romans 12:20, and James 4:6. Whereas human proverbs, like those of Franklin and others, demonstrate human common sense, the Book of Proverbs is a source of heavenly wisdom by which men and women can model their lives so as to attain wisdom and internal peace.

Wisdom literature does not deny nor dilute the value of human wisdom or common sense—biblical wisdom offers divine advice and guidance for daily living as well as eternal happiness. The fact that some Proverbs show similarities to wisdom literature of Egyptian, Persian, or Babylonian writings does not detract from their inspired status. Biblical wisdom has eternal and celestial reward as motivation.

Ecclesiastes

"Vanity of vanities, says the Preacher, vanity of vanities! All is vanity." This is how many versions (KJV, RSV, NAB, and others) open the Book of Ecclesiastes (1:2). The NIV reads: "Meaningless! Meaningless! says the Teacher. Utterly meaningless! Everything is meaningless." No matter how it is said, Ecclesiastes repeats this theme several times. It is considered a kind of "tough wisdom" where what has to be said, is said. This book seeks to impart a different wisdom from that of the folksy proverbs to these diamonds in the rough, so to speak.

At first glance Ecclesiastes 3 may appear a bit fatalistic: "Things happen, get used to it" sort of motto. When examined more closely, however, the third chapter was not only put to music by The Byrds in 1965 ("Turn, Turn, Turn"), but it also speaks of humility. When the believer is confronted with paradoxes, such as life and death, health and sickness, joy and sorrow, Ecclesiastes 3 reminds the reader that none of these will last since time keeps on turning.

"There is a time for everything, and a season for every activity under heaven: a time to be born and a time to die, a time to plant and a time to uproot, a time to kill and a time to heal, a time to tear down and a time to build, a time to weep and a time to laugh, a time to mourn and a time to dance, a time to scatter stones and a time to gather them, a time to embrace and a time to refrain, a time to search and a time to give up, a time to keep and a time to throw away, a time to tear and a time to mend, a time to be silent and a time to speak, a time to love and a time to hate, a time for war and a time for peace."

The Book of Wisdom

The Book of Wisdom is one of the seven deuterocanonical/apocryphal books sometimes found in the Apocrypha section of the Bible. Often called the Wisdom of Solomon, it is unlikely that King Solomon wrote this book as it appears to be an encouragement for Diaspora Israelites in exile during the Babylonian Captivity. Two main points are supposedly made in Wisdom. The first is not to abandon the faith and traditions of your faith just to fit in with your neighbors. And the second (the only time it explicitly appears in the Old Testament) is that there is an afterlife where good is rewarded and evil punished.

Wisdom is spoken of in Ecclesiasticus (Sirach) and in the Book of Wisdom with a feminine pronoun, "she." The Hebrew, Greek, and Latin words for wisdom are *chokmah*, *Sophia*, and *sapientia*, which have feminine gender.

Sirach

The Book of Sirach is also known as Ecclesiasticus from the Latin for "church book" since it was used a lot by the early church fathers. Like the Book of Wisdom, it is one of the seven deuterocanonical/apocryphal books. It offers some practical wisdom for everyday life, as in the case with 6:14–19 on the value of a friend, which is often found on greeting cards.

"A faithful friend is a sturdy shelter: he that has found one has found a treasure. There is nothing so precious as a faithful friend, and no scales can measure his excellence. A faithful friend is an elixir of life; and those who fear the Lord will find him. Whoever fears the Lord directs his friendship aright, for as he is, so is his neighbor also. My son, from your youth up choose instruction, and until you are old you will keep finding wisdom. Come to her like one who plows and sows, and wait for her good harvest."

Chapter 12
Prophetic Writings

This chapter looks at the major and minor prophets. Isaiah, Jeremiah, Ezekiel, and Daniel comprise the four major prophets. Hosea, Joel, Amos, Obadiah, Jonah, Micah, Nahum, Habakkuk, Zephaniah, Haggai, Zechariah, and Malachi are considered the twelve minor prophets. Lamentations (attributed to Jeremiah) and Baruch (a scribe of Jeremiah and one of the seven deuterocanonical/apocryphal books) are included as part of prophetic books because of their connection to Jeremiah and their placement in the Septuagint.

What Really Is a Prophet?

A biblical prophet is not someone who predicts the future, reads minds, or communicates with the dead. The English term "prophet" originated from the Greek word *Prophetes*, which simply means to speak on behalf of someone else. God chose and sent the prophets to speak on His behalf, as in the case of Jonah. The prophet's primary mission was to teach—to inform the people of what message God was sending them.

FACT

The titles "major" and "minor" do not delineate importance; rather, they simply mean that the books of the major prophets are longer than the books of the minor prophets.

The Great Prophet Isaiah

The Book of Isaiah is divided into two parts, the first being chapters 1 to 39 and the second being chapters 40 to 66. The book spans the time frame of three monarchies: King Jotham (742–735 B.C.), King Ahaz (735–715 B.C.), and King Hezekiah (715–687 B.C.). Chapter 1 sets the tone for the entire book, namely judgment and salvation. Isaiah's very name means "the Lord saves." He lived under the reign of King Uzziah (792–740 B.C.) but was not called to be a prophet until the death of this monarch.

Isaiah Warns Judah

The first half of Isaiah (thirty-nine chapters) paints a dark, cloudy horizon over the kingdom of Judah. The people have become mechanical in their worship. They have followed the prescribed rituals and ceremonies of the law, but they did not have their hearts in it. Their external rites were supposed to be accompanied by virtuous and charitable acts of love, but instead they were accused of immorality and neglect of the widows and orphans.

According to the Bible, because of these sinful ways, God sent Isaiah to warn the people to change their hearts or suffer the consequences of their actions. Despite the numerous sacrifices of offering up animals, the hearts of the people had grown cold toward God and toward their neighbors. External acts of religion without internal acts of faith and love proved to be shallow, and Isaiah reminded the people of this, saying:

"Hear the Word of the Lord, you rulers of Sodom; listen to the law of our God, you people of Gomorrah! 'The multitude of your sacrifices— what are they to me?' says the Lord. 'I have more than enough of burnt offerings, of rams and the fat of fattened animals; I have no pleasure in the blood of bulls and lambs and goats. When you come to appear before me, who has asked this of you, this trampling of my courts? Stop bringing meaningless offerings! Your incense is detestable to me. New Moons, Sabbaths and convocations—I cannot bear your evil assemblies. Your New Moon festivals and your appointed feasts my soul hates. They have become a burden to me; I am weary of bearing them. When you spread out your hands in prayer, I will hide my eyes from you; even if you offer many prayers, I will not listen. Your hands are full of blood; wash and make yourselves clean. Take your evil deeds out of my sight! Stop doing wrong, learn to do right! Seek justice, encourage the oppressed, defend the cause of the fatherless, plead the case of the widow. Come now, let us reason together,' says the Lord. 'Though your sins are like scarlet, they shall be as white as snow; though they are red as crimson, they shall be like wool. If you are willing and obedient, you will eat the best from the land; but if you resist and rebel, you will be devoured by the sword.' For the mouth of the Lord has spoken. See how the faithful city has become a harlot! She once was full of justice; righteousness used to dwell in her— but now murderers! Your silver has become dross, your choice wine is diluted with water. Your rulers are rebels, companions of thieves; they all love bribes and chase after gifts. They do not defend the cause of the fatherless; the widow's case does not come before them. Therefore the Lord, the Lord Almighty, the Mighty One of Israel, declares: 'Ah, I will get relief from my foes and avenge myself on my enemies. I will turn my hand against you; I will thoroughly purge away your dross and remove all your impurities. I will restore your judges as in days of old, your counselors as at the beginning. Afterward you will be called the City of Righteousness, the Faithful City.'"

(Isaiah 1:10–26)

Isaiah's Prophesies

Isaiah also gave dire predictions unless the people of Judah would repent and renew their hearts and spirit. He not only prophesized chastisement and judgment, but also foretold of hope and salvation and a time of true peace to the land, both internally and externally. "They will beat their swords into plowshares and their spears into pruning hooks. Nation will not take up sword against nation, nor will they train for war anymore" (Isaiah 2:4). But the real prophecy is in chapter 7: "Therefore the Lord himself will give you a sign: The virgin will be with child and will give birth to a son, and will call him Immanuel" (Isaiah 7:14). This was later interpreted by Christian scholars as a foretelling of the coming of the Messiah.

The Hebrew word *almah* can mean either a "virgin" or a "young unmarried maiden." The Greek Septuagint translated it as *parthenos* (virgin), which is the word "retained" in most of the English translations (KJV, NAB, NIV, and so forth). Matthew 1:22 quotes this passage of Isaiah when telling of the virgin birth of Jesus: "to fulfill what the Lord had said through the prophet."

Jeremiah

Jeremiah lived from 643 to around 560 B.C., and under the reigns of Kings Manasseh, Amon, Josiah, Jehoahaz, Jehoiakim, Jehoiachin, and Zedekiah. The Babylonian Captivity took place after the fall of Jerusalem in 586 B.C., and thus ending the southern kingdom of Judah. Israel, the northern kingdom, had fallen in 722 B.C. to the Assyrians. Jeremiah is known as the "weeping prophet" since he lived during the tragic fall of Jerusalem, which could have been averted had his prophecies been heeded.

The Judgment Against Jerusalem

Like Isaiah, God sent Jeremiah to correct the people who had gone astray. "Go up and down the streets of Jerusalem, look around and consider, search through her squares. If you can find but one person who deals honestly and seeks the truth, I will forgive this city" (Jeremiah 5:1). Jeremiah, however, could not find a single one.

FACT

The phrase "eating sour grapes" comes from Jeremiah 31:29 and Ezekiel 18:2. The proverb was used to blame one's ancestors' sins for the person's own misery. The meaning was that the father's sins are felt through the sufferings of the children. If a man ate sour grapes, it made him bitter and nasty and his ill temper resulted in his children being on edge.

Jeremiah was a reluctant prophet. He did not want to bring the bad news of judgment to the people for he knew they would react with denial and anger. He felt the brunt of their displeasure and wanted no part of it, but God prevailed nonetheless. Chapters 42 and 43 tell how after the fall of Jerusalem, the people came to Jeremiah, crying that they should have paid attention to his words. When Jeremiah warned them not to go to Egypt, however, the people took him hostage.

God warned the people that there would be dire consequences if they ignored His command to avoid Egypt rather than to stay and trust that God would allow them to coexist with the Babylonians. The leaders, however, arrested Jeremiah under the pretext that he was a false prophet and the move to Egypt went as planned.

Jeremiah's message was simple. Trust God, who asked that the people and leaders trust the Babylonian King Nebuchadnezzar. Political intrigue and power plays won out and the choice to side with Egypt was made and thus Jerusalem fell. Jeremiah would be more influential after his death, since no one listened while he was alive. Later generations, on the other hand, would learn that being unfaithful to the Lord by ignoring His true prophet and foolishly following the false ones will inevitably lead to ruin. Jeremiah's fidelity, although it resulted in his own death, was a sign of perseverance in the midst of opposition.

Lamentations and Baruch

Lamentations is sometimes called the Lamentations of Jeremiah because it shows Jeremiah's sorrow for the fall of Jerusalem. After the fall of the city, the conditions were so bad that some of the survivors resorted to cannibalism. This is the reason why the book is called Lamentations. The Greek Septuagint calls it *Threnoi*, which means "dirges."

Baruch was a scribe or secretary to Jeremiah. This deuterocanonical/apocryphal book continues the themes found in Jeremiah and Lamentations. It contains a prayer of contrition, in which the people acknowledged their guilt—individually and corporately. Baruch also praised wisdom and attempted to encourage those in exile not to give up and not to lose hope.

Even though there was discouragement and lament over the fall of Jerusalem, these prophetic books teach that there was still time left to repent and there is always hope. Whether or not the people responded was up to them, but according to the covenant, it is not God who gives up.

Ezekiel

An exiled priest in Babylon, Ezekiel was one of 10,000 expelled from his homeland before the fall of Jerusalem. He is noted for his vivid visions, like the four creatures: "each of the four had the face of a man, and on the right side each had the face of a lion, and on the left the face of an ox; each also had the face of an eagle" (Ezekiel 1:10). These images parallel Revelation (Apocalypse) 4:7: "The first living creature was like a lion, the second was like an ox, the third had a face like a man, the fourth was like a flying eagle." Sacred art has used these to represent the four evangelists (Gospel Writers) of Matthew (man), Mark (lion), Luke (ox), and John (eagle).

The Dry Bones Vision

Chapters 1 to 24 of Ezekiel warn the exiles about the fate of Jerusalem; chapters 25 to 32 contain warnings against the nations; chapters 33 to 37 promise the restoration; chapters 38 to 39 are prophecies against Gog; and chapters 40 to 48 speak of the new city and new Temple. In Ezekiel 37:4, it describes the vision of the dry bones: "Then he said to me, 'Prophesy to these bones and say to them, Dry bones, hear the Word of the Lord!'" This was the basis for the familiar children's song many have learned in Bible school.

The prophecy of the revivification of dead, dry bones is a message to the Israelites that even though the kingdom will be destroyed (including the holy city of Jerusalem), God has the power to reanimate, resurrect, and bring back to life. The dried bones represent the post–Babylonian Exile Israel, which was politically and geographically dissolved. Yet, the faith would continue and like a Phoenix rising from its ashes, a new Jerusalem would eventually emerge.

Daniel

The Book of the Prophet Daniel is written in a unique style—much like that of Revelation (Apocalypse), hence the name apocalyptic literature. This is a special kind of prophecy, which uses colorful imagery, allegory, and metaphor in an almost secret-code of sorts. Just as John wrote his Apocalypse during the reigns of Emperors Domitian, Nerva, and Trajan (A.D. 81–117), this book is probably written during the vicious persecution of the Israelites by the Seleucid King Antiochus IV Epiphanes (167–164 B.C.).

Servant of King's Court

According to this book, King Nebuchadnezzar took Daniel captive during the Babylonian Captivity (586–538 B.C.), and made him a servant of the imperial court, along with some other young men: Hananiah,

Mishael, and Azariah (or the Babylonian names of Shadrach, Meshach, and Abednego). Daniel was given the Babylonian name of Belteshazzar. Although they lost their Hebrew names, the four men refused to eat the defiled food from the royal kitchen, and instead ate vegetables and drank only water. For their faithfulness, God blessed them with wisdom and knowledge.

Nebuchadnezzar's Dream

Chapter 2 tells of the dream Nebuchadnezzar had, which robbed him of his sleep and bothered him during the day. He ordered his court's wizards, visionaries, magicians, and soothsayers to interpret the dream, but they claimed they could only interpret it if he told them what it was about. King Nebuchadnezzar realized they were fakes, and executed them. Then Daniel approached Nebuchadnezzar and fulfilled his request. He told the king that it was the one true God who gave the king the dream and only He can interpret it. Daniel was merely His messenger.

Some scholars claim the elements of gold, silver, bronze, and iron represent the Babylonian, the Medo-Persian, the Greco-Seleucid, and the Roman Empires, respectively. Others claim they symbolize the Babylonians, Medes, Persians, and Greeks.

Daniel told Nebuchadnezzar he had dreamt of a great statue: "The head of the statue was made of pure gold, its chest and arms of silver, its belly and thighs of bronze, its legs of iron, its feet partly of iron and partly of baked clay" (Daniel 2:32–33). The elements of gold, silver, bronze, and iron correlated to four Ages of the world but also to four powerful empires.

Fiery Furnace

Chapter 3 tells how Nebuchadnezzar erected a ninety-foot gold statue of his god and ordered the kingdom to worship it. Faithful

Israelites, like Daniel's three companions, refused to commit idolatry and the king was infuriated that they refused the order. Nebuchadnezzar was so enraged that he had a fiery furnace heated white hot, and Shadrach, Meshach, and Abednego were thrown into it. The heat was so great that the soldiers, who threw the three young men into the furnace, were burned alive as well. The three Israelites, however, remained unharmed.

After Daniel 3:23, the Catholic Bible includes another sixty-five verses from the deuterocanonical/apocryphal section of the Septuagint. These verses (3:24–90) include the Prayer of Azariah (Abednego) and the Song of the Three Young Men. Verses 91 to 100 in the New American Bible (Catholic) correspond to verses 24 to 30 in the Protestant versions—NIV, KJV, and so forth.

FACT

On Sunday mornings, in the Liturgy of Hours (also known as the Divine Office or Breviary), the Catholic clergy and laity pray the Canticle or Song of the Three Young Men (Daniel 3:56–88) from the deuterocanonical/apocryphal fragment in the Septuagint. It is often referred to from the first two words in Latin (from the Vulgate): *Benedicite Dominum* ("Bless the Lord").

The Lions' Den

Chapter 6 shows the famous scene of Daniel being thrown into the lions' den. After Darius had succeeded Nebuchadnezzar as king, he was so pleased with Daniel that he was about to promote him to general of the armies when jealous contemporaries conspired to get rid of Daniel. Knowing he was a faithful Jew, Daniel's enemies convinced the king to issue a law that all in the kingdom had to worship Darius for one month. When Daniel refused, he was thrown into the lions' den. The next morning, when the stone covering the den was removed, there was Daniel safe and sound—the lions had not touched a hair on his head. The king released Daniel and instead threw the conspirators into the den.

"At the first light of dawn, the king got up and hurried to the lions' den. When he came near the den, he called to Daniel in an anguished voice, 'Daniel, servant of the living God, has your God, whom you serve continually, been able to rescue you from the lions?' Daniel answered, 'O king, live forever! My God sent his angel, and he shut the mouths of the lions. They have not hurt me, because I was found innocent in his sight. Nor have I ever done any wrong before you, O king.' The king was overjoyed and gave orders to lift Daniel out of the den. And when Daniel was lifted from the den, no wound was found on him, because he had trusted in his God. At the king's command, the men who had falsely accused Daniel were brought in and thrown into the lions' den, along with their wives and children. And before they reached the floor of the den, the lions overpowered them and crushed all their bones."

(Daniel 6:19–24)

Daniel, Part Two

Chapters 7, 8, 9, and 10 through 12 compose the second half of the Book of Daniel and contain four apocalypses. These correspond with four successive empires that will control the Land and yet will disintegrate one by one. The Babylonian, Median, Persian and Greek empires are represented in chapter 7 by a vision of four beasts: a lion, a bear, a leopard, and a ten-horned iron-toothed beast, respectively. Apocalyptic literature uses graphic imagery to convey powerful and sometimes controversial information. An occupied territory does not want writings that speak of the dissolution of the status quo being spread freely among the populace. Symbolic language, on the other hand, could appear harmless and yet to the trained eye and ear, give hope to the oppressed that the tide will eventually be turned.

The older Antiochean (Greek) canon from 250 B.C. has an extra two chapters in Daniel (13 and 14), which are not found in the Palestinian (Hebrew) canon of 100 A.D. This section tells of a young Israelite woman Susannah who is falsely accused of adultery. Two dirty old men who also happen to be judges of the people are scorned by this virtuous woman when they attempt to seduce her. They retaliate with charges that she has a secret lover.

In a scene that could have appeared in an episode of Perry Mason, the prophet Daniel proves in court Susannah's innocence by exposing the perjury of the two false witnesses.

The Minor Prophets

The twelve minor prophets are not small in importance, just short in length. The current arrangement in the Bible is not in chronological order, however. The order is: Amos, Hosea, Micah, Zephaniah, Nahum, Habakkuk, Haggai, Zechariah, Malachi, Obadiah, Joel, and Jonah. In 1947, copies of the minor prophets were found among the Dead Sea Scrolls in the caves of Qumran (near Jerusalem), which confirmed the authenticity of these Hebrew texts. The discovery provided better insight into the culture out of which emerged both Judaism and Christianity, and became the subject of great scholarly and public interest.

Hosea and Joel

Hosea lived in the eighth century B.C. and was commanded by God to marry a prostitute named Gomer. This bizarre order is meant to poignantly show Israel how unfaithful the nation had become. God is represented by Hosea, as the faithful husband who kept taking his wife back despite her numerous and adulterous infidelities, while Gomer represents Israel. Idolatry and worship of false gods (sometimes called "religious syncretism") is considered prostituting the faith; hence, the prophet was to marry the unfaithful harlot. Just as Hosea kept taking his cheating wife back, God will take Israel back as soon as the people realize their infidelity and come back to the Lord and their rightful ways.

ESSENTIAL

Idolatry, especially Baal worship, was rampant among the Israelites during the time of Hosea. His marriage to a prostitute is not meant as an approval of her adultery and fornication; rather, it was a graphic reminder to the people that they were just as unfaithful to the Lord as Gomer was to Hosea.

Three hundred and fifty years after Hosea, the prophet Joel warned about the Day of the Lord, or in other words, the Judgment Day. An invasion of locusts will be the omen of upcoming disasters like "the sun will be turned to darkness and the moon to blood before the coming of the great and dreadful day of the Lord" (Joel 2:31). The faithful have nothing to fear, however, for God will protect them. Only the unrighteous have need to repent or be afraid.

Amos and Obadiah

Amos lived in the mid-eighth century B.C., during the reign of King Jeroboam II. His prophecy has been classified as one of social justice. He warned both Israel and Judah to stop taking advantage of the poor. He spoke out against common but immoral practices, such as financial and economic corruption at the expense of the poor, laying heavy debts on those who cannot repay them, exploiting others, promiscuity, pagan temple prostitution, and other debauchery. Amos denounced these sins as the people hypocritically continued their religious rituals and ceremonies according to the law of Moses while defrauding their neighbor and ignoring the poor, the orphans, and the widows.

Israel took its name after the younger son of Isaac, Jacob, who after wrestling with an angel was called "Israel." Edom was the country south of Judah and was named after a descendant of Esau, the older son of Isaac, who forfeited his birthright to Jacob. The Edomites and Israelites did not get along for obvious reasons. Obadiah rebuked Edom for staying neutral when Judah was conquered by the Babylonians in 586 B.C., and for looting and pillaging it afterwards.

Jonah

The most remembered of the minor prophets, Jonah is like Jeremiah in that he was an unwilling recruit. God sent him to Nineveh (future capital of the Assyrian Empire) to preach repentance. Nineveh was the enemy, and Jonah preferred that God destroy it, like Sodom and Gomorrah. So, instead of heading east toward Nineveh, Jonah went west to Tarshish. He traveled by boat and while at sea, a violent storm ensued.

The sailors realized that they had a draft-dodger on board and so they threw him into the sea. According to the Bible, a whale swallowed Jonah, and after three days in his belly, the fish regurgitated Jonah upon land.

ALERT!

Jonah's reluctance and procrastination did not go unnoticed nor unpunished. This book teaches the value of obedience and surrendering one's own feelings, opinions, and judgments, and embracing the will of God instead. To believers, it shows that you can run from the Lord, but you cannot hide.

Learning his lesson, he went to Nineveh, which was so large it took three days to walk it. Jonah reluctantly and unenthusiastically prophesized "forty more days and Nineveh will be overturned" (Jonah 3:4). The King of Nineveh and all the inhabitants heeded the warning, and ordered everyone—from monarch to peasant, including all the animals, pets, and livestock—to put on sackcloth and ashes. God forgave the citizens of Ninevah and canceled the impending doom.

After God spared Ninevah, Jonah traveled east of the city to see if God might change his mind about punishing the people. God provided a plant with leaves to give Jonah some shade. Then He sent a worm to eat the plant, which withered and allowed the scorching sun to burn Jonah's head. Jonah complained, and God replied that instead of being concerned about one plant, there were 120,000 people at stake in Ninevah who warranted God's concern first.

Micah and Nahum

A contemporary of Isaiah and Amos, Micah rebuked the practice of neglecting or abusing the poor. He saw social injustice running rampant and denounced it as evil in the sight of God. Political corruption, graft, greed, and nepotism were abominations to the Lord since they resulted in making victims of the poor. He identified corruption and fraud in the marketplace, in the courts, and in the palace.

Nineveh went back to its old habits a century after being spared through the preaching of Jonah. It was then Nahum who took it to task for breaking the covenant with God. Unfortunately, Jerusalem did not learn from Nineveh's mistakes and suffered the consequences later.

The minor prophets spoke often about social justice, particularly concern for the poor and for treating them justly. This resulted in opposition, persecution, isolation, and sometimes death of these prophets. The prophets told the people what they needed to hear, not what they wanted or expected to hear. Ritual sacrifices meant nothing if people's hearts were turned toward greed, lust, envy, and pride.

Habakkuk and Zephaniah

A contemporary of Jeremiah, Habakkuk prophesied under King Jehoiakim that Judah would be chastised by the notorious Babylonians. God responded that Judah's sins were just as grave as Babylon's since its people should have known better, being the Chosen People of the covenant.

Great-grandson of King Hezekiah, Zephaniah prophesized under the reign of King Josiah of Judah in the later mid-seventh century B.C. Like Joel, he warned about the Day of the Lord. The idolatry of Judah will merit punishment but Jerusalem will be restored some day as well.

Haggai, Zechariah, and Malachi

A prophet of the mid-sixth century, Haggai called for the rebuilding of the Temple in Jerusalem after Judean exiles returned to the city. The Lord was displeased that the returning refugees built their own lovely homes and estates first and left the Temple for last. Haggai reminded them of their priorities.

A contemporary of Haggai, Zechariah was of the priestly class. He, too, prophesied about the restoration of the Temple. Chapter 9 is a Messianic prophesy that the Messiah-King would restore what had been destroyed (Jerusalem) and that it would endure forever. Christians interpret the church as the heavenly Jerusalem, which fulfills this prediction.

Writing perhaps around 425 B.C., Malachi is a postexilic prophet. He mentioned the efficacy of tithing where one tenth of one's possessions and wealth should go to God. Malachi also predicted the return of Elijah. Christians would interpret the ministry of John the Baptist as the fulfillment of this prophecy.

The Sound of Silence

Aside from the two deuterocanonical/apocryphal books of 1 and 2 Maccabees (150–100 B.C.), there was a pronounced silence after the prophet Malachi. This is often called the intertestamental period, which buffers the Old and New Testament time periods. Several of the apocryphal/ pseudepigraphical books, which never made it into any Bible, were written during the 200- to 400-year span of the intertestamental era. The absence of substantial amounts of inspired writings is the reason why this is considered a silent epoch. ⓔ

Chapter 13

The New Testament

This chapter looks at the New Testament in relation to the Old Testament, which came before it. It is a general overview of the second half of the Bible, where Christianity emerged as a new religion, with roots clearly visible in the Hebrew faith. From the Gospels to the Epistles, the documents of the New Testament are examined from their origin, purpose, and impact, at home and abroad.

The Ancient Promise

The word "Messiah" comes from the Hebrew word *mashiyach*, which means "anointed one." Greek uses the word *christos* to mean the same thing. This anointed one would be the one who would save the people. Moses was the "deliverer" who freed the Israelities from their physical slavery in Egypt, but he was not the Savior nor the Messiah. The anointed one would be a king who would establish a kingdom that would never end.

There are three types or visions of a Messiah, which developed over the Old Testament period. Prophetic, apocalyptic, and revolutionary Messianism independently developed side by side, influenced by the social, political, economic, and religious experiences of the diverse group of Hebrew people. After the disintegration of the single state (Saul, David, and Solomon) into two separate kingdoms, Judah (southern kingdom) and Israel (northern kingdom) take different paths. The Babylonian Captivity and Diaspora will further complicate matter as more Israelites would come to live and worship outside their native land.

Prophetic Messiah

This type of Messianism looked for a sign of the coming of an earthly king, who would establish an earthly (temporal) kingdom of God on earth. The first king, Saul, raised hopes since he was anointed by the prophet Samuel, but later proved a disappointment. The great King David and his son, the wise King Solomon, also had raised high but false expectations that an earthly reign would be the fulfillment of the Promise. Once the kingdom was divided between north (Israel) and south (Judah), the hopes attenuated until the Babylonian exile and Diaspora, which put them to rest.

Apocalyptic Messiah

Unlike prophetic Messianism, apocalyptic did not expect the kingdom of God to just happen one day through the efforts of an earthly king. This type looked for something more supernatural and less ordinary. A chastisement called the Day of the Lord would bring the wrath of God upon those who violated the covenant. Those who remained faithful would be rewarded by staying alive and living in the new kingdom governed by the anointed one (Messiah). This gave hope to the Israelites in captivity or exile.

FACT

Whether it was the Babylonians or Syrians, displaced Israelites longed for a major turn of the tables when their king would be the imperial power to reckon with, instead of the status quo.

Revolutionary or Political Messiah

Both prophetic and apocalyptic Messianism depended solely on God to choose the man, the day, the time, the hour, and the place for it to happen. Revolutionary or political Messianism, on the other hand, realized that while God would be the one who established the Messiah's reign, He would also want the cooperation and assistance of the people. Just as the Israelites had to fight their way into the Promised Land of Canaan, so, too, this flavor of Messianism called for drastic measures. The Maccabean victories over the Syrians and the recapture of old territory gave some credibility to this model. Defeat by the Romans, however, took a lot of steam out of their popular support.

The Preparation Period

Judaism was not a homogenous monolithic religion. Within the Hebrew faith were many divisions and sects and no one group represented all Jews. The four principal and major players who set the stage for the arrival of the Messiah in the person of Jesus Christ were the Pharisees, Sadducees, Essenes, and the Zealot Party.

ESSENTIAL

The Scribes were a very small group of religious lawyers who associated with the Pharisees. They organized synagogue worship whereas the Priests had been reserved for temple sacrifices and prayers. As experts in the law, they advised the Pharisees in the Sanhedrin, the supreme tribunal, and council for the postexilic Jews.

Pharisees

The Pharisees were the largest and most powerful group. The name comes from the Aramaic word for separate (*peras*), and comprised the descendants of the Hasidaeans, a society of religious and pious men who sought to separate (hence the term Pharisee) from the tainted and syncretistic Hellenizers. Pharisees were predominantly laymen who isolated themselves from the Gentiles (name given to people who are not Jewish), and especially from the influence of Greek culture since it was pagan. Purity of religion was their goal, which was achieved by scrupulous observance of the law of Moses. Other characteristics were their acceptance and reverence for the oral tradition on the same level as the written law, and their belief in the immortality of the soul, the afterlife, and the resurrection of the dead.

Sadducees

This smaller group is named after the Hebrew word *tsaddiqim*, meaning righteous ones. They were descendants of the Hellenizers, and thus bitter rivals with the Pharisees. Sadducees were clerics, that is, of the priestly class (Levites) and although a few did join the Pharisees or Scribes, only Levites could become priests since it was hereditary. They were more fundamentalist in the sense that they only accepted the teachings contained in the written scrolls, and unlike the Pharisees, did not accept oral tradition as equal. This also meant that they rejected the immortality of the soul, resurrection of the dead, and so on.

Essenes

This esoteric group of Jewish mystics gets its name from the Aramaic "asayya," meaning healer. Shortly after the Maccabean Wars, the Essenes devoted themselves to prayer and study, almost the precursor to Christian monasticism. Many gathered away from the cities and towns and sought solace near the Dead Sea. The famous Dead Sea Scrolls are reputed to be written by the Essenes since they devoted themselves to prayer and copying the sacred writings. They cloistered themselves from Jerusalem, which they believed had become defiled by unbelievers.

Zealots

Political or Revolutionary Messianism produced what is known as the Zealot Party, or simply the Zealots. These people sought an activist role in bringing about the liberation from foreign occupation, be it Persian, Greek, or Roman. Simon was called the Zealot for two reasons. One, he formerly belonged to this group before becoming an apostle, and two, to distinguish him from Simon Peter, the head of the apostles.

FACT

The Zealots admired and emulated Mattathias, the first Maccabee, who led a revolt against foreign occupiers. The last bastion of the Zealots was Masada, which fell to the Romans in A.D. 74, just three years after the Temple in Jerusalem had been destroyed.

Jesus' Birth and Childhood

Technically speaking, one could presume that Jesus of Nazareth was born on January 1st, in the year A.D. 1, since the Christian calendar is based on the notion of B.C. being "before Christ" and A.D. being the *Anno Domini* (Latin for "year of the Lord"). Actually, no one knows the exact month or day of His birth, and the year was slightly miscalculated. The Bible says that Jesus was born during the reign of Herod the Great, who ordered all infant boys slaughtered after the Magi saw an uncommon star and came looking for the Messiah. Herod's reign, according to Flavius Josephus, was from 37–4 B.C. Many scholars propose that Jesus was born closer to the year 4 B.C., as Herod's reign came to an end. All that is known is that the cousin of Jesus, John the Baptist, was born six months before Him.

Little is known about Jesus' childhood. Matthew 2:13–16 tells of the Flight into Egypt when Joseph and Mary had to hide the infant from Herod:

"When they had gone, an angel of the Lord appeared to Joseph in a dream. 'Get up,' he said, 'take the child and his mother and escape to Egypt. Stay there until I tell you, for Herod is going to search for the child to kill him.' So he got up, took the child and his mother during the night and left for Egypt, where he stayed until the death of Herod. And so was fulfilled what the Lord had said through the prophet: 'Out of Egypt I called my son.' When Herod realized that he had been outwitted by the Magi, he was furious, and he gave orders to kill all the boys in Bethlehem and its vicinity who were two years old and under, in accordance with the time he had learned from the Magi."

Luke 2:41–52 tells of twelve-year-old Jesus instructing the teachers in the Temple of Jerusalem. Other than that, He lived in Nazareth as the adopted son of a carpenter (Joseph, the husband of Mary). According to Jewish custom, Jesus would have spent most of his infancy and childhood with His mother until He had His bar mitzvah at the age of twelve. From then on, He would have spent more time with Joseph, the head of the family, who happened to be a carpenter.

QUESTION?

Why do Christians celebrate Jesus' birth on December 25th? Saint Augustine claims it is because Jesus said in John 8:12, "I am the light of the world" and John the Baptist said in John 3:30, "He must become greater; I must become less." Based on those passages, the church celebrated the birth of Christ around the winter solstice (after the shortest day of the year, when daylight starts to increase) and the birth of John the Baptist around the summer solstice (after the longest day, when daylight begins to decrease).

Public Life and Ministry

According to the New Testament of the Bible, Jesus lived a quiet and obscure life from the age of twelve until He turned thirty. Then He was baptized by His cousin John (the Baptist) in the River Jordan and went into the desert for forty days to fast and pray. While there, the devil tempted Him (Matthew 3:13–17; Mark 1:9–11; Luke 3:21–22) and successfully resisting that, Jesus proceeded to his public ministry. Only John's Gospel relates the first public miracle of Christ, the changing of the water into wine at the wedding feast of Cana.

Jesus' Preaching

The sermons of Jesus—found in the New Testament Gospels—form what biblical scholars call "the preaching," or in Greek, the *kerygma* of Christ. There are ten sermons in Matthew, five in Mark, thirteen in Luke, and eight in John. They cover issues such as divorce, forgiveness, discipleship, brotherly love, and others. The most famous of Jesus' sermons was the Sermon on the Mount (Matthew 5:1–7:29), which is very similar to His Sermon on the Plain (Luke 6:17–49). Turn the other cheek, love those who hate you, pray for those who persecute you, do unto others as you would have them do unto you—these are some of the principal elements of Jesus' preaching.

Jesus' Teaching

The doctrine or teachings of Christ are found in His preaching. They are almost inseparable. Where *kerygma* focuses on what Jesus said, *didache* (teaching) focuses on what His words mean. Since in Matthew 5:17, it is written "I have not come to abolish them but to fulfill them [the Law]," the moral law—as contained in the Commandments—still applied when He explained about divorce, adultery, murder, anger, and so on. What is different in His teaching from that of the Old Testament is that forgiveness is possible and available through Him.

The term *didache* should not be confused with the book Didache or "The Teaching of the Twelve Apostles." One of the oldest non-biblical documents on the Christian faith, the book Didache speaks of Christian ethics, morality, and piety. The term *didache* in reference to the Gospels simply means the teachings of Christ.

Jesus' Miracles

The miraculous healings by Jesus—the raising of Lazarus and Jairus' daughter from the dead; the curing of Peter's mother-in-law; the exorcism of the possessed; the healing of the blind, the deaf, the mute, and the lame—showed that God had compassion on those who suffered and authenticated the credentials of Jesus that He was the Son of God. According to the New Testament, Jesus' main mission was to save and redeem humankind from sin. The miraculous healings were a vindication of His power and authority to forgive sin.

FACT

The only place Jesus encountered obstinate resistance to His preaching and teaching was in His hometown, Nazareth. "Jesus said to them, 'Only in his hometown and in his own house is a prophet without honor.' And he did not do many miracles there because of their lack of faith" (Matthew 13:57–58).

Development of the Gospels

The four Gospel accounts of Matthew, Mark, Luke, and John came about in three stages, though not all at the same time. The first phase was the actual sayings, healings, and miracles of Jesus—what He said and what He did. Phase two was the oral tradition whereby His disciples and apostles preached and told by word of mouth what Jesus said and did. The final phase was the inspired writing of the Gospel by the evangelist. No one took notes or dictation while Jesus preached, taught, or performed His miracles. The written Word came many years after the preached or unwritten (spoken) Word.

Comparing the Gospels

Matthew, Mark, and Luke's accounts of Jesus' life are so similar that they are called the Synoptic Gospels—from the Greek *synopsis*, meaning sharing the same content, style, and sequence of events. John's Gospel, on the other hand, is quite different. However, there are not four separate Gospels as if there were four different Jesuses being described. Also, each evangelist (Gospel writer) did not intend to tell you everything Jesus said or did, just those sayings and deeds he felt were important and critical for his intended audience.

ESSENTIAL

> At the end of his Gospel, John tells us that, "Jesus did many other things as well. If every one of them were written down, I suppose that even the whole world would not have room for the books that would be written" (John 21:25).

You may wish to consider the four Gospel accounts like four newspapers. One is written for a Jewish audience in a Jewish neighborhood; one for a Gentile audience in a Greek neighborhood; one for a Roman audience in a Roman province; and one for a Christian audience in a Christian environment. Just as the *New York Times*, *The Wall Street Journal*, *The Harrisburg Patriot-News*, and the *Hershey Chronicle* are all newspapers, each one often covers the very same stories but for very different audiences. Those audiences influence what the reporter includes or omits in his or her article. A national or international paper is going to give different coverage from a local or financial paper. Likewise, Matthew will write for a Jewish audience, Luke for a Gentile, Mark for a Roman, and John for a Christian, and that will affect what, how much, and in what manner things Jesus said and did are related.

Saint Ignatius of Loyola devised a method for praying the Gospels. When you read one of the four Gospel accounts, imagine you are one of the people, spectators, at the event. Using your imagination, envision yourself in a native costume. Feel the breeze on your face, smell the fresh flowers of the field, listen to the birds chirping or the crowd murmuring. As you read the text of Jesus' sermons, imagine you are there hearing them with your own ears. By engaging as many of the five senses as possible and applying them to as many parts of the Gospel as possible, you will not only remember more, you will also get more out of it as well.

The Epistles

The Epistles (from *epistola* meaning "letter") of the early Christian leaders (the apostles and their successors, and the bishops) make up the other half of the New Testament. Each individual letter or Epistle was written for a specific location and group of people, either under the spiritual care of the author or having affiliations with him. Just as pastors write columns in their weekly bulletins—bishops to their flock in the diocese and popes to their faithful around the world—men like Paul, James, John, Peter, and Jude wrote similar letters to encourage, correct, teach, explain, and guide.

FACT

In order to be placed in the Bible, a book had to be considered inspired since inspiration carries with it the gift of inerrancy, and the written Word, along with the spoken Word, comprise what is called "Divine Revelation."

However, just as there are apocryphal/pseudepigraphical Gospels, such as Thomas and Peter, so, too, there are noninspired and noncanonical Epistles, which never made it into the Bible. These include the Letters of Lentulus, the Epistle to the Laodiceans, the Correspondence of Paul and Seneca, the Epistle to the Alexandrians, and the Epistle of the Apostles.

The Early Christian Church

The Acts of the Apostles chronicle the early days and beginnings of the Christian church. Remember, no written text existed yet since the oldest Gospel was not written until A.D. 45, or A.D. 50 at the very earliest. Some scholars push the dates even further from A.D. 55 to A.D. 69 and John did not finish his until close to A.D. 100. That means there was no written Bible, no written Gospels, just the oral tradition of the apostles and disciples preaching Jesus' message to the people by word of mouth. The early church also had to make some decisions and modifications to deal with new situations, which did not occur while Jesus was alive.

Christ called Jews to be His apostles. According to the Bible, after His death, Resurrection, and Ascension, more Gentiles became interested in following his teaching. Some of the questions that came up were: Should Gentiles first become Jews before becoming Christian? Should Gentile Christian men be circumcised like Jewish Christian men? Should someone replace the apostle Judas? What about all the Jewish dietary laws from the Old Testament; do they apply to Gentile converts? These questions were all addressed and answered in the Book of Acts.

Chapter 14

The Gospel of Matthew

The first book of the New Testament is the Gospel according to Saint Matthew, which has also been coined the "Gospel of fulfillment." One of the original twelve apostles, Matthew writes for a Hebrew audience and makes numerous parallels with the Old Testament to show its fulfillment in the person of Jesus Christ. He gives more attention to what Jesus said than what He did, even though both are present in the text.

Jewish Audience

Matthew was a tax collector (Matthew 9:9) by trade, but was also of the Jewish faith. His knowledge of the Hebrew religion was used to introduce his fellow Jews to Jesus of Nazareth whom the Christians believed to be the Messiah (Aramaic for "the anointed one"; in Greek, *Christos*). Bible scholars have traditionally described Matthew's account of the Gospel as being written for a Jewish audience, but that doesn't mean that Gentiles and non-Jews should avoid Matthew. On the contrary, it is crucial for Christians to see the roots and foundations of their faith—in the religion of their founder and His disciples who were also Jews. Sacred art depicts Matthew as a man with wings since he begins with the human origins of Christ.

Connect the Dots

In comparison to the other Synoptics (Mark and Luke), this Gospel makes parallel connections between the two major protagonists of the Bible—Moses (Old Testament) and Jesus Christ (New Testament). Matthew does not "create" a connection; he merely identifies and emphasizes it. Hence, the genealogy in his Gospel goes from Abraham to Jesus in descending order, whereas in Luke, the lineage goes in ascending order from Jesus all the way to Adam. The former is a shorter list yet does not deny the continuation given in the latter; however, it is the emphasis on the point of origin and the point of termination that makes the difference. A Jewish audience would be most attentive to the demonstration that the Christian Messiah is indeed a branch of the family tree of Abraham, since it was "Father Abraham" with whom God made the covenant.

ESSENTIAL

When opponents of Jesus accused him of contempt for the Law of Moses, the reply in Matthew is: "Do not think that I have come to abolish the Law or the Prophets; I have not come to abolish them but to fulfill them. I tell you the truth, until heaven and earth disappear, not the smallest letter, not the least stroke of a pen, will by any means disappear from the Law until everything is accomplished" (Matthew 5:17–18).

The famous Sermon on the Mount is given in Matthew (5:1–7:29) but a very similar sermon is also in Luke (6:17–49), yet in that instance the location is identified as a level plain. A Jewish audience would know and remember that God gave the law to Moses on Mount Sinai (Exodus 19). That same audience would be interested in listening to a sermon given on a mount and hopefully make the connection between Moses and Jesus.

When Was It Written?

Matthew's account of the Gospel was probably first written in Hebrew or Aramaic, ancient sources tell us; but no copy exists, only references to it. The Greek text, however, was penned sometime between A.D. 50 and 69 since no mention is made of the destruction of the Temple of Jerusalem, which the Romans did in A.D. 70 in response to an uprising. Some scholars date the Gospel well after that event by ten or more years.

Genealogy and Infancy (Matthew 1–2)

Everyone has at least one relative who is interested in their family tree. This is the person who painstakingly researches the genealogy of the ancestors, from mom and dad, to grandma and grandpa who came over on the boat from the "old country," and so on. Jesus had a family tree just like everyone else, and Matthew traces the lineage of Christ back to Abraham. Actually, the Gospel begins with "Abraham was the father of Isaac, Isaac the father of Jacob, Jacob the father of Judah and his brothers . . ." (Matthew 1:2). This continues through to King David "and Jesse the father of King David. David was the father of Solomon, whose mother had been Uriah's wife . . ." (Matthew 1:6). The genealogy concludes with "and Jacob the father of Joseph, the husband of Mary, of whom was born Jesus, who is called Christ" (Matthew 1:16).

This list is important to Matthew and to his intended audience. Abraham is the patriarch of the Hebrew nation. "Father Abraham" is one of the central figures of Judaism since it is through Abraham that the covenant is first made between God and His Chosen People. Showing the connection, then, between Jesus, whom Matthew is asserting is the Messiah, and Abraham, the father of the Hebrew religion, is not just a little tidbit of information; it is a fundamental cornerstone.

How does Matthew try to connect the two Testaments?
Matthew wants to connect the old covenant with the new by presenting the New Testament as the fulfillment of the Old Testament.

QUESTION?

Scripture Fulfillment

Fulfillment is a major theme in Matthew's Gospel as he continues in verse 22–23 of chapter 1: "All this took place to fulfill what the Lord had said through the prophet [Isaiah]: 'The virgin will be with child and will give birth to a son, and they will call him Immanuel,' which means, 'God with us.'" Matthew matter-of-factly ends chapter 1 with the description of Mary (the mother of Jesus) as being engaged/betrothed to Joseph, though not yet living together as husband and wife and that she was "with child" (pregnant) "through the Holy Spirit" (Matthew 1:18). Joseph at first intends to quietly divorce Mary when he discovers she is with child and he knows he is not the father. Matthew tells us that an angel speaks to Joseph, in a dream, not to be afraid since she was not unfaithful; rather it was by the Holy Spirit she conceived. "When Joseph woke up, he did what the angel of the Lord had commanded him and took Mary home as his wife. But he had no union with her until she gave birth to a son. And he gave him the name Jesus" (Matthew 1:24–25).

FACT

A Jewish audience would be sensitive that Joseph intends to divorce Mary quietly since the Mosaic law only had two alternatives for infidelity—stoning or divorce. He knew he was not the biological father, having no idea of how Mary conceived until he was told by the angel, but being a just man, he gives her the benefit of the doubt and opts for the less painful remedy.

Chapter 2 deals with Jesus' early infancy. The story of the Wise Men (also known as the Magi, Astrologers, or Kings) from the East is mentioned only in Matthew's Gospel. He points out that these Gentile (non-Jewish) travelers came to King Herod who was not popular with the Jews since he was a puppet ruler for Rome. As the story continues, we discover that evil Herod was jealous of the newborn "king of the Jews" (as the infant Jesus is referred to by the Magi), and so he plotted to kill the child. He asked the Magi to offer homage to the baby Jesus and then inform him of his location.

Popular piety and pious tradition have given the Magi three names: Caspar, Melchior, and Balthasar. The reason for three kings was to correspond with the three gifts given to the Christ-child of gold, frankincense, and myrrh (Matthew 2:11), as well as to fulfill the prophecy of Isaiah: "Nations will come to your light, and kings to the brightness of your dawn" (Isaiah 60:3).

Herod, the Evil King

When the Magi told Herod about the birth of the "new king of the Jews," he ordered the slaughter of every male infant, two years old or younger. Again, a Jewish audience would see parallels with the story in Exodus where Pharaoh ordered the killing of all the male Hebrew babies. Moses survived that bloodbath and Jesus survived this one. Matthew makes more connections in verses 5–6 and 18 of chapter 2 when the Old Testament prophets Micah and Jeremiah are quoted and presented as fulfilled prophecies.

The Proclamation (Matthew 3–7)

This section deals with the period before the public ministry of Jesus. Matthew jumps from infancy to adulthood, leaving out the childhood and adolescence of Christ. Bible scholars call this part of the Gospel the "Proclamation," since it contains sayings and sermons of Jesus in preparation for His public ministry—when He would travel, preach, and perform miracles. The stage is different in that it describes the preliminary work, which had to be done before Jesus would venture out "on the road," so to speak.

Baptism

Matthew begins chapter 3 with "In those days John the Baptist came, preaching in the Desert of Judea and saying, 'Repent, for the kingdom of heaven is near.' This is he who was spoken of through the prophet Isaiah: A voice of one calling in the desert, 'Prepare the way for the Lord, make straight paths for him'" (Matthew 3:1–3).

The phrase "kingdom of heaven" is unique to Matthew, whereas the other Gospel accounts use "kingdom of God." John was performing a symbolic baptism of repentance and conversion. When Jesus appeared, Matthew says that John at first protested: "I need to be baptized by you, and do you come to me?" (Matthew 3:14). But then he relented since it was meant to fulfill Scripture, and so he baptized Jesus in the River Jordan.

Temptation

The three temptations the devil made toward Jesus are succinctly handled in this Gospel account. The first temptation to turn stones into bread (Matthew 4:3–4) receives the retort: "man does not live on bread alone, but on every word that comes from the mouth of God" as quoted by Jesus from Deuteronomy 8:3. It was an appeal to succumb to physical wants and needs, whereas Christ replied that the spiritual sustenance from God is superior.

In the second temptation (Matthew 4:5–7), Satan (the devil) asked Jesus to throw Himself off the Temple so that the angels could rescue Him. Jesus responded: "Do not put the Lord your God to the test" (Matthew 4:7). In the third and last temptation of Christ (Matthew 4:8–10), the devil offered the world in return for worship. Jesus sternly reprimanded the tempter with: "Away from me, Satan! For it is written: 'Worship the Lord your God, and serve him only'" (Matthew 4:10).

QUESTION?

What is the significance of the number "forty" in the Bible? Forty is a special number in the Bible, especially in the Old Testament. It rained forty days and forty nights during the Flood of Noah, the Israelites were lost in the desert for forty years before entering the Promised Land, Moses spent forty days on Mount Sinai before receiving the Ten Commandments, and Jesus spent forty days in the desert in preparation of His public ministry.

The Call

Verses 18–22 of chapter 4 mention Jesus choosing the first four apostles, Peter and his brother Andrew, as well as James and his brother John. All four were fishermen tending their nets when Jesus said: "come, follow me . . . and I will make you fishers of men." Matthew says they "immediately" (*eutheos* in Greek) left their boat and followed Him.

Sermon on the Mount

This is the most famous of Jesus' sermons. The interesting detail in Matthew is that this sermon was given on a Mount, which a Jewish audience would hopefully associate with Moses receiving the Ten Commandments on Mount Sinai. The first part of it has been given the name the *Beatitudes* since the first word of every line in the Latin Vulgate of Saint Jerome reads *beati* or "blessed." These phrases give comfort and courage to those who lack the transitory power, wealth, or comfort in this world to seek the eternal happiness of heaven. There are nine beatitudes in Matthew 5:

1. Blessed are the poor in spirit, for theirs is the kingdom of heaven.
2. Blessed are those who mourn, for they will be comforted.
3. Blessed are the meek, for they will inherit the earth.
4. Blessed are those who hunger and thirst for righteousness, for they will be filled.
5. Blessed are the merciful, for they will be shown mercy.
6. Blessed are the pure in heart, for they will see God.

7. Blessed are the peacemakers, for they will be called sons of God.

8. Blessed are those who are persecuted because of righteousness, for theirs is the kingdom of heaven.

9. Blessed are you when people insult you, persecute you and falsely say all kinds of evil against you because of me. Rejoice and be glad, because great is your reward in heaven, for in the same way they persecuted the prophets who were before you.

The Ministry (Matthew 8–10)

The second part of Matthew's Gospel moves from the sermons to the active ministry. Chapter 8 begins with Jesus coming down from the Mount and curing a leper. There are also ten miracles that Jesus performs and then, in chapter 10, He sends out the twelve disciples (who later become Jesus' apostles) and gives them detailed instructions for their mission.

ESSENTIAL

According to believers, Jesus preached forgiveness and taught mercy. Forgiving one's enemies and not seeking revenge nor judging others, either, were part of his message. He also taught the value of redemptive suffering, that is, making sacrifices and enduring hardship (taking up the cross) not as punishment but for holiness sake.

The First Four Miracles

The first miracle involved a leper. After the miraculous healing, Jesus said to the man: "show yourself to the priest and offer the gift Moses commanded, as a testimony to them" (Matthew 8:4), something a Jewish audience would like to know since one of the charges made by His enemies was that Jesus repudiated and denounced the old law of Moses.

The second miracle was different from the first in that it was more of an affirmation of the faith present in the person making the request. The Centurion (Roman soldier) told Jesus there is no need for Him to come to the house because he did not need to "see" the miracle to believe. He already believed and all Jesus need do was "say the word." As a soldier, the Roman knew that orders are obeyed. The fact that the Centurion did not need to witness the event showed great faith on his part, which Jesus affirmed in this section.

In the third miracle, Jesus' disciple Simon Peter's mother-in-law was sick, and Jesus healed her. As soon as she got better, she "ministered" unto them. The Greek word Matthew uses is *diakoneo* for service, the same word the Acts of Apostles will appropriate for the office of deacon—those men and women chosen by the apostles and their successors to serve/minister unto the needs of the widows and orphans in the early church.

The fourth miracle presented in the Gospel of Matthew simply stated that "many who were demon possessed were brought to him, and he drove out the spirits with a word and healed all the sick" (Matthew 8:16). This is a bit matter-of-fact but to the point, namely, that Jesus had authority and power over both physical and spiritual maladies.

Calming of the Sea

The fifth miracle is referred to as "the calming of the sea." When a large crowd gathered around Jesus to hear him preach, Jesus got into a boat with his disciples. A storm came and the boat began shipping water. The disciples were scared and asked Jesus to save them. Jesus "got up and rebuked the winds and the waves, and it was completely calm" (Matthew 8:26). This miracle showed His authority and power over nature itself.

Two Demoniacs and the Paralytic

Jesus' healing of the two possessed men in the sixth miracle showed that the powers of darkness knew with whom they are dealing when they shouted, "What do you want with us, Son of God?" (Matthew 8:29). Even though most men and women at this time are unaware of Jesus' Divinity, the demons recognized it and were repulsed by it. Jesus cast the demons from the men into a herd of swine.

In the seventh miracle, Jesus healed a man suffering from palsy (called a paralytic in many translations) and forgave his sins. This act showed that the spiritual healing was more urgent than the physical. However, some reacted to Jesus' miracle, claiming, "This fellow is blaspheming!" (Matthew 9:3) since Jesus was healing during the Sabbath (Jewish Holy Day).

E ALERT!

The physical cure of the paralytic in this case was meant as evidence to the audience that Jesus had the authority to forgive sins just as He had power over illness, demons, and nature.

The Last Three Miracles

In the eighth miracle, a synagogue official (named Jairus in other Gospel accounts) had a sick daughter, who died, but he still asked Jesus to come to his home and "put your hand on her, and she will live" (Matthew 9:18). The official's faith that even death is no obstacle for Jesus was the main point of this miracle. When He arrived at the house, Jesus confronted the mourners and said, "The girl is not dead but asleep" (Matthew 9:24), which bewildered them. Jesus indeed restored the girl to life, as soon as He took her by the hand. The idea of death as "sleep" was later adopted by early Christians, who referred to their dead as "the sleepers."

The ninth miracle presented by Matthew in his Gospel is placed during the miraculous cure of the official's dead daughter. A woman has been plagued with a blood disease for twelve years, and was cured merely by touching Jesus' cloak. Matthew shows that it was not a magic garment that healed her but rather her faith. Jesus said: "'Your faith has healed you.' And the woman was healed from that moment" (Matthew 9:22).

The last of the ten miracles has two parts. The first deals with the cure of two blind men, the second with a man possessed by a mute spirit. The irony appears after the man is exorcised of his demon when the Pharisees shout, "It is by the prince of demons that he drives out demons." The saying "no good deed goes unpunished" could apply here. No matter what good Jesus did, whether it was healing the sick, expelling demons, or calming storms, his enemies twisted it around and claimed it as evidence of diabolical power.

The twelve disciples that Jesus picked were ordinary men; there was nothing outstanding about them. They were not the brightest, the strongest, nor the most educated. Despite their personal or professional shortcomings, Jesus gives them a chance to be His followers.

The Twelve Disciples

After visiting many towns where Jesus went about teaching, preaching, and healing, Matthew points out that He was moved with compassion seeing the multitude "harassed and helpless, like sheep without a shepherd" (Matthew 9:36). Jesus then appointed the twelve disciples to take care of these people's needs. Matthew listed the twelve disciples as follows:

1. Simon (who is called Peter)
2. his brother Andrew
3. James son of Zebedee
4. his brother John
5. Philip
6. Bartholomew
7. Thomas
8. Matthew the tax collector
9. James son of Alphaeus
10. (Jude) Thaddaeus
11. Simon the Zealot
12. Judas Iscariot

Jesus gave His disciples a three-part instruction. The first (Matthew 10:5–15) dealt with the immediate present, the second (Matthew 10:16–23) with the near future, and the third (Matthew 10:24–42) with the final destination. Phase one involved "the lost sheep of Israel," and not the Gentiles nor the Samaritans. Phase two involved the opposition and persecution that followed the first part. "Be as shrewd as snakes and as innocent as doves," or in other words, use your wits, be careful, and be clever. Phase three gave hope that all their trial and tribulation would be rewarded. In the last section (Matthew 10:28), Jesus told them, "Do not be afraid," for their efforts would not go unnoticed in the next world.

The Parables (Matthew 11–13)

In his Gospel, Matthew retells six of Jesus' parables. These lessons in morality are a common tool used by rabbis and teachers at the time of Jesus. Just as Plato and Socrates would give examples to their students, Jesus gave homespun stories, which had a moral ending for the audience.

The first parable is the one of the sower (Matthew 13:1–9) who threw seeds onto his property. Some fell on the ground and were eaten by birds, some on the rocks where no roots could be established, some among thorns (which choked off the plants), but some seed fell on good soil where it produced much fruit. Jesus later explained that God represented the sower, and the seeds were the Word of God.

FACT

According to the parable of the sower, those who hear the Word but do not understand it are like the seeds eaten by the birds. Those who accept the Word at first but don't let it take root will be scorched like the seeds on rocky ground. Those who receive the Word but do not live according to it are like the seeds among thorns that choke them to death. Finally, those who hear the Word and understand it are like the seeds on good soil; they will produce a rich harvest.

The second parable is the one of the weeds (Matthew 13:24–30). A farmer sowed seeds in his field but at night his enemy planted weeds among the wheat. This act went unnoticed until the plants began to sprout and then the servants realized that there were weeds among the wheat. The farmer told the servants to wait until harvest time, when the two will be separated and then the weeds will be burned and the wheat taken into the barn.

The third parable concerned the mustard seed (Matthew 13:31–32), which was the smallest seed but produced the largest plant. It is followed by the fourth parable of the yeast (Matthew 13:33), which likewise described the kingdom of heaven—small beginnings but tremendous results. The fifth parable (Matthew 13:44–46) dealt with hidden treasure and found pearls. When a person discovered them, he sold what he had to possess the pearls.

Here the message is that the kingdom of heaven requires a total commitment and complete surrender. The sixth parable (Matthew 13:47–52) was about a net, which collected all kinds of fish. However, the fishermen had to separate the good from the bad when they hauled in the net. This parable symbolized the end of the world when the angels will separate the wicked from the righteous.

The Disciples (Matthew 14–18)

This part of Matthew's Gospel account concerns the disciples of Jesus as He continues His public ministry with them. It begins with the death of John the Baptist and culminates in His departure for Jerusalem. This section includes the Feeding of the 5,000, the Walking on Water, Peter's Confession of Faith, Jesus' Prediction of His own death, and the Transfiguration.

Beheading of John the Baptist

King Herod held a birthday party for himself and was delighted by a seductive dance from his wife's (Herodias) daughter so much that he granted her any wish. Since John the Baptist had been jailed for speaking out against the adulterous marriage of Herod and Herodias (formerly married to his brother), the mother convinced her daughter to ask for the head of the Baptist on a platter. The request had to be granted since the king had made his oath before all the guests.

Following the death of John the Baptist, Matthew tells of the miracle (Matthew 14:13–21) where Jesus blessed five loaves of bread and two fish, and fed 5,000 men, not counting women and children. Twelve baskets of leftovers were then collected. This is followed by the miracle (Matthew 14:22–36) of Jesus walking on the water, which at first terrified His disciples, who thought they were seeing a ghost. But Jesus reassured them, "Take courage! It is I. Don't be afraid."

Peter's Confession of Faith

Matthew is the only Synoptic Gospel to include what the Catholic Church considers the Petrine Promise (Peter's Promise). Luke and Mark briefly recount the same scene of Jesus asking the question, "Who do people say the Son of Man is?" And Peter alone replies, "You are the Christ, the Son of the Living God." But only Matthew 16 has the lines "I tell you that you are Peter, and on this rock I will build my church, and the gates of Hades will not overcome it. I will give you the keys of the kingdom of heaven; whatever you bind on earth will be bound in heaven, and whatever you loose on earth will be loosed in heaven."

Here is a play on words: *Petros*, which is a Greek proper name for "Peter," and *petra*, which is Greek for "rock." Catholicism sees it as a biblical foundation for the office (vis-à-vis the "keys") and ministry of Peter and his successors—the popes (bishops of Rome), whereas other Christian denominations (Eastern Orthodox and Protestant) dispute this and claim it is Peter's faith, which Jesus is using to build the church, and not his position.

FACT

Moses and Elijah are the epitome of the Old Testament, representing the law and the prophets, respectively. They are two central figures to the Hebrew religion.

Chapter 17 includes the scene of the Transfiguration (Matthew 17:1–13) in which Jesus took Peter, James, and John with Him to a mountain (Tabor or Hermon), where He was transfigured before them and out of nowhere appeared Moses and Elijah. When the two disappear mysteriously, a voice from the clouds proclaims, "this is my Son . . . listen to Him." They are told to keep this quiet "until the Son of Man has been raised from the dead."

Jerusalem (Matthew 19–25)

This section describes Jesus' entry into Jerusalem on Palm Sunday coupled with the expulsion of the money-changers in the Temple in chapter 22. Jesus chastises the hypocrisy of the religious leaders in chapter 23 and Matthew concludes chapter 25 with the parables of the ten virgins, the parable of the talents, and the depiction of Judgment Day as the separation of sheep from goats.

Matthew 19 quotes the prohibition against divorce and remarriage "what God has joined together, let man not separate" (Matthew 19:6). There is debate on the statement in verse 9: "I tell you that anyone who divorces his wife, except for marital unfaithfulness, and marries another woman commits adultery." The Greek word used is *porneia*, which the New International Version renders as marital infidelity, but other versions translate it as illicit sexual relations (incest, bestiality, etc.) since the more proper and accurate Greek word for adultery is *moicheia*.

In verse 21 of chapter 19, Jesus disappointed the rich young man who had faithfully kept all the Commandments but wanted to know how to get into God's kingdom. Jesus replied: "If you want to be perfect, go, sell your possessions and give to the poor, and you will have treasure in heaven." However, this answer does not sit well with the young man since he had many possessions. In chapter 21, Matthew shows Jesus entering Jerusalem while riding a donkey and then entering the Temple and throwing out the money-changers. This act angered the chief priests and elders who questioned Jesus' authority.

The phrase "if you want to be perfect" uses the Greek word *teleios*, which can also be translated to say, "If you want to be made whole" or "morally complete." The sense here is one of ethical and moral integration and not perfection in a metaphysical sense.

Passion and Death (Matthew 26–27)

The next to last section of Matthew's Gospel account begins with chapter 26 where the chief priests and elders began to plot against Jesus to have Him arrested and executed. This was made possible through the treachery of Judas Iscariot (one of Jesus' apostles), who was given thirty pieces of silver to betray Jesus at the right time and place. In just two chapters, Matthew writes about the Last Supper on Holy Thursday, and the Crucifixion and Death on Good Friday.

Chapter 26:17–30 recounts the Last Supper exactly as do Mark and Luke regarding the words spoken over the bread and wine, "this is my body" and "this is my blood." Verse 31 has the prediction of Peter's denial of Jesus, which is fulfilled in verses 69–75. Jesus is arrested and brought before the High Priest Caiaphas, who directly asks if He is the Christ, the Son of God, to which Jesus answers, "Yes, it is as you say." That seals His fate as the Sanhedrin send their prisoner to the Roman Governor, Pontius Pilate, in chapter 27. Next follows the details of the crucifixion, death, and burial of Jesus.

Resurrection (Matthew 28)

This last chapter is but twenty verses long. It is noteworthy that Mary Magdalene is the first one to see the empty tomb on Easter Sunday, "after the Sabbath, at dawn on the first day of the week," and she and the other women go tell the apostles that the Lord had risen. Matthew concludes with Jesus commissioning the apostles: "go and make disciples of all nations, baptizing them in the name of the Father and of the Son and of the Holy Spirit." There is not as much post-Resurrection dialogue in Matthew as in Luke or John, but only Matthew includes the parenthetical story of the guards being bribed to say the body was stolen after the burial in an attempt to refute the reports of Resurrection. Ⓔ

Chapter 15

The Gospel of Mark

Saint Mark was not one of the original twelve apostles and his Gospel is the shortest of the four Gospel accounts. It focuses on what Jesus did, more than on what He said, sort of the opposite of Matthew's version. Mark lets the actions and deeds speak for themselves and the miracles of Jesus are the means by which the authenticity, veracity, and origin of Jesus' mission are established.

Roman Audience

Mark is a Roman name (Marcus) and the evangelist was also known as John Mark. His audience is mainly Roman, and there is a lot of action and fewer sermons in this Gospel. Sacred art depicts Mark as a lion with wings since he begins with a regal or royal power of Christ and His kingdom of God. Potential Roman converts to Christianity would be more impressed with mighty deeds, like miracles, more so than with eloquent sermons or elaborate genealogies as one finds in Matthew. Mark begins most paragraphs with "at that time" or "and then" or "immediately" to keep the pace brisk and always moving.

FACT

Modern scholars claim that the shorter the document, the older it is, since over time there is the tendency to embellish the original story. Mark is the shortest Gospel, so some claim it is the oldest. Yet, others claim its brevity is due to the audience for which it is directed. Romans were not interested in sermons and dialogues as much as in action.

Who's First?

Mark's account of the Gospel was written between A.D. 60 and A.D. 69. A debate ensues among Bible scholars as to which evangelist (Gospel writer) wrote first: Matthew or Mark. Evidence exists for an early Hebrew or Aramaic Matthew, which predates Mark, but no copies exist today, only references to it. The Greek (also called the "canonical") version of Matthew could have been written shortly before or shortly after Mark, as it appears both have more similarities than any others. Despite the continuing debate, Bibles of all denominations still retain the traditional order St. Jerome established of Matthew, Mark, Luke, and John.

Prep Time (Mark 1:1–13)

Mark only briefly describes the preliminary activity to the public ministry of Jesus. There are no lengthy genealogy, no infancy narratives, no childhood stories of shepherds and three kings in Mark's account of Jesus' life. His Gospel account begins with Jesus as an adult meeting John the Baptist at the River Jordan and being baptized by him. Many paragraphs begin with "And" (*kai* in the original Greek), which keeps the action (and movement) almost continuous. As soon as John baptizes Jesus, Mark says in verse 12, "at once the Spirit sent him out into the desert."

Ministry in Galilee (Mark 1:14–7:23)

In Mark's account, following the forty days in the desert, Jesus began His ministry by calling the first four disciples—Peter and his brother Andrew, and James and his brother John. Almost immediately there is a miraculous cure of a demoniac in Capernaum. When the demon, who was possessing the man, said to Jesus that he knew He is the "Holy One of God," the rebuke is swift: "Be quiet!" and then "come out of him." Here is where Bible scholars came up with the term *Messianic Secret* since in verse 34 it also says, "He also drove out many demons, but he would not let the demons speak because they knew who he was."

Whereas Matthew details the dialogue of the temptation of Christ by Satan, Mark merely states that it happened with very simple descriptions: "he was baptized by John"; "the Spirit sent him"; "he was in the desert for forty days being tempted by Satan."

The Miracles

Next, Jesus cured Peter's mother-in-law and then a man with leprosy. The miraculous healings are immediate, swift, and complete. Mark sees this as evidence of divine authority and so he wants his audience to know that Jesus was more than a healer, since many before and after Him could also cure the sick but no one else could achieve such an instantaneous and total cure.

Jesus cured a paralytic and a man with a shriveled hand in the same immediate fashion in chapters 2 and 3, and He quieted down the wind and waves during a storm in chapter 4. One man was plagued by several demons in chapter 5 and Jesus cast them out into a herd of swine, which drowned themselves in the nearby lake. This is followed by the raising from the dead of the daughter of Jairus, a synagogue official (unnamed in Matthew), and the cure of the woman with a hemorrhage. Five thousand are miraculously fed with five loaves and two fish by Jesus in chapter 6, which concludes with Jesus walking on the water.

The Journeys (Mark 7:24–9:49, 10:1–52)

This section covers Jesus' journeys to Tyre and Sidon, the Decapolis, and the return to Galilee. The area being visited is filled with Greeks and Gentiles and those who are cured in these chapters show that Jesus not only cured Jews and non-Jews alike, He also went after both. A Jewish rabbi who cares for both Gentile and Jew would definitely grab the attention of a first-century crowd. A Roman audience would feel comfortable, then, seeing a universal dimension to the Messiah.

The Syrophoenician Woman

A Greek woman, born in Syrian Phoenicia, came to Jesus in chapter 7, pleading for her daughter who was possessed by a demon. At first glance, it appears that Jesus rebuked the woman: "it is not right to take the children's bread and toss it to their dogs" (Mark 7:27). An alleged insult was then turned around (in verse 28) into an act of preserving faith on her part as she replied, "but even the dogs under the table eat the children's crumbs." Jesus rewarded her courage by healing her daughter. Some in His company, perhaps even some of His own disciples, would have looked down at this woman since she was a Gentile and not a believing Jew.

After curing the possessed daughter, Jesus left Tyre for Sidon. He healed a deaf mute at the close of chapter 7, and then miraculously fed 4,000 people with seven loaves of bread and a few fish in the beginning of chapter 8—much like He did with the 5,000 previously in chapter 6. Verse 6 says Jesus had taken the bread and "given thanks"—which is *eucharisteo* in Greek, the root word for "Eucharist" that many Christians use to this day to call their Sunday worship where bread and wine are blessed and consecrated.

FACT

Jesus and the woman both used a play on words, which was typical for Greeks back then. Rather than the regular Greek word for "dogs" (*kynas*), as in the case of wild hounds and junkyard dogs, Jesus used the affectionate term "puppies" (*kynariois*).

Tough Love

In chapter 10, Mark recounts some of Jesus' hard sayings. In the first section, He denounced divorce and remarriage by saying, "anyone who divorces his wife and marries another woman commits adultery against her. And if she divorces her husband and marries another man, she commits adultery" (Mark 10:11–12). This is then followed by the famous reply to the rich young man, "it is easier for a camel to go through the eye of a needle than for a rich man to enter the kingdom of God" (Mark 10:25). In both cases, Mark shows that Jesus is willing to take the tough road Himself when He predicts His own death and says that the Son of Man will be betrayed, condemned, and killed (after being mocked, flogged, and spit at), and will rise three days later (10:33–34).

Jerusalem Ministry (Mark 11:1–13:37)

In chapter 11 of Mark's account of the Gospel, Jesus proceeds to the Holy City (Jerusalem). This section describes His entrance into the city, gives a parable or two, and concludes with sober words about Judgment Day and the end of the world. Parenthetically, there is a little incident where Jesus cursed a barren fig tree, which many Bible scholars propose is a metaphor for those who profess to have faith but do nothing with it; in other words, produce no fruit (Mark 11:12–14).

The Vineyard Parable

In chapter 12, Jesus tells the parable of the vineyard tenants. It is a tale of an owner who planted a vineyard and leased it to tenants. At harvest time, he sent his servants to collect his portion, one by one, but the tenants mistreated each one of the servants. They beat one, wounded another, and killed a third. Finally, the owner sent his son, thinking the tenants would respect the boy. But the tenants seized the boy, and beat and killed him as well.

"A man planted a vineyard. He put a wall around it, dug a pit for the winepress and built a watchtower. Then he rented the vineyard to some farmers and went away on a journey. At harvest time he sent a servant to the tenants to collect from them some of the fruit of the vineyard. But they seized him, beat him and sent him away empty-handed. Then he sent another servant to them; they struck this man on the head and treated him shamefully. He sent still another, and that one they killed. He sent many others; some of them they beat, others they killed. He had one left to send, a son, whom he loved. He sent him last of all, saying, 'They will respect my son.' But the tenants said to one another, 'This is the heir. Come, let's kill him, and the inheritance will be ours.' So they took him and killed him, and threw him out of the vineyard. What then will the owner of the vineyard do? He will come and kill those tenants and give the vineyard to others. Haven't you read this Scripture: 'The stone the builders rejected has become the capstone; the Lord has done this, and it is marvelous in our eyes'?"

(Mark 12:1–11)

Jesus uses this parable to describe His fate. Just as God's people rejected the true Prophets, beating some, killing others, so, too, many believe God's Son did not fare any better than the owner's son in the parable. The tenants captured the boy and killed him for his inheritance. Likewise, Mark reminds his audience that God's people rejected His Son and put Him to death.

The Eschatological Discourse

Chapter 13 includes the "eschatological discourse" (from the Greek word *eschaton* for "last"), which is a fancy and technical term for talking about the last things (i.e., the end of the world, doomsday, Armageddon, etc.). "Brother will betray brother to death, and a father his child. Children will rebel against their parents and have them put to death. All men will hate you because of me, but he who stands firm to the end will be saved" (Mark 13:12–13). It gets worse: "following that distress, 'the sun will be darkened, and the moon will not give its light; the stars will fall from the sky, and the heavenly bodies will be shaken'" (Mark 13:24–25). Since no one knows the day nor the hour when the world will end, Jesus reminds His followers to be prepared and be ready; be on guard and watch.

Passion, Death, and Resurrection (Mark 14:1–16:8)

The gesture of the woman who poured perfumed oil on the head of Jesus speaks volumes. More than just words, her action of anointing Him showed her great faith that He was the Anointed One, the Messiah, the Christ. The words of the disciples: "Why this waste of perfume? . . . the money [could have been] given to the poor" (Mark 14:4–5) are dismissed by the actions of the woman, "she has done a beautiful thing to me" (Mark 14:6). "I tell you the truth, wherever the gospel is preached throughout the world, what she has done will also be told, in memory of her" (Mark 14:9).

FACT

The Greek word Mark uses to describe what the woman did for Jesus in anointing Him is *kalos*, which means "good." *Agathos* is used in other places in Mark to describe "good" as in a benedicial way, but *kalos* means more than that. It is "good" as in excellent, lovely, generously excessive, and so forth.

The Lord's Supper and Betrayal

Verses 12 to 26 of chapter 14 relate to the events of the Last Supper, sometimes called the Lord's Supper. The same four actions occur in all three Synoptic (Matthew, Mark, and Luke) Gospel accounts of the Last Supper: Jesus took, blessed, broke, and gave the bread and then the wine (*labon, eulogesas, eklasen, edoken* in Greek; *accepit, benedixit, fregit, dedit* in Latin).

Three poignant betrayals take place in Mark 14:32–72. The first is by Judas who sold out Jesus for money; the second is by Peter who thrice denied knowing Jesus; the third is by His disciples who abandoned Him. In verse 10, Judas went to the chief priests with the intention of betraying Christ and then in verse 45, he identified Jesus with a kiss, which ironically was a sign of friendship. Peter, James, and John fell asleep while Jesus asked them to pray with Him in verse 32, even though He said, "My soul is overwhelmed with sorrow to the point of death," in verse 34. The betrayal of His disciples is finalized in verse 50 when "everyone deserted him and fled." The ultimate betrayal, however, is not by Judas, nor by the group of apostles, but by Peter to whom Jesus had placed authority and respect. Verses 66 to 72 tell of his three denials of ever knowing Jesus.

ESSENTIAL

Only Mark mentions "a young man, wearing nothing but a linen garment, was following Jesus. When they seized him, he fled naked, leaving his garment behind" (Mark 14:51–52). Many believe that the young man was the same who wrote the Gospel and at whose family's home the Last Supper took place.

Pilate

Pontius Pilate was the Roman Governor of Judea, and he was not totally convinced that Jesus was a threat to the Caesar in terms of claiming to be an "earthly" king. However, in accordance with Roman law, Pilate proceeded with the trial. When the governor posed the question to the crowd, "What crime has he committed?" the mob demanded crucifixion. Wanting to avoid an ugly scene, Pilate handed Jesus over to be scourged (flogged) and crucified.

Crucifixion

Following the condemnation and scourging, Jesus was to be crucified. Roman soldiers bullied the convicted criminals and Mark mentioned the details of a mocking chant the Romans would give, "Hail, King of the Jews." According to Roman custom, the condemned carried his own cross, usually just the cross-beam, which would later be fastened to the vertical pole inserted in the ground. After a brutal scourging, Mark tells his audience that the soldiers pressed an innocent bystander, Simon of Cyrene, to help Jesus carry the cross. The gory and brutal death by crucifixion was the Roman deterrence to future acts of sedition. It was such a horrible means of execution that the fear of crucifixion alone terrorized many into submission to Roman rule.

After suffering for many hours, Jesus died on the cross. The soldiers offered him wine mixed with myrrh, which was a common practice to numb the excruciating pain of the crucifixion, but Jesus refused to drink it once He realized what had been offered. Mark concluded the death of Jesus with "and when the centurion, who stood there in front of Jesus, heard his cry and saw how he died, he said, 'Surely this man was the Son of God!'" (Mark 15: 39). Here, a Roman was making the proclamation of Jesus' divinity.

E ALERT!

Mark is the only one to use the Greek word *kenturion*, which is directly taken from the Latin *centurion* (centurion in English), meaning a commander of 100 soldiers. The other Gospel writers use the word *hekatontarchos*, which is the common Greek equivalent.

Since Jesus died on Friday, the day before the Sabbath (Saturday), Mark tells that it was Joseph of Arimathea who asked Pilate for Jesus' body so He could be buried before sundown. Only Mark offers confirmation of death asked for and given to the governor. Once verified, Pilate released the body to Joseph.

The Endings (Mark 16:9–20)

Mark's last chapter 16 is the most controversial. The problem is that since there is no existing autograph, some manuscripts end at verse 8; others end with 20. Hence the dilemma of a longer and a shorter ending. There is a subtle difference in style after verse 8, which some use as evidence to say that the shorter ending is what Mark intended; yet others point out that Saint Jerome and others mention the omission in some Greek manuscripts but cite its presence in others. Also, many of the church fathers quote from the longer ending. Every Bible has all twenty verses, but some bracket the last twelve in an attempt to indicate the textual variant.

Shorter Ending

Chapter 16 begins with Mary Magdalene (Jesus' friend) going to the tomb very early the day after the Sabbath to finish the ritual anointing of Jesus' dead body. She went to the tomb, expecting to find nothing more than a corpse. Instead, she and Mary, the mother of James (relative of Jesus) and Salome, arrived to find an empty grave. An angel told them not to be afraid: "You are looking for Jesus the Nazarene, who was crucified. He has risen! He is not here. See the place where they laid him. But go, tell his disciples and Peter, 'He is going ahead of you into Galilee. There you will see him, just as he told you.' Trembling and bewildered, the women went out and fled from the tomb. They said nothing to anyone, because they were afraid" (Mark 16:6–8).

Longer Ending

The next twelve verses make up the longer ending of Mark. The risen Christ appeared to Mary Magdalene and to the eleven disciples (Judas had killed himself by now). Verse 15 shows Jesus commissioning His Apostles to "go into all the world and preach the good news to all creation." This section ends with the Ascension of Jesus into heaven and the preaching of the disciples.

Chapter 16

The Gospel of Luke

It is believed that Saint Luke was a physician by trade just as Saint Peter was a fisherman and Saint Matthew a tax collector. This chapter looks at the Gospel of Luke, often called the Gospel of Women, or the Gospel of Mercy. Luke uses his physician skills and his Gentile background to present an image of the Messiah and Savior, which non-Jewish listeners and readers can appreciate.

Gentile Audience

Fluent in both Hebrew and Greek, acquainted with the Septuagint, Luke was not a Jew but one of the many Hellenists-Greek sympathizers who accepted and believed most of the Mosaic law without the final plunge of being circumcised nor being prohibited to eat pork or other nonkosher foods. Next to John, he is known for his eloquent use of language throughout the text. His is also the longest of the four Gospel accounts. A universality (catholicity) is evident in Luke as he portrays Christ as the Savior of the entire human race and of the whole world.

From the Start (Luke 1:1–4)

Luke opens his account with "many have undertaken to draw up an account of the things that have been fulfilled among us, just as they were *handed down* to us by those who from the first were eyewitnesses and servants of the word. Therefore, since I myself have carefully investigated everything from the beginning, it seemed good also to me to write an orderly account for you." Luke uses the Greek word *paradosis*, which is the equivalent of the Latin *traditio* (where we get the word "tradition") meaning "to hand down."

QUESTION?

From where did Luke obtain information for his Gospel?
Luke wasn't one of the twelve apostles, and so he depended on oral tradition and existing written texts when compiling his account.

The Infancy Narrative (Luke 1:5–2:52)

Sometimes called the "infancy narrative," this section of Luke deals with Mary's pregnancy and the birth of Jesus. Luke's Gentile audience was accustomed to hearing extraordinary circumstances of the births of major historical figures, from Alexander the Great to Julius Caesar. Some scholars believe it is probable that Luke received a good portion of his information from the mother of Jesus herself.

Double Announcement

Chapter 1 contains the announcements of the births of John the Baptist and Jesus Christ. Verses 5 to 25 chronicle the arrival of the former, while verses 26 to 38 concern the latter. The angel Gabriel separately appeared to Zechariah (John the Baptist's father) and to Mary (Jesus' mother), and told them, "Be not afraid." Because both he and his wife Elizabeth were old, Zechariah had doubts: "How can I be sure of this?" (Luke 1:18), whereas Mary welcomed the announcement with faith: "I am the Lord's servant, May it be to me as you have said" (Luke 1:38). Because of his wavering faith, Zechariah is reprimanded with being struck silent until his son is born. However, this is the sign he sought from God, and from that moment on, he believed that he and his barren wife would become parents.

FACT

Many Christians refer to the angel Gabriel's announcement to Mary that she will have a son and name him Jesus as "the Annunciation." The visit Mary made to her pregnant cousin Elizabeth (Zechariah's wife) is called "the Visitation." The first half of the ancient prayer known as the *Hail Mary* or *Ave Maria* is taken directly from Luke 1:28,42.

Two Baby Boys

Chapter 1 closes with the birth of John the Baptist (verses 57 to 80), and chapter 2 opens with the birth of Jesus (verses 1 to 20). Each pregnancy was miraculous: Elizabeth's because of her old age and infertility, and Mary because of her virginity. Elizabeth then gave birth to John the Baptist, who was to "prepare the way" for the Messiah, and Mary gave birth to Jesus, whom Christians consider the Messiah Himself.

Luke then goes into details like the imperial census, which forced

Joseph and Mary to leave Nazareth and register in Bethlehem as she is about to give birth; the angels and shepherds at the birth itself; the circumcision of the baby Jesus eight days later; and the adolescent (twelve-year-old) Jesus being lost for three days in the Temple of Jerusalem.

John the Baptist and Jesus (Luke 3:1–4:13)

Chapter 3 opens with another historical context. "In the fifteenth year of the reign of Tiberius Caesar—when Pontius Pilate was governor of Judea, Herod tetrarch of Galilee, his brother Philip tetrarch of Iturea and Traconitis, and Lysanias tetrarch of Abilen—during the high priesthood of Annas and Caiaphas, the Word of God came to John son of Zechariah in the desert." Luke situates the time frame within political and religious points of reference to emphasize the reality and the impact of what happened. Ancient peoples would often refer to historical events as ways of dating (e.g., during the reign of Caesar Augustus).

Luke the physician carefully points out that the birth of Jesus took place during the reign of the Roman Emperor Caesar Augustus and the governorship of Quirinius of Syria. He wants his Gentile audience to know that this birth is a historical fact.

John's Mission

Verses 1 to 20 of chapter 3 focus on the preaching of John the Baptist. He was the last prophet who prepared the people for the coming of the Messiah, and the only prophet to see Him as well. The name Baptist does not refer to John's religious affiliation. He was a Jew, but was called the Baptist since he baptized people in the River Jordan. Unlike the Christian sacrament of Baptism, where a person (adult or infant) is immersed in water or has water poured over the head while the Holy Trinity is invoked ("I baptize you in the name of the Father and of the Son and of the Holy Spirit"), John's baptism is interpreted by some as merely a symbolic gesture; a call to repentance in preparation for the coming of the Messiah.

John called the people to abandon greed and embrace generosity: "The man with two tunics should share with him who has none, and the one who has food should do the same" (Luke 3:11). He urged tax collectors to be fair rather than dishonest, and soldiers to not abuse their authority or resort to extortion. What got him in big trouble, however, was his denunciation of King Herod who was living with his brother's wife, Herodias, in an adulterous relationship.

Jesus' Baptism

Luke uses genealogy to show the ancestry of Jesus, just like Matthew did in his account. The only difference is that the Book of Luke goes all the way back to Adam, whereas Matthew only goes as far as Abraham. Remember, Matthew wrote for a Jewish audience, and Abraham was the patriarch par excellence of the Hebrew religion since God made the first covenant with him. Luke, writing for a Gentile audience, had more affinity for the common man, Adam, than Father Abraham.

FACT

Emperor Tiberius Caesar reigned from A.D. 14–37. Pontius Pilate was governor of Judea from A.D. 26–36. Herod Antipas (son of Herod the Great) was tetrarch (a sort of governor) of Galilee from 4 B.C.–A.D. 39. Caiaphas (son-in-law to Annas) held office as High Priest from A.D. 18–37. The fifteenth year of Tiberius Caesar's reign would have been between A.D. 27 and 28.

Jesus' divinity (that He is the Son of God) is evidenced at His baptism. Luke tells that immediately after John baptized Jesus, the "Holy Spirit descended on him in bodily form like a dove. And a voice came from heaven: 'You are my Son, whom I love; with you I am well pleased'" (Luke 3:22). Such a passage is often seen as a subtle reference to the Holy Trinity (Father, Son, and Holy Spirit), which later became the primary doctrine of Christianity, differentiating it from the other two monotheistic religions of Judaism and Islam.

The Temptation

In his Gospel, Luke also includes a detailed account of Jesus' temptations. This account is similar to Matthew, with a slightly different order. Like Matthew, Luke first writes about the temptation of Jesus in the desert, where the devil asks Him to turn stones into bread. The second one in Luke, though, is the temptation to worship the devil in exchange for all the kingdoms of the earth. In Matthew, this appears as the third temptation. In the last temptation, the devil orders Jesus to throw Himself off the pinnacle of the Temple so the angels can catch Him.

Galilean Ministry (Luke 4:14–9:50)

This section covers the ministry of Jesus from His preaching in Nazareth (in Israel), to the call of the disciples, several miraculous healings, the feeding of 5,000, some exorcisms, and the Transfiguration. In this section, Luke shows Jesus as a teacher, giving pearls of wisdom to enlighten the human mind. Chapter 6 goes into further detail with the Sermon on the Plain, or as is sometimes called, the Great Discourse. It is the first phase of the public ministry, which will continue until Jesus' entrance into Jerusalem.

Jesus intentionally fasted for forty days in the desert and to break that fast by acquiescing to the request of the devil would have defeated the whole purpose of making a fast in the first place. The question was not whether Jesus had the power to do it, but rather, the reason for using His divine powers? The devil was tempting Jesus to overshadow His human nature by overexposing His divine nature.

Hometown Crowd

Born in Bethlehem, Jesus was raised in Nazareth, and that's where he began to spread God's word. The beginnings of Jesus' preaching were not easy, however. After reading to the people of Nazareth from Isaiah 61 ("The Spirit of the Lord is on me, because he has anointed me . . ."), the crowd grew furious and physically attempted to hurl Jesus off the brow of the hill into the cliff. Ironically, the message Jesus gave was one of hope, not doom: "to preach good news to the poor . . . to proclaim freedom for the prisoners and recovery of sight for the blind, to release the oppressed, to proclaim the year of the Lord's favor" (Luke 4:18–19). Jesus, however, acknowledged that, "no prophet is accepted in his hometown" (Luke 4:24).

First Draft Pick

Chapter 5 begins with Jesus calling His first disciples. Simon Peter, the fisherman, took Jesus out on his boat into deep water and Jesus taught the crowds from that vantage point. When finished, He asked Simon to lower his nets, to which the seasoned sailor said, "Master, we've worked hard all night and haven't caught anything" (Luke 5:5). Complying with Jesus' wishes anyway, Simon lowered the nets and hauled in so many fish the net almost broke. Jesus then said to Simon Peter: "from now on you will catch men" (Luke 5:11), meaning that He wanted Simon Peter to follow him and spread His message to others. In chapter 6, Jesus picks his twelve apostles: Simon Peter, Andrew, James, John, Philip, Bartholomew, Matthew, Thomas, James son of Alphaeus, Simon the Zealot, Jude, and Judas Iscariot.

FACT

One of the twelve disciples, Judas Iscariot, betrayed Jesus by selling him out to the Jewish priests for thirty silver pieces. Later, the guilt-ridden Judas returned the coins (the bribe) to the priests and committed suicide. The disciples then chose Matthias to fill Judas' place.

Blessings and Woes

Matthew was the first to give the account of the Sermon on the Mount, where Jesus preached the Beatitudes (Matthew 5:3–12), but Luke tells of a slightly different version in chapter 6. Along with the blessings are the "woes":

Blessed are you who are poor, for yours is the kingdom of God . . . But woe to you who are rich, for you have already received your comfort.

Blessed are you who hunger now, for you will be satisfied . . . Woe to you who are well fed now, for you will go hungry.

Blessed are you who weep now, for you will laugh . . . Woe to you who laugh now, for you will mourn and weep.

Blessed are you when men hate you, when they exclude you and insult you and reject your name as evil, because of the Son of Man. Rejoice in that day and leap for joy, because great is your reward in heaven. For that is how their fathers treated the prophets . . . Woe to you when all men speak well of you, for that is how their fathers treated the false prophets.

While Luke gives the positive blessings first, and then follows with the corresponding woes, Matthew does not include the woes. Gentiles, especially Greeks, would appreciate a dichotomy in the Socratic tradition. Many believe it wasn't unusual for Jesus to give the same sermon with a few modifications and in two different locations.

Luke's identification of the Sermon on the Plain is noteworthy. The Greeks loved philosophical debate and when it occurred, it is believed that the orators would not use elevated podiums; rather, they were on an even level with the audience to avoid overemphasis.

On the Road to Jerusalem (Luke 9:51–19:28)

This section concerns the duties and privileges of discipleship, and the journey of Jesus toward Jerusalem through Samaritan towns. The

Samaritans were Israelites who survived the Assyrian captivity of the northern kingdom of Israel in 721 B.C. After the Babylonian Captivity in 586 B.C., the returning Jews in the south found the Samaritan Jews in the north had a different expression of Hebrew religion, and thus the animosity grew.

The Seventy-Two

Luke mentions that Jesus also sent out seventy-two (seventy in some manuscripts) disciples, in distinction with the mission of the twelve apostles. Some believe Luke himself may have been one of those disciples since neither he nor Mark were original apostles like Matthew and John. These seventy-some disciples were sent two by two to towns ahead of Jesus to prepare them for His arrival. They were warned, "Do not take a purse or bag or sandals; and do not greet anyone on the road . . . Do not move around from house to house" (Luke 10:4,7).

The Good Samaritan

Only the Gospel of Luke contains the parable of the Good Samaritan. Verses 29 to 37 of chapter 10 tell the story of a man who is mugged and beaten. A priest of the Temple and a Levite passed him by and offered no assistance, but a stranger, a Samaritan, came to his aid. He bandaged his wounds, took him to an inn, and gave money to the innkeeper to cover the expenses of his recovery. This parable is meant to answer the question of "Who is my neighbor?"

FACT

The Scripture says, "'Love the Lord your God with all your heart and with all your soul and with all your strength and with all your mind'; and, 'Love your neighbor as yourself'" (Luke 10:27). But a student of the Mosaic law asked Jesus "Who is my neighbor?" and Jesus then offered the parable of the Good Samaritan to show that everyone is a neighbor.

Martha and Mary

Luke is often called the "Gospel of Women" since he shows women as key players in Jesus' life. Martha and Mary, sisters of Lazarus, were Jesus' friends and Luke writes about Jesus' visit with them at the end of chapter 10. While Martha busied herself with hospitality concerns, Mary sat attentively listening to Jesus' words of wisdom.

The Lord's Prayer

When Jesus was praying, one of his disciples asked Him to teach the disciples how to pray. And so Jesus gathered His disciples and taught them the "Lord's Prayer." Luke has a shorter version of the "Our Father" than does Matthew:

"Father, hallowed be your name, your kingdom come. Give us each day our daily bread. Forgive us our sins, for we also forgive everyone who sins against us. And lead us not into temptation" (Luke 11:2–4).

"Our Father in heaven, hallowed be your name, your kingdom come, your will be done on earth as it is in heaven. Give us today our daily bread. Forgive us our debts, as we also have forgiven our debtors. And lead us not into temptation, but deliver us from the evil one" (Matthew 6:9–13).

ALERT!

The familiar ending of the Lord's Prayer "For thine is the kingdom, the power and the glory. For ever and ever" is not found at all in Luke nor in most versions of Matthew's Gospel. Most of the older manuscripts do not have it, while a few later ones do.

The Palm Procession (Luke 19:29–21:38)

These sections deal with Jesus' entrance into Jerusalem, which was his final arrival in the city before his death. Like Matthew and Mark, Luke describes the Palm Sunday procession into the city with Jesus riding on a donkey, while the people shout, sing, and throw palm branches before His feet. It includes a prediction about the destruction of Jerusalem, which did not actually take place until around A.D. 70.

While teaching in the Temple during the day, Jesus attracted great crowds. This, however, infuriated His enemies, who sought to get rid of Jesus through any possible means. The religious leaders feared and envied His popularity, and the more He spoke, the more they plotted against Him.

Passion, Death, and Resurrection (Luke 22:1–24:53)

These final sections incorporate the Last Supper, arrest, trial, and crucifixion of Jesus, followed by His burial and Resurrection. Luke follows the same outline as that seen in the Gospels of Matthew and Mark, in terms of the words spoken at the meal and the sequence of events. Shortly after the meal (which is commonly referred to as the Last Supper), Jesus predicted that Peter would deny Him three times. He then went into the Garden of Olives and experienced His bitter agony. Only Luke mentions, "an angel from heaven appeared to him and strengthened him" (Luke 22:43), while the other Gospels omit it completely. Ironically, only Matthew and Mark mention angels waiting on Jesus after the devil tempted Him in the desert.

FACT

The Gospels only tell of two occasions when Jesus wept. The first is in Luke 19:41 when He weeps over the impending destruction of Jerusalem. The second is in John 11:35 when He weeps at the tomb of His dear friend Lazarus.

Before Pontius Pilate

The crowd accused Jesus of treason, and brought him before Pontius Pilate. The crowd said, "He opposes payment of taxes to Caesar" (Luke 23:2); yet when asked if it is lawful to pay taxes, it was also Jesus who said, "give to Caesar what is Caesar's, and to God what is God's" (Luke 20:25). The crowd then asked Pilate to release the criminal Barnabas for Jesus. Fearing the people, Pontius Pilate handed Jesus over for crucifixion.

Death on the Cross

Unlike Matthew and John, who show that the passion (suffering) and death of Jesus by crucifixion fulfilled the Old Testament prophecies, Luke, on the other hand, highlights His mercy and forgiveness from the cross. In chapter 23, Jesus forgives the soldiers who were torturing Him: "Father, forgive them, for they do not know what they are doing" (Luke 23:34), as well as one of the two thieves crucified alongside him: "today you will be with me in paradise" (Luke 23:43). Jesus then died and was buried.

According to legend, the thief who ridiculed Jesus was known as Gestas, while the good thief who repented was known as Dismas, patron of prisoners. An apocryphal gospel tells the tale of Dismas and Gestas as partners in crime who stumble upon Mary and Joseph and baby Jesus fleeing into Egypt. Dismas allegedly convinced Gestas to let the poor family go by without robbing them.

Resurrection

According to Luke's Gospel, when the women came to Jesus' tomb to finish the ceremonial anointing of the body, they didn't find Jesus, but there were two men in white robes who said, "Why do you look for the living among the dead?" (Luke 24:5). Luke makes a point to mention the women were first to come to the empty tomb. Jesus' disciples followed next. The Gospel ends with the Ascension of Jesus into heaven shortly after His appearance on the road to Emmaus. (E)

Chapter 17

The Gospel of John

Often called the Gospel of Light, John's account is the most sublime, theological, and sophisticated of the four. The employment of Greek philosophy is evident in the first chapter and in the consistent dichotomy made between the "light" and the "darkness." John also emphasizes the concept of the "hour," which is not sixty minutes but a reference to "the moment" or "the time."

Christian Audience

Written around A.D. 90, and before the Book of Revelation, or the Apocalypse, this last of the four Gospels can be divided into the Book of Signs and the Book of Glory. Whereas Matthew wrote for a Jewish audience, Mark for the Romans, and Luke for Gentiles, John wrote for a Christian audience. The three Gospels of Matthew, Mark, and Luke are like Christianity 101 in college, while John can be compared to the advanced graduate level Christianity 501. Called the most theological of the four Gospel accounts, John directed his book to new Christian converts, whether they were Jewish, Gentile, or Romans.

The Prologue (John 1:1–18)

John's Gospel opens as does the first book of the Bible, Genesis: "In the beginning . . ." Whereas Matthew and Luke use human genealogies to trace Jesus' lineage to Abraham or Adam, John uses a similar tool to establish Jesus' divine lineage. "In the beginning was the Word, and the Word was with God, and the Word was God."

FACT

The Greek word John used for "word" was *logos*, which is the reflection of what is in the mind of the speaker. Here, "word" is more than mere letters put together; it is a thought, an idea, and more than that, it is a glimpse into the mind of the author. *Logos* reveals the reasoning and the reason present in the mind of the speaker.

Genesis describes Creation in this way: "And God said, 'Let there be light,' and there was light" (Genesis 1:3). The phrase "God said" is used nine times in Genesis and whenever it's used, things immediately are created or things happen. Likewise, John opens his Gospel account with the phrase "In the beginning" and goes on to say, "the Word was with God, and the Word was God." Verse 3 affirms the presence of the Word at Creation: "through him all things were made; without him nothing was made that has been made." John puts the Word on equality with God:

"the Word was God." Jesus, as God the Son, is the Eternal Word of God the Father. The Father speaks the Word, which is the Son.

The Word Became Flesh

Verse 14 is key to understanding John. Not only is the Word divine, it is also human (god and man): "The Word became flesh and made his dwelling among us" (John 1:14). The Greek word *sarx* is used for "flesh," and the Latin uses *caro* from which we get the word "incarnation," meaning the moment at which God the Son took on human flesh and was conceived inside his human mother's (Mary) womb.

Book of Signs: New Creation (John 1:19–2:11)

The first half of John's account of the Gospel can be called the Book of Signs since it incorporates seven miracles of Jesus. These supernatural wonders are "signs" for John of Jesus' true identity as the Son of God. The Synoptics (Matthew, Mark, and Luke) spent time showing the humanity of Christ, that He was a real man with a real human nature, yet they also acknowledged His divinity. John, while acknowledging the humanity of Jesus, gives emphasis to His divinity, and especially His divine origins. Here is a list of the seven miraculous signs in John's Gospel:

1. Water into wine at Cana
2. Cure of royal official's son
3. Healing of paralytic at pool of Bethesda
4. Multiplication of loaves and fish
5. Walking on the water
6. Healing of young man born blind
7. Raising of Lazarus from the dead

The connection that John keeps making is with the creative Word found in Genesis ("and God said . . . and then there was . . ."), with the Word made flesh (Jesus Christ). Just as Genesis had a seven-day week of Creation (one day of rest), so, too, John presents seven miracles as "signs" of the creative and divine power of Jesus.

John's "seven signs" are also very sacramental in that sacraments are outwards signs of invisible grace. Waters of baptism, oil of anointing, and so forth are external signs of the unseen, invisible grace being given by God.

Miracle at Cana

Jesus, His mother, and His disciples were invited to a wedding in Cana of Galilee. At one point the wine ran out. Mary noticed the situation and said to her Son, "They have no more wine." Jesus replied, "Woman, why do you involve me? My time has not yet come" (John 2:4). Yet, Mary proceeded to say to the servants, "Do whatever he tells you" (John 2:5). Jesus then instructed the servants to fill six water jars, each holding twenty to thirty gallons. He then said, "Now draw some out and take it to the master of the banquet" (John 2:8).

When the headwaiter tasted it, instead of water, there was wine—the best choice vintage of wine. In those days, it was customary to serve the good wine first, and so when Jesus presented this delicious wine, the headwaiter had to make mention of it. Jesus turning water into wine was a sign of God using the ordinary and making it extraordinary—a sign of new creation.

The Mother/Son Relationship

After Mary, the mother of Jesus, said, "They have no more wine," Jesus replied, "Woman, why do you involve me?" The original Greek, however, is *ti emoi kai soi gynai*, which is literally translated "What to me and to you woman?" Rather than a rebuke (since Jesus responded to Mary's request), it is a statement of relationship. Mary is the human mother of Jesus but she is also a disciple insofar as she is to follow her Son and obey Him like all believers are asked to do. Her role of Mother is subservient to her role as faithful disciple, hence the title "woman."

Before the wedding feast at Cana, Jesus and Mary lived as Mother and Son. After the miraculous change of water into wine, Mary accepted the role of a disciple, and listened, followed, and obeyed Jesus.

FACT

Mary's advice to the servants—"Do whatever he tells you"—can be seen as sound advice to all followers of Jesus even today, and not just the hired help at the catered wedding reception. Her maternal relationship takes second place to her now primary role, and that of all believers, to be a true disciple.

Book of Signs: New Life (John 2:12–4:54)

This section zeroes in on the idea of new life, whereas the previous looked at new creation (water into wine). The new life is the life of grace. When Jesus chases the money-changers out of the Temple, He proclaims, "Destroy this temple, and I will raise it again in three days" (John 2:19). Not only was He speaking of His physical body as being the temple that will be destroyed through death and then rise up on the third day, but also an allusion to the terrible fate of the Temple of Jerusalem, which would be demolished by the Romans in A.D. 70.

Born Again

New life is represented in the idea of being born again. Jesus has a discourse with Nicodemus, a member of the Sanhedrin, the Jewish religious leadership council. "I tell you the truth, no one can enter the kingdom of God unless he is born of water and the Spirit" (John 3:5). *Gennethe anothen* is the Greek for being "born again" or "born from above."

ESSENTIAL

Some Christian denominations interpret this passage (of being born again) to mean an adult, conscious decision to accept Jesus Christ as your Lord and Savior. Other Christian religions see the sacrament of baptism as the moment of spiritually being reborn into the life of grace, whether as an adult or as an infant.

Woman at the Well

After telling Nicodemus that in order to enter the kingdom of God, one must be born again of water and the Spirit, Jesus encountered a Samaritan woman at a drinking well. Jews never associated with Samaritans—especially Jewish men with Samaritan women. But, here was Jesus asking a Samaritan for a drink of water. While He requested physical water, Jesus also offered spiritual water (divine grace), which is the source of new life. Jesus said to the woman: "Whoever drinks the water I give him will never thirst. Indeed, the water I give him will become in him a spring of water welling up to eternal life" (John 4:14). The woman was further amazed when Jesus revealed that He knew she had been married seven times and was now living with a man who wasn't her husband.

Healing of the Official's Son

This second sign in John concerns Jesus healing an army official's son who was deadly ill. When the boy's father came to Jesus who had returned to Cana in Galilee, Jesus said: "You may go. Your son will live" (John 4:40). The man then believed Jesus, and went home, where he found his son miraculously cured. The servants told him that it happened at the seventh-hour, which was the exact moment Jesus had told him, "your son will live."

Book of Signs: Light and Darkness (John 5:1–10:42)

This section highlights the struggle between good and evil as symbolized in the signs of light and darkness. Those who plot to betray and kill Jesus do their scheming at night when it is dark, whereas Jesus preaches openly in the daylight. Chapter 9 concludes with a dialogue between Jesus and some Pharisees where He equates sin with voluntary moral blindness, warning that sin is the intentional refusal to look and see what is true, preferring the blindness of ignorance and evil.

QUESTION?

What is the Christian Liturgical Year?
The Christian Liturgical Year focuses on two themes: Christ as Light and Christ as Life. The themes become pillars to which the faith is anchored. Advent and Christmas season use the symbol of light (star of Bethlehem), while Lent and Easter season use the symbol of life (Resurrection from the dead).

Healing of the Paralytic

This third sign occured at the Sheep Gate pool, also known in Aramaic as Bethesda. Like the famous grotto of Lourdes is for the Catholics, or the Ganges River is for the Hindus, the Pool at Bethesda was for the Jews a place of healing and purification. One poor fellow (who was lame) was unable to physically get into the river as the waters were stirred up. By the time he crawled near, someone else jumped in ahead of him. Jesus encountered him and said, "Pick up your mat and walk" (John 5:8). "At once the man was cured; he picked up his mat and walked" (John 5:9). This miracle happened on the Sabbath, a Jewish holy day.

Curing a man on the Sabbath irritated the enemies of Jesus, but his response to the criticism angered them even more for they considered it a blasphemy: "My Father is always at his work to this very day, and I, too, am working" (John 5:17). Here, Jesus identifies Himself as the Son of the Father, which his enemies considered blasphemous because they didn't believe He was the Son of God, or the Messiah.

Multiplication of Loaves and Fish

In his fourth sign, Jesus miraculously fed 5,000 people with just five barley loaves and two fish. After the crowd had eaten, the disciples collected twelve baskets of leftovers. This miracle made Jesus enormously popular, for many who didn't believe in Him, started to believe, and told others about the miracle: "After the people saw the miraculous sign that Jesus did, they began to say, 'Surely this is the Prophet who is to come into the world'" (John 6:14).

Walking on Water

After feeding the crowd with the loaves and fish, the disciples got into the boat and set off across the lake. Jesus was not with them and when He finally arrived they were already away from the shore. He then began to walk on the water toward them. They were terrified, but He reassured them, "It is I; don't be afraid" (John 6:20). This is considered the fifth sign.

ESSENTIAL

The Gospel of Matthew offers a different version. When Jesus was walking on water, Peter said, "'Lord, if it's you . . . tell me to come to you on the water . . . .' Then Peter got . . . out of the boat, walked on the water and came toward Jesus. But when he saw the wind, he was afraid, and, beginning to sink . . . . Jesus reached out his hand and caught him. 'You of little faith,' he said, 'why did you doubt?'" (Matthew 14:28–31)

Bread of Life Discourse

The feeding of the multitude with physical bread was a sign for John of the spiritual food Jesus would later give in the Holy Eucharist. Jesus called Himself the "bread of life" (John 6:35) and made a parallel with the manna from heaven, by which Moses fed the Israelites in the desert. Whereas the ancestors who ate that manna eventually died, "But here is the bread that comes down from heaven, which a man may eat and not die. I am the living bread that came down from heaven. If anyone eats of this bread, he will live forever" (John 6:49–51). John is the only one who goes into great length and depth in chapter 6 with the theme of the bread of life.

"Unless you eat the flesh of the Son of Man and drink his blood, you have no life in you. Whoever eats my flesh and drinks my blood has eternal life, and I will raise him up at the last day. For my flesh is real food and my blood is real drink. Whoever eats my flesh and drinks my blood remains in me, and I in him. Just as the living Father sent me and I live because of the Father, so the one who feeds on me will live because of me."

(John 6:53–57)

The sixth chapter of John is fundamental to the Christian doctrine on the Eucharist, with some churches taking a very literal interpretation (Catholic, Orthodox), others a more mystical or symbolic meaning (Presbyterian, Methodist, Baptist), and some in between the two (Anglican, Episcopalian, Lutheran). Nevertheless, the fact that every Christian church has some form of Eucharistic service, from daily and weekly to occasionally or rarely, still shows the fact that it was never abandoned completely. Baptism and Eucharist are two sacraments or ordinances that all Christian denominations practice, though they do not share the same theology or liturgy. Called the Lord's Supper, Divine Liturgy, Communion Service, Holy Eucharist, or Sacrifice of the Mass, this Christian act of worship is rooted in John 6 and in the Last Supper accounts of the three Synoptic Gospels.

Healing of a Blind Man

This sixth sign occurs in the ninth chapter of John. The disciples came upon a man blind since birth and asked Jesus if it was his sins or his parents' sins that caused this to happen. At the time of Jesus, many believed that good luck and fortune, health, and wealth were rewards from God for being good, whereas poverty, illness, bad luck, misfortune, and every kind of suffering were punishments for any evil committed. Jesus responded to the inquiry, "this happened so that the work of God might be displayed in his life" (John 9:3).

FACT

The *Sanhedrin* was the highest Jewish judicial and administrative council. According to Jewish tradition, the Sanhedrin was set up with the seventy elders chosen by God through Moses, while the Israelites were on their journey from Egypt to the Promised Land. During Jesus' time, the Sanhedrin had great authority, and the council consisted of seventy-one members. The Sanhedrin members were bitter opponents of Jesus.

After spitting on the ground and making mud with the saliva, Jesus applied it to the man's eyes and told him to wash in the Pool of

Siloam. The blind man did as Jesus ordered and his sight was miraculously restored. Later, the Sanhedrin questioned the man and his parents since the healing took place on the Sabbath. They would use this as another excuse to accuse Jesus of violating the Mosaic Law.

Book of Signs: Last Journey (John 11:1–12:50)

Chapter 11 contains the seventh and last sign of Jesus, which only appears in John's Gospel. It is the raising of Lazarus from the dead. Lazarus was the brother of Martha and Mary, and the three were close friends of Jesus as He often visited them in Bethany (near Jerusalem). The Bible only mentions two occasions on which Jesus wept and one of them was at the death of His dear friend Lazarus. Arriving four days after the burial, Jesus came to the tomb and ordered that the stone be rolled back, at which Martha objected, "by this time there is a bad odor, for he has been there four days" (John 11:39). Jesus called out Lazarus' name and the dead man came back to life and exited the tomb, covered in burial cloths. This is what Jesus meant in his earlier dialogue with Martha: "I am the resurrection and the life. He who believes in me will live, even though he dies; and whoever lives and believes in me will never die" (John 11:25–26).

Although Jesus used His divinity to raise Lazarus from the dead, His humanity brought Him tears at the death of Lazarus. This along with His passion, suffering, and death showed His human nature while the miracles and His Resurrection showed His divine.

Book of Glory: The Last Supper (John 13:1–17:26)

The Book of Signs concludes with chapter 12, and chapter 13 opens the Book of Glory. The main theme here is the glorification of the Son by

His obedient acceptance of the passion, death, and Resurrection. He must endure for the salvation of humankind. It is called the Book of Glory since the power of God is manifested through enduring a horrible death and by divinely rising from the dead on the third day, something no human being could ever duplicate.

Foot Washing

Chapter 13 opens with an act of complete humility. It was just before the Passover meal and Jesus got down on His knees with a bowl of water and began to wash the feet of His disciples. This was a symbolic act. Jesus' greatest foe was the devil, who is the epitome of pride, and the opposite of pride is humility. Therefore, by washing His disciples' feet Jesus practiced humility to conquer pride (the devil).

FACT

Even though Jesus said: "Now that I, your Lord and Teacher, have washed your feet, you also should wash one another's feet. I have set you an example that you should do as I have done for you" (John 13:14–15), only the Anabaptist and Seventh Day Adventist churches regard this as a sacrament/ordinance that must be done, as in the case of Baptism or Eucharist. Other Christians may do this minor ritual as an option on Holy Thursday.

The ensuing dialogue between Jesus and Peter is equally as critical as the actual foot washing. Symbolically, the washing of feet was to represent service since "the Son of Man came not to be served, but to serve" (Mark 10:45). However, the disciple Peter at first refused to allow Jesus to bathe his feet. But Jesus told him, "unless I wash you, you have no part with me" (John 13:8). Peter impetuously replied by asking Jesus to wash his hands and head as well. Jesus then replied: "A person who has had a bath needs only to wash his feet; his whole body is clean" (John 13:10). Many Bible scholars believe this symbolic washing of just the feet when a person has already had a bath refers to repentance in the Christian after his or her washing in baptism. It is only the dirty feet that need washing, not the whole body.

Final Discourse

Chapters 14 to 17 comprise the final discourse Jesus gave to His disciples before being arrested, condemned, and crucified. They entail words of encouragement since the men were discouraged and sad after hearing from Jesus that He would die, that one of them would betray Him, that Satan was after them, and that they would all be scattered around the world. More than a pep rally, these discourses were meant to edify, encourage, and aspire the disciples to be His true and faithful followers.

There are seven "I AM" sayings of Jesus in John's account of the Gospel. I am: the Bread of Life (John 6:35); the Light of the World (John 8:12); the Good Shepherd (John 10:14); the Resurrection and the Life (John 11:25); the Way, the Truth and the Life (John 14:6); the True Vine (John 15:1); and just I AM (John 8:58 and 18:5).

The most comforting of words spoken at this time are very often used at Christian funerals: "Do not let your hearts be troubled. Trust in God; trust also in me. In my Father's house are many rooms; if it were not so, I would have told you. I am going there to prepare a place for you. And if I go and prepare a place for you, I will come back and take you to be with me that you also may be where I am" (John 14:1–3).

Another passage that brings consolation is:

"As the Father has loved me, so have I loved you. Now remain in my love. If you obey my commands, you will remain in my love, just as I have obeyed my Father's commands and remain in his love. I have told you this so that my joy may be in you and that your joy may be complete. My command is this: Love each other as I have loved you. Greater love has no one than this, that he lay down his life for his friends. You are my friends if you do what I command. I no longer call you servants, because a servant does not know his master's business. Instead, I have called you friends, for everything that I learned from my Father I have made known to you. You did not choose me, but I chose you and appointed you to go and bear fruit—fruit that will last. Then the Father will give you whatever you ask in my name. This is my command: Love each other."

(John 15:9–17)

Book of Glory: Trial and Death (John 18:1–19:42)

This section deals with the arrest, trial, and sentence of Jesus to death by crucifixion. This is the "hour" He has prepared for. Again, not sixty minutes as we know it, but an hour insofar as the proper time, the right moment for Him to do what He was born to do—to die for sinners and save them.

Chapter 18 begins with the betrayer Judas identifying Jesus in the Garden to a cohort of soldiers who arrest Him. When asked whom they want, the soldiers replied, "Jesus of Nazareth." Then Jesus uttered the response "I am" (*ego eimi* in Greek, which is how the Septuagint translates the sacred name of God [*ego eimi ho on*], in Hebrew [*Ehye aser eyhe*], or in English, "I am Who Am").

Crucifixion

Like the Synoptics, John follows the same story of Jesus' crucifixion, except he adds an intimate dialogue between Jesus and His mother Mary at the foot of the cross just before He dies. "When Jesus saw his mother there, and the disciple whom he loved standing nearby, he said to his mother, 'Woman, here is your son,' and to the disciple, 'Here is your mother'" (John 19:26–27). Some scholars maintain that the "woman" here represents the church and the disciple represents all believers. Others propose that Mary, the Woman at the Cross, is also the Woman of Genesis 3:15 and Revelation 12:1, so that John 19:26–27 is a spiritual adoption of sorts—as adopted brothers and sisters in Christ, His mother becomes our mother by adoption as well. This view is held by the Eastern Orthodox Church and the Roman Catholics.

Book of Glory: Resurrection
(John 20:1–31)

This last section concerns the Resurrection, empty tomb, the miraculous draft of fish, and the commissioning of Peter. It concludes the Gospel with the line: "Jesus did many other things as well. If every one of them were written down, I suppose that even the whole world would not have room for the books that would be written" (John 21:25). This indicates that beyond the written word is also the unwritten or spoken word, sometimes called oral tradition, which did not get set to pen and ink. Many scholars consider Chapter 21 to be a later addition to John.

FACT

John uses two different Greek words: the first two times, *agapas*, then *phileis*. English translations merely give the same question three times, "do you love me?" *Agapas me* should be "do you care for me?" whereas *phileis me* would be "do you really love me?" Latin uses *diligis* and *amas*, respectively.

Commissioning of Peter

After denying knowing Jesus three times as predicted (John 13:38), it is not unexpected that Jesus would ask for a sign of repentance. Hence, the risen Jesus asked Peter three times: "Simon, do you love me?" It is called the commissioning since the election of Peter is considered to have happened in Matthew 16:18 and now that same Peter is told "feed my sheep; feed my lambs" (John 21:15–17). An allusion is also made to Peter's own death in verse 18 of chapter 21.

Chapter 18

Acts of the Apostles

The Acts of the Apostles is the first book after the Gospels in the New Testament. It is a chronicle of the early, ancient church, and a sequel to the Gospel according to Luke. The first chapters describe the big debate over church membership, such as who can be a Christian? The second half concerns Paul's journeys, his argument with Barnabas, and his arrest and arrival in Rome.

Preparation for Mission (Acts 1:1–2:13)

Luke, the author of the third Gospel account and the Book of Acts of the Apostles, opens both with a first person singular address to Theophilus, a possible patron. This first section of the Acts starts with the Ascension of Christ into heaven and ends with the Pentecost—the descent of the Holy Spirit upon the apostles. It is above all else a book of the church since it details how the Christian community functioned as an assembly of the faithful. The English word "church" is often used to denote the building where the faithful gather to worship, but the original and fuller meaning of "church" is the body or assembly of believers united by faith and not necessarily by language or place (territory).

Luke, a disciple and not an original apostle, gives this brief but eyewitness account of early church history to show the development of the ecclesial community. More than just an aggregate or union of believers, the church is the coming together of the faithful who believe in Christ and who are led by the apostles and their successors. Christianity will seek to blend the individual need to communicate with God and the social need to relate with one's neighbor. Communal worship and organized leadership become hallmarks of the new religion even though its Jewish roots are clearly shown in Acts.

ESSENTIAL

Ekklesia is Greek for "assembly" (*ecclesia* in Latin, where we get the word "ecclesiastical" meaning church-related). The word is used throughout Acts, the Epistles, and in Revelation to designate the organic unity of the body of believers. It is not an informal, accidental, or amorphous/nebulous union, but a structured one nonetheless.

Election Day

Since Judas committed suicide after betraying Jesus, the apostles were down to eleven in number. Jesus left no by-laws, manuals, constitutions, or written/verbal instructions on what to do about the organizational and operational aspects of the church. Since the founder never explicitly said to replace missing leaders, Peter and the other apostles had to interpret the known and available Scriptures. Many believe they interpreted Psalm 109 ("may another take his place of leadership") to mean that someone should replace Judas Iscariot as an apostle.

The apostles then selected two men from among the 120 who could fulfill the criteria of a disciple. They selected Joseph, called Barsabbas or Justus, and Matthias. Casting lots, it was decided that Matthias would take the place of Judas.

Pentecost

Fifty days after Easter and ten days after Jesus' Ascension into heaven, the twelve apostles (including Matthias) gathered at their meeting place when a great wind and sound entered the room and tongues of fire appeared over their heads. Filled with the Holy Spirit, they began to speak in different tongues (languages).

"When they heard this sound, a crowd came together in bewilderment, because each one heard them speaking in his own language. Utterly amazed, they asked: 'Are not all these men who are speaking Galileans? Then how is it that each of us hears them in his own native language? Parthians, Medes and Elamites; residents of Mesopotamia, Judea and Cappadocia, Pontus and Asia, Phrygia and Pamphylia, Egypt and the parts of Libya near Cyrene; visitors from Rome (both Jews and converts to Judaism); Cretans and Arabs—we hear them declaring the wonders of God in our own tongues!' Amazed and perplexed, they asked one another, 'What does this mean?'

Some, however, made fun of them and said, 'They have had too much wine.'"

(Acts 2:5–13)

Mission in Jerusalem (Acts 2:14–8:3)

After the Holy Spirit descended unto the apostles, Peter told them what they ought to do. "Repent and be baptized, every one of you, in the name of Jesus Christ for the forgiveness of your sins. And you will receive the gift of the Holy Spirit." This section then moves on to persecution, selecting deacons, and the first Christian martyr.

The Arrest

Peter and John were arrested after healing a man crippled from birth: "Silver or gold I do not have, but what I have I give you. In the name of Jesus Christ of Nazareth, walk" (Acts 3:6). The phrase "the name" will appear twenty-two times in Acts. It is "in the name" of Jesus Christ or "in the name" of the Lord that the apostles were able to perform miracles. This is why some scholars refer to them as "ambassadors of Christ." When the Sanhedrin ordered them to stop using and invoking the name of Jesus, Peter and John replied that it is better to obey God than man.

Deacons

Chapter 6 opens with a dispute among the Hellenistic (Greek-speaking) Jewish Christians and the Hebrew-speaking Jewish Christians. The argument was over the treatment of their widows and orphans. The twelve apostles gathered and decided that it was necessary to select seven good men to take care of the temporal/physical needs while they devoted themselves to the spiritual needs of the community. They prayed and laid hands on Stephen, Philip, Procorus, Nicanor, Timon, Parmenas, and Nicolas from Antioch and thus ordained them deacons.

Stephen's Death

After appearing before the Jewish Sanhedrin, the deacon Stephen was taken outside and stoned to death. Ironically, it was Saul of Tarsus, the vehement anti-Christian, who gave his approval to the stoning of Stephen for his blasphemy. This same Saul later became Saint Paul, the apostle and ardent defender of the Christian faith. Because he was the very first martyr to die for the church, Stephen is often called the "proto-martyr."

Mission in Judea and Samaria (Acts 8:4–9:43)

This section covers Simon Magus, Philip and the Ethiopian, and the Conversion of Saint Paul. It shows the infant Christian church branching out beyond the confines of Jerusalem. The death of Stephen led to a persecution of the church, which in turn helped it grow and flourish despite the intentions and efforts to eradicate the religion.

Simony

The sin of simony happens when someone tries to buy or sell spiritual benefits or graces—for example, when some clerics attempted to sell indulgences during the sixteenth century. The name itself comes from Simon Magus, a magician and sorcerer who attempted to bribe Peter and John. "When Simon saw that the Spirit was given at the laying on of the apostles' hands, he offered them money and said, 'Give me also this ability so that everyone on whom I lay my hands may receive the Holy Spirit.'" Peter answered: "May your money perish with you, because you thought you could buy the gift of God with money! You have no part or share in this ministry, because your heart is not right before God" (Acts 8:18–21).

Legend has it that Simon Magus challenged Saint Peter to a contest before Emperor Nero. He tried to create an illusion and fake rising from the dead or being able to fly. Either way, according to the story, he failed and died in the attempt.

Saul Becomes Paul

Saul was born in the port city of Tarsus in Cilicia, Asia Minor (modern-day southern Turkey), of the tribe of Benjamin, and was educated at Jerusalem in the school of Gamaliel. He was a member of the Pharisee party (part of the Sanhedrin) in terms of his Judaism, but also a Roman citizen by birth. In approximately A.D. 34, he had his conversion experience and fourteen years later changed his name from Saul (Hebrew) to Paul (Roman).

Saul had been on a mission to expose, arrest, and incarcerate Christians whom he regarded as a dangerous breakaway sect of Judaism. While on the road to Damascus one day, he was struck down to the ground and heard a voice saying, "Saul, Saul, why do you persecute me?" When Saul asked who the voice was, the response came back, "I am Jesus, whom you are persecuting" (Acts 9:4–5). Saul then got up from the ground but was unable to see. He was taken to the disciple Ananias in Damascus who at first had reservations about this notorious enemy of Christianity. But God spoke to Ananias: "Go! This man is my chosen instrument to carry my name before the Gentiles and their kings and before the people of Israel. I will show him how much he must suffer for my name" (Acts 9:15).

E FACT

Legend has it that Saul was knocked off his horse when Jesus called out to him, "Saul, Saul, why do you persecute me?" Yet, the Bible never mentions the horse (Acts 9:4) or how Saul was traveling for that matter. It is presumed that he was on horseback but the Scriptures never affirm nor deny it. Christian art has traditionally portrayed the scene with him falling off his horse.

When Ananias finally met Saul, he placed his hands on him and immediately scales fell off from Saul's eyes and he was able to see again. Saul was then baptized and instructed in all that the disciples could teach him about Jesus. He became as fierce and zealous a Christian as he had formerly been its chief opponent. Barnabas introduced him to the apostles. The Jewish leaders in Jerusalem heard of his conversion and plotted to kill him.

Gentile Mission (Acts 10:1–15:35)

This section deals with the expansion of Christianity from Jewish converts to Gentiles. As the Jewish leaders became more antagonistic toward Christianity, the apostles continued to convert the Gentiles. Acts 10 concentrates on the Roman Centurion Cornelius, Peter's vision, and his visit at Cornelius' house. Acts 11 covers Barnabas' and Paul's travels to Antioch and Tarsus, and Acts 12 details Peter's escape from prison and Herod's death. In Acts 13 and 14, Jesus' disciples continue to preach in Cyprus and Syria, among other places, and Acts 15 concentrates on the Council in Jerusalem.

Peter, Cornelius, and the Gentile Question

Cornelius was a Roman Centurion who was also a God-fearing and devout man. At the time of the apostles, there were three kinds of believers: Jews (Hebrew-speaking), Hellenists (Greek-speaking), and the God-fearers (Gentiles who intellectually accepted the Jewish faith but did not embrace the rituals or Mosaic Law). These same three groups would also become the first converts to Christianity. Jewish-Christian converts were often at odds with the Hellenistic Jewish-Christian converts, who allied themselves with the God-fearing Christian converts. Cornelius was a God-fearer, which meant that he was sympathetic to the Jewish faith but was not circumcised nor did he follow the Jewish dietary laws.

Some Christian churches use the example of Peter and Cornelius (Acts 10:48) and that of the Jailor of Paul and Silas (Acts 16:33)—with his entire family and household being baptized—as a justification for baptizing infants and not just adults.

Both Peter and Cornelius had dreams sent from God, and Cornelius called for Peter and asked to be baptized. This is the first time a noncircumcised God-fearer was seeking baptism. Before, only Hellenistic (Greek-speaking) circumcised Jews and Hebrew-speaking circumcised

Jews had been baptized. Peter's vision earlier had been that it was not the outside that made a man unclean, but what was inside his heart. Hence, despite the fact that Cornelius and his household ate food forbidden in Mosaic Law and none of the males had been circumcised, their hearts were pure and God-fearing. Peter baptized Cornelius, his family, and the entire household (men, women, and children).

Peter's baptism of Cornelius caused big problems. The circumcised believers (Jewish and Hellenistic) jumped on his back and asked why Peter would visit the home and eat with uncircumcised men. Once he told the details of his vision and the true faith found in Cornelius and his household, many came to believe that God was calling both Jews and Gentiles to the new Christian Way of Life.

The Fugitive

King Herod killed James, John's brother, with a sword and then arrested Peter. The night before his trial, an angel visited Peter. Chains fell off his wrists, locked doors and gates opened by themselves, and Peter passed safely by every guard in the prison. He then went to the home of John Mark (evangelist who wrote the second Gospel) and his mother Mary.

Paul and Barnabas

Paul and Barnabas became friends and preachers. John Mark, the young cousin of Barnabas, who may have been the Gospel writer and probably fled the Garden of Olives when Jesus was arrested. When Paul was ready to sail to Pamphylia (ancient name for the fertile coastal plain in southern Turkey), John fled again to Jerusalem (Acts 13:13). This irked Paul so much that when Barnabas suggested his cousin John Mark join them again (Acts 15:37–41), Paul became angry, and the two separated on unfriendly terms. Barnabas took Mark to Cyprus, while Paul took Silas to Syria and Cilicia.

QUESTION?

Was Barnabas an apostle?

Although Paul never openly calls Barnabas an apostle, he tends to use the title "apostle" in a wider sense than Luke. It is also evident from Scripture that Barnabas was a gifted orator. It was common for Paul and Barnabas to visit the synagogues of the cities in which they evangelized and debated with various religious groups.

Council of Jerusalem

Chapter 15 opens with: "Some men came down from Judea to Antioch and were teaching the brothers: 'Unless you are circumcised, according to the custom taught by Moses, you cannot be saved.' This brought Paul and Barnabas into sharp dispute and debate with them" (Acts 15:1–2). Thus, a meeting of the apostles and disciples was convened in Jerusalem to settle the dispute. Peter, who had just recently baptized the God-fearing and uncircumcised Cornelius, as well as his family and household, spoke up: "Now then, why do you try to test God by putting on the necks of the disciples a yoke that neither we nor our fathers have been able to bear? We believe it is through the grace of our Lord Jesus that we are saved, just as they are" (Acts 15:10–11).

James then added his opinion in the debate: "It is my judgment, therefore, that we should not make it difficult for the Gentiles who are turning to God. Instead we should write to them, telling them to abstain from food polluted by idols, from sexual immorality, from the meat of strangled animals and from blood. For Moses has been preached in every city from the earliest times and is read in the synagogues on every Sabbath" (Acts 15:19–21).

This was a watershed for the Christian church in three ways:

1. It was the final straw, which broke any hope of reconciliation with the Jewish faith now that the Gentiles were allowed to be baptized without circumcision.

2. It opened the door to conversions for Greeks, Gentiles, and Romans who previously had no desire to embrace the Mosaic Law regarding circumcision and dietary regulations, yet were very willing to embrace the new Christian religion.

3. It showed that within the Bible (Acts of the Apostles), the church leadership (apostles and their successors) had to exercise authority and make decisions where Scripture had been silent or ambiguous.

Paul's Mission (Acts 15:36–28:31)

After the quarrel between Paul and Barnabas over his cousin John Mark, Paul decided to go separately. His travelling companions were Silas and later Timothy. Their travels began in Derbe and Lystra, and continued through Philippi, Thessalonica, Athens, Corinth, Ephesus, Macedonia and Greece, Jerusalem, Caesarea, and finally Rome. The time period was around A.D. 50–64 and marked an era where Gentiles joined the Christian church in large numbers.

Some Bible scholars believe that the Acts of the Apostles may have been a legal brief based on the recollections of Paul and Luke's diary, to help in Paul's trial defense before the Emperor. However, neither the Acts nor Paul's surviving letters reveal the results of that trial.

Paul and Silas (Acts 16:16–40)

After converting Lydia, the purple cloth dealer in Philippi, Paul and Silas encountered a slave girl who was possessed by a demon, but could predict the future. She earned a comfortable living for her owners as a fortune-teller and soothsayer. She pestered Paul and Silas so much with her episodes of clairvoyance that Paul finally said: "In the name of Jesus Christ I command you to come out of her!" The evil spirit left and so did her "psychic" abilities, which angered her owners. Beaten and flogged, Paul and Silas were thrown into prison.

A mysterious earthquake shook all the prison doors open and popped off all the chains of the prisoners. The jailor feared he would be blamed for the ensuing escape and was about to throw himself on the sword when Paul stopped him. The grateful guard took Paul and Silas home and cared for their wounds. He and his entire household were baptized that night and became devout Christians. Paul and Silas returned to their cells.

The next morning the magistrates wanted to release the prisoners quietly when Paul and Silas announced, "They beat us publicly without a trial, even though we are Roman citizens, and threw us into prison. And now do they want to get rid of us quietly? No! Let them come themselves and escort us out." The revelation of their citizenship scared the officials into escorting them out as requested.

Why was Paul's Roman citizenship important?
Because Roman citizens could not be crucified nor should they be imprisoned without trial.

QUESTION?

Athens and the Unknown God (Acts 17:16–34)

While waiting for Silas and Timothy to return from Berea, Paul stayed in Athens. He noticed the numerous idols, gods, and goddesses the Greeks worshipped. The Areopagus was a place where philosophers met and debated, and was the seat of the highest judicial and legislative council. Paul debated with them about their worship, and Stoics (who exalted reason and logic) and Epicureans (who glorified physical pleasure) were intrigued by his preaching. Paul played on the fact that among the pantheon of deities, there was an altar to the "unknown god." He said:

"Now what you worship as something unknown I am going to proclaim to you. The God who made the world and everything in it is the Lord of heaven and earth and does not live in temples built by hands. And he is not served by human hands, as if he needed anything, because he himself gives all men life and breath and everything else. From one man he made every nation of men, that they should inhabit the whole earth; and he determined the times set for them and the exact places where they should live. God did this so that men would seek him and perhaps reach out for him and find him, though he is not far from each one of us. For in him we live and move and have our being. As some of your own poets have said, 'We are his offspring.' Therefore since we are God's offspring, we should not think that the divine being is like gold or silver or stone—an image made by man's design and skill. In the past God overlooked such ignorance, but now he commands all people everywhere to repent. For he has set a day when he will judge the world with justice by the man he has appointed. He has given proof of this to all men by raising him from the dead."

(Acts 17:23–31)

After hearing Paul's eloquent preaching on the one true God, some laughed at him, while others believed his words and became his followers. Among the ones impressed were Dionysius, a member of the Areopagus, a woman named Damaris, and other members. After the sermon, Paul left Athens and traveled to the Greek city of Corinth.

Third Missionary Journey (Acts 21:37–28:31)

In his third missionary journey, Paul returned to Jerusalem to report his apostolic work in Gentile territory. While preaching in the Temple area, Paul's enemies incited a mob riot and a Roman commander arrested him. He asked for permission to speak to the crowd one more time. He explained his Jewish heritage, education, and religious background. He then told of his conversion and his conviction that Jesus is the Messiah and of his commission to preach to the Gentiles. The audience was shocked and the Roman commander ordered him to be scourged. Paul then announced his Roman citizenship, which prevented him from being scourged and entitled him to a trial.

He was transferred to Caesarea where the Roman Governor Felix and then his successor Festus ruled in the name of Caesar. Paul's enemies wanted him sent back to Jerusalem for trial. As a Roman citizen, however, Paul invoked his final right of appeal before Caesar and was automatically sent to Rome. He encountered a huge storm, a shipwreck, and was bitten by a snake on Malta only to be switched to another ship and headed for Rome. The Book of Acts ends with Paul's arrival in Rome and a two-year house arrest where he preached often and vigorously. No mention, however, is made of his death. Ⓔ

Chapter 19
The Pauline Epistles

The letters or Epistles (from the Latin *epistula* meaning "written communication" or "letter") of Paul were written to the various Christian communities and churches he visited during his missionary work. There are traditionally fourteen Pauline Epistles but contemporary scholars debate whether Paul was the author of all of them. Next to the four Gospel accounts (Matthew, Mark, Luke, and John), the Pauline Epistles are the second most influential documents of Christianity.

Romans

Paul's letter to the Romans was most likely written around A.D. 57, during his third missionary journey. He wrote this letter to the church in Rome and to a community he himself had not founded. Here he teaches about justification by faith and not through the mere observance of the law. He also invokes the principle of the natural moral law: "Indeed, when Gentiles, who do not have the law, do by nature things required by the law, they are a law for themselves, even though they do not have the law, since they show that the requirements of the law are written on their hearts, their consciences also bearing witness, and their thoughts now accusing, now even defending them" (Romans 2:14–15).

In his letter to the Romans, Paul reminds the Christian community that all men and women of all creeds and cultures are capable of knowing right from wrong. This capacity to discern basic ethical norms is given by reason to all human beings, and it is accented by those ethical norms common to all cultures and civilizations.

Paul does not want the Romans (and Christians in general) to take their salvation for granted. He claims that living a moral life is the duty of all believers since even the pagans know rudimentary right from wrong. According to him, Christians not only have the moral law to inform them, but by faith have the love of Christ to motivate them. Paul's message is to trust in God and place hope in Christ.

Justification by Faith

Romans 3:23–24 states: "for all have sinned and fall short of the glory of God, and are justified freely by his grace through the redemption that came by Christ Jesus." This became the hallmark of Martin Luther and the Protestant Reformers in the sixteenth century A.D. Paul goes on in chapter 4 to explain that Abraham was not justified by works but "[he] believed God, and it was credited to him as righteousness" (Romans 4:3).

Original Sin

Chapter 5 of the letter to the Romans gave Saint Augustine the foundation for his theology of Original Sin. "Therefore, just as sin entered the world through one man, and death through sin, and in this way death came to all men, because all sinned" (Romans 5:12). "For just as through the disobedience of the one man the many were made sinners, so also through the obedience of the one man the many will be made righteous" (Romans 5:19).

FACT

Augustine saw the connection Paul was making with the first man, Adam, by which Original Sin was transmitted to all human beings via wounded human nature and the Second Adam, Christ, who saved all human beings by redeeming human nature.

Comfort

Chapter 8 gives great comfort to the Christians during time of trial and tribulation. "If God is for us, who can be against us? He who did not spare his own Son, but gave him up for us all—how will he not also, along with him, graciously give us all things? . . . For I am convinced that neither death nor life, neither angels nor demons, neither the present nor the future, nor any powers, neither height nor depth, nor anything else in all Creation, will be able to separate us from the love of God that is in Christ Jesus our Lord" (Romans 8:31–32, 38–39).

Corinthians 1 and 2

Paul may have written his two Epistles to the church in Corinth around A.D. 57. He was the one who established the Christian church there among the Corinthians sometime about seven years earlier. Concerns he addresses are internal division, sexual immorality, marriage problems, paganism, liturgical abuse, and the resurrection of the dead. Where 1 Corinthians is a letter of fraternal correction, 2 Corinthians is a letter of instruction on how to do even better than before, as well as on Paul's love for the community. He addresses concerns like almsgiving, forgiveness, and a self-defense of his ministry and authority.

First Corinthians

The first issue Paul deals with is divisions within the church. "One of you says, 'I follow Paul'; another, 'I follow Apollos'; another, 'I follow Cephas'; still another, 'I follow Christ.' Is Christ divided? Was Paul crucified for you? Were you baptized into the name of Paul?" (1 Corinthians 1:12–13). Here he battles the focus on personality and reminds the Corinthians that the preacher or pastor is not the focus but the message and the Lord Jesus are what should be the center of attention.

Then he moves on to sexual immorality. "It is actually reported that there is sexual immorality among you, and of a kind that does not occur even among pagans: A man has his father's wife" (1 Corinthians 5:1). "Do you not know that the wicked will not inherit the kingdom of God? Do not be deceived: Neither the sexually immoral nor idolaters nor adulterers nor male prostitutes nor homosexual offenders nor thieves nor the greedy nor drunkards nor slanderers nor swindlers will inherit the kingdom of God" (1 Corinthians 6:9).

QUESTION?

What does Paul say about marriage?
His teaching on marriage is found in chapter 7: "Now to the unmarried and the widows I say: It is good for them to stay unmarried, as I am. But if they cannot control themselves, they should marry, for it is better to marry than to burn with passion. To the married I give this command (not I, but the Lord): A wife must not separate from her husband. But if she does, she must remain unmarried or else be reconciled to her husband. And a husband must not divorce his wife" (1 Corinthians 7:8–11).

Chapter 11, verses 23–25 reiterate the words of the Last Supper and also the very same words spoken at the Christian Eucharistic Liturgy.

"For I received from the Lord what I also passed on to you: The Lord Jesus, on the night he was betrayed, took bread, and when he had given thanks, he broke it and said, 'This is my body, which is for you; do this in remembrance of me.' In the same way, after supper he took the cup, saying, 'This cup is the new covenant in my blood; do this, whenever you drink it, in remembrance of me.'"

Second Corinthians

This follow-up letter is intended to balance the chastisement of the previous with compassion and mercy. He reminds the Corinthians to show forgiveness after a sinner repents. "You ought to forgive and comfort him, so that he will not be overwhelmed by excessive sorrow" (2 Corinthians 2:7). He also repudiates those that question his credentials, in other words, the sufferings he has already endured for the Gospel:

"In great endurance; in troubles, hardships and distresses; in beatings, imprisonments and riots; in hard work, sleepless nights and hunger; in purity, understanding, patience and kindness; in the Holy Spirit and in sincere love; in truthful speech and in the power of God; with weapons of righteousness in the right hand and in the left; through glory and dishonor, bad report and good report; genuine, yet regarded as impostors; known, yet regarded as unknown; dying, and yet we live on; beaten, and yet not killed; sorrowful, yet always rejoicing; poor, yet making many rich; having nothing, and yet possessing everything."

(2 Corinthians 6:4–10)

Galatians

Written between A.D. 50 and A.D. 55, this letter is to the community in Galatia, warning them against the attempts of the Judaizers to impose their personal piety on everyone else. The Judaizers were zealous Jewish-Christian converts, who thought that all Christians should retain the Mosaic Law, especially the dietary regulations and the requirement of circumcision. Paul chastised Peter (Cephas) for allegedly flip-flopping and eating with Gentiles at one moment and then avoiding their table when Jewish Christians came to town.

In the letter to the Galatians, Paul gives a partial list of sins that he is concerned about among the Galatians: "The acts of the sinful nature are obvious: sexual immorality, impurity and debauchery; idolatry and witchcraft; hatred, discord, jealousy, fits of rage, selfish ambition, dissensions, factions and envy; drunkenness, orgies, and the like. I warn you, as I did before, that those who live like this will not inherit the kingdom of God" (Galatians 5:19–21).

Ephesians

The letter to the Ephesians was probably written around A.D. 60. By that time, Paul was already imprisoned in Rome. While addressed to the church community in Ephesus, this Epistle, like all that are in the New Testament, has global and perennial importance and impact. This letter reminds the reader that the church is an organic unity and not an optional, accidental association of individuals. According to Saint Paul, the church is the mystical body of Christ—an analogy he uses in more than one Epistle.

Unity in the Body

"There is one body and one Spirit—just as you were called to one hope when you were called—one Lord, one faith, one baptism; one God and Father of all, who is over all and through all and in all" (Ephesians 4:4–6). Division for Paul is the work of the devil since God wishes all His children to be one with Him. The Body of Christ (i.e., the church) is not just an institution, but an organic unity. It is a unity within diversity so that unity does not equate with uniformity. "It was he who gave some to be apostles, some to be prophets, some to be evangelists, and some to be pastors and teachers" (Ephesians 4:11).

Married Life

The most controversial passage from Paul's Epistle to the Ephesians is: "Wives, submit to your husbands as to the Lord. For the husband is the head of the wife as Christ is the head of the church, his body, of which he is the Savior. Now as the church submits to Christ, so also wives should submit to their husbands in everything" (Ephesians 5:22–24). Whenever a Scripture passage is taken out of context you get a pretext. All of Scripture is inspired and inerrant but it must be taken in context with the whole of Scripture. This passage only makes real sense when you read the rest of the story. "Husbands, love your wives, just as Christ loved the church and gave himself up for her" (Ephesians 5:25). "Husbands ought to love their wives as their own bodies. He who loves his wife loves himself" (Ephesians 5:28). The complete passage shows that both the husband and wife have obligations to each other.

FACT

The image of a spousal relationship, bride and groom, is endemic to Paul. He makes the analogy that Christ loves the church as a groom loves his bride. The church is often spoken of in feminine terms, with feminine pronouns, since she is considered the Bride of Christ and Jesus being male is described in masculine terms and pronouns. This same marital relationship was portrayed in the Old Testament covenant of God and the Hebrew People.

Parents and Children; Slaves and Masters

Chapter 6 describes the proper behavior for children toward their parents and slaves toward their masters. "Children, obey your parents in the Lord, for this is right" (Ephesians 6:1). "Fathers, do not exasperate your children; instead, bring them up in the training and instruction of the Lord" (Ephesians 6:4).

Another controversial section in this Epistle is: "Slaves, obey your earthly masters with respect and fear, and with sincerity of heart, just as you would obey Christ. Obey them not only to win their favor when their eye is on you, but like slaves of Christ, doing the will of God from your heart. Serve wholeheartedly, as if you were serving the Lord, not men, because you know that the Lord will reward everyone for whatever good he does, whether he is slave or free. And masters, treat your slaves in the same way. Do not threaten them, since you know that he who is both their Master and yours is in heaven, and there is no favoritism with him" (Ephesians 6:5–9).

QUESTION?

Is Paul justifying slavery?
Paul is neither justifying nor endorsing slavery. However, slavery at the time was not often as heinous as it was in the New World when Africans were enslaved and shipped to America. The historical context is one element of accurately interpreting Scripture.

At the time of Paul, society was patriarchal and imperial—almost akin to the idea of "necessary evils" in the sense that as a result of Original Sin, the previous equality of all people of all genders, races, nationalities, and cultures was disrupted. Division and inequality are results of sin. Genesis uses the Tower of Babel to explain why there are different languages in the world instead of just one. The sin of pride destroyed the unity of speech. Paul is also not using the Bible to justify patriarchy anymore than slavery. Nevertheless, the historical context, just like the erroneous notion of the geocentric universe, is part of the context of the sacred author.

Philippians

An optimistic and upbeat Epistle, the letter to the church community in Philippi was most likely meant to show encouragement despite the fact that at that time Paul was under house arrest in Rome. His imprisonment was a blessing in disguise, he tells the Philippians, since his captivity has given courage and zeal to others to take up the torch and continue evangelizing. He tells them not to worry about his predicament. All his discomfort, pain, and suffering is worth it since being united to Christ is what gives him real joy. He also warns them not to become complacent since many of them enjoy the privileges of Roman citizenship, just as he does. It won't save his life nor his soul but it will be of some advantage nonetheless.

One of the most sublime and edifying hymns found in Paul's Epistles is Ephesians 2:5–11, which is meant to extol the virtue of humility. As Jesus was humble, even in surrendering some of His divine prerogatives while not diminishing His divinity, so, too, the Christian is to seek a life of humility. Here is the pertinent passage:

"Your attitude should be the same as that of Christ Jesus: Who, being in very nature God, did not consider equality with God something to be grasped, but made himself nothing, taking the very nature of a servant, being made in human likeness. And being found in appearance as a man, he humbled himself and became obedient to death—even death on a cross! Therefore God exalted him to the highest place and gave him the name that is above every name, that at the name of Jesus every knee should bow, in heaven and on earth and under the earth, and every tongue confess that Jesus Christ is Lord, to the glory of God the Father."

Colossians

Though Paul did not visit nor found the church in Colossae (east of Ephesus), it still was dear to him. He wrote the letter to the Colossians to correct some errors that had been infiltrating their Christian church. The most likely culprits were the Gnostics, who preached a secret knowledge of salvation, which contradicted the universal (*catholic* with a small "c") gospel. Their unorthodox teachings diluted some of the Christian doctrines Paul now had to reaffirm: Jesus Christ is true God and true man; He has a real divine nature and a real human nature. He is not half-god and half-human, but possesses full divinity and full humanity. The central doctrine of Christianity—which distinguishes it from the other two monotheistic religions, Judaism and Islam—is the notion of a Triune God (one God in three Persons).

"He is the image of the invisible God, the firstborn over all creation. For by him all things were created: things in heaven and on earth, visible and invisible, whether thrones or powers or rulers or authorities; all things were created by him and for him. He is before all things, and in him all things hold together. And he is the head of the body, the church; he is the beginning and the firstborn from among the dead, so that in everything he might have the supremacy. For God was pleased to have all his fullness dwell in him, and through him to reconcile to himself all things, whether things on earth or things in heaven, by making peace through his blood, shed on the cross."

(Colossians 1:15–20)

In his letter to the Colossians, Paul also reiterates his social teaching on family and civil life (as found in Ephesians). "Wives, submit to your husbands, as is fitting in the Lord. Husbands, love your wives and do not be harsh with them. Children, obey your parents in everything, for this pleases the Lord. Fathers, do not embitter your children, or they will become discouraged. Slaves, obey your earthly masters in everything; and do it, not only when their eye is on you and to win their favor, but with sincerity of heart and reverence for the Lord" (Colossians 3:18–22). Here, he encourages the Colossians not only to abandon false teachings but also to embrace and pursue a life of holiness.

Thessalonians 1 and 2

These two Epistles concern the Christian church in Thessalonica, a city in northeast Greece. Paul preached there during his second missionary journey. Acts 17 shows that Paul did not stay long (three weeks) among the Thessalonians due to the unrest and civil disturbance caused by their enemies in that town. The main thrust of both Epistles, however, deals with the Second Coming of Christ (called the *Parousia* in Greek) at the end of the world. Many of the Thessalonians thought the Second Coming was extremely immanent, so that meant there was little for them to do but wait and others thought it had already happened and they had somehow missed it.

"Brothers, we do not want you to be ignorant about those who fall asleep, or to grieve like the rest of men, who have no hope" (1 Thessalonians 4:13). The early Christians called the dead "sleepers" since death was seen as falling asleep and not the final end.

First Thessalonians

Probably the oldest and first of Paul's letters (possibly written around A.D. 50–52), this Epistle deals with a doctrine uniquely Christian in origin and meaning—the Second Coming of Christ. The first coming of Christ took place when He was conceived in His mother's womb and was then born in Bethlehem nine months later. After His death and Resurrection, He ascended into heaven but promised He would return. That return of the risen and glorified Christ is called the Second Coming, or *Parousia*.

Paul reminds the Thessalonians that neither the dead nor the living will have an advantage over the other at the Second Coming of Christ.

"According to the Lord's own word, we tell you that we who are still alive, who are left till the coming of the Lord, will certainly not precede those who have fallen asleep. For the Lord himself will come down from heaven, with a loud command, with the voice of the archangel and with the trumpet call of God, and the dead in Christ will rise first. After that, we who are still alive and are left will be caught up together with them in the clouds to meet the Lord in the air. And so we will be with the Lord forever."

(1 Thessalonians 4:15–17)

Rapture

The Greek word *harpag^sometha* used in 1 Thessalonians 4:17, means "to be caught up; to be seized; to be snatched up." Saint Jerome's Latin Vulgate used the word *rapiemur*, the root being *rapere* from which the English word "rapture" has its origin. The "rapture" is a popular teaching among some Christian denominations. Manuel de

Lecunza y Diaz (eighteenth century) was the first to espouse the doctrine, later modified by John Nelson Darby (nineteenth century) and embraced by Cyrus I. Scofield (twentieth century), author of the Scofield Bible. The doctrine is that prior to the Second Coming of Christ, there will be a seven-year period of great tribulation (suffering) on earth. The saints of Christ (believers) will not experience this great tribulation since they will be "caught or taken up" (raptured) and meet Christ in the sky.

Second Thessalonians

Evidently, the first letter was not taken to heart. Some of the Thessalonians still worried that the Second Coming was so imminent that they stopped working, thinking the end was very near. That meant nothing got done, at home or at work. People did not marry nor have kids, fearing the end was at hand and the world would soon end. "If a man will not work, he shall not eat" (2 Thessalonians 3:10). This was directed at those Christians who no longer went to work.

FACT

The branches of Christianity, that believe in the literal rapture, have variations on the event. *Pretribulational* rapture is the notion that the rapture occurs before the seven years of tribulation; *Posttribulational* is that the rapture happens after the tribulation; *Premillenialism* is the notion that the Second Coming precedes the Millennium (1,000-year reign of Christ on earth with His believers; Satan vanquished to hell); *Postmillenialism* is that the Millennium precedes the Second Coming.

Timothy 1 and 2

Timothy traveled with Paul since his second journey. His father was a Gentile but his mother was Jewish, which was why Paul circumcised Timothy (Acts 16:3) to appease the sensitivities of some Hebrew speaking Christians. These letters contain advice from an old friend on how to refute false teachings and defend the true faith, how to manage the relationships and appoint the worthy pastors (presbyters or priests), deacons, and bishops (successors to the apostles).

"Now the overseer must be above reproach, the husband of but one wife, temperate, self-controlled, respectable, hospitable, able to teach, not given to drunkenness, not violent but gentle, not quarrelsome, not a lover of money. He must manage his own family well and see that his children obey him with proper respect. (If anyone does not know how to manage his own family, how can he take care of God's church?) He must not be a recent convert, or he may become conceited and fall under the same judgment as the devil. He must also have a good reputation with outsiders, so that he will not fall into disgrace and into the devil's trap."

(1 Timothy 3:2–7)

Then he gives the qualifications for the deacon: "Deacons, likewise, are to be men worthy of respect, sincere, not indulging in much wine, and not pursuing dishonest gain. They must keep hold of the deep truths of the faith with a clear conscience . . . A deacon must be the husband of but one wife and must manage his children and his household well" (1 Timothy 3:8–9,12).

Paul also warns about worldliness. Many Christians became complacent when they also became successful, financially speaking. He never advocated a total and radical poverty as a precondition to the spiritual life and in fact he is often misquoted. The saying "money is the root of all evil" is an inaccurate quotation. What Paul did say to Timothy was "for the love of money is a root of all kinds of evil" (1 Timothy 6:10).

ALERT!

Paul uses three Greek words—*episkopos* (bishop), *diakonos* (deacon), and *presbuteros* (priest or elder)—for three offices of spiritual leadership in the church. Catholicism, Eastern Orthodoxy, and the Anglican churches see these as three tiers of the sacrament of Holy Orders.

Titus and Philemon

Titus was a Gentile (Greek) convert and a travelling companion of Paul. Around A.D. 63–64, and after Timothy stayed in Ephesus, Paul and Titus continued to Crete. Titus remained to establish the Christian church while Paul continued his missionary journey. Philemon was a prestigious and well-respected Christian in Colossae. Philemon's Epistle is a personal letter from Paul addressed to him concerning his runaway slave, Onesimus.

Titus

Paul asks Titus to take care of some unfinished business, namely, to select, appoint, and ordain local leaders, bishops (overseers), and priests (elders or presbyters). The bishop would be in charge of the larger area (e.g., the entire town), while the priest or elder would be the equivalent of the local neighborhood pastor as there could be several or more in one town. "An elder [priest or presbyter] must be blameless, the husband of but one wife, a man whose children believe and are not open to the charge of being wild and disobedient" (Titus 1:6).

FACT

Paul warns, "Do not be hasty in the laying on of hands" (1 Timothy 5:22). The "laying on of hands" is synonymous with ordination. The gesture is an invocation of the Holy Spirit upon the person, but when done by the bishop, it is part of the ordination ritual to the episcopacy (bishop), diaconate (deacon), or priesthood (presbyter or elder). It is a Christian sacrament (ordinance), like baptism and the Eucharist (Lord's Supper).

The bishop, on the other hand, has more qualifications to fulfill since he has a larger responsibility. "Since an overseer [bishop] is entrusted with God's work, he must be blameless—not overbearing, not quick-tempered, not given to drunkenness, not violent, not pursuing dishonest gain. Rather he must be hospitable, one who loves what is good, who is self-controlled, upright, holy and disciplined. He must hold firmly to the trustworthy message as it has been taught, so that he can encourage others by sound doctrine and refute those who oppose it" (Titus 1:7–9).

While sounding a little jaundiced, Paul warns Titus about the local recruits from which to appoint bishops and priests (elders). "Even one of their own prophets has said, 'Cretans are always liars, evil brutes, lazy gluttons'" (Titus 1:12).

Philemon

Onesimus was a slave who belonged to Philemon and then escaped. He fled to Rome and wound up in jail with Paul. Onesimus embraces the Christian faith while imprisoned with Paul. Paul now writes to Philemon asking him to take Onesimus back but not to mistreat, abuse, or punish him for his escape. He may have even stolen some money from Philemon, in which case Paul tells the owner to charge it to his account instead. "If he has done you any wrong or owes you anything, charge it to me" (Philemon 18). In ancient times, an escaped slave could be brutally beaten, abused, or even killed. Since Onesimus was now a believer and Philemon had been one for a while, Paul counted on his Christian sense of mercy. He did not, however, ask for his emancipation.

Hebrews

Scholars continue to debate as to the identity of the author and the intended audience of the Epistle to the Hebrews. Some maintain it is Paul who wrote it; others say it is one of his students. Some say it was written for Jewish converts before the destruction of the Temple of Jerusalem (A.D. 70); others claim it was written afterwards. Martin Luther hypothesized that Apollos was the author, Tertullian thought it was actually Barnabas, while Clement of Alexandria and Origen credit it to Paul.

The Epistle to the Hebrews contains highly developed theology on Christ (known as Christology), especially the notion of Jesus Christ as the eternal High Priest. Paul explains that Jesus Christ is the new High Priest, not by birth (He was of a different clan and tribe) but by election (i.e., God the Father chose Him). Secondly, His priesthood is not symbolic. John the Baptist calls Jesus "the Lamb of God." On the cross, Jesus was both the priest who offered the sacrifice and the victim being sacrificed. The author, Paul, makes the analogy of Melchizedek, King of Salem and Priest. Unlike the hereditary Levitical priesthood, Melchizedek is priest by nature not by birth. He offers up bread and wine just as Jesus did at the Last Supper.

Paul quotes Psalm 110: "You are a priest forever, in the order of Melchizedek" (Hebrews 5:6). Formerly, priests were taken from among men who were weak, imperfect, and sinful, and so the sacrifices they offered on behalf of the people, they also offered for their own sins as well. Jesus—being the Son of God—has no sin and therefore does not offer up sacrifice for His behalf but totally for our benefit. The sacrifice is not something symbolic like a lamb; it is His very own life, which Jesus sacrifices on the altar of the cross at Calvary.

"If perfection could have been attained through the Levitical priesthood (for on the basis of it the law was given to the people), why was there still need for another priest to come—one in the order of Melchizedek, not in the order of Aaron? For when there is a change of the priesthood, there must also be a change of the law. He of whom these things are said belonged to a different tribe, and no one from that tribe has ever served at the altar. For it is clear that our Lord descended from Judah, and in regard to that tribe Moses said nothing about priests. And what we have said is even more clear if another priest like Melchizedek appears, one who has become a priest not on the basis of a regulation as to his ancestry but on the basis of the power of an indestructible life. For it is declared: 'You are a priest forever, in the order of Melchizedek.'"

(Hebrews 7:11–17)

The author of Hebrews points out that the priesthood of Christ is eternal. A priest is one who offers sacrifice to God on behalf and in the name of the people. The Old Testament priesthood was imperfect but symbolic as it pointed to the real priesthood of Jesus, which would not be symbolic (i.e., no animal sacrifice but the very Son Himself is sacrificed in atonement for our sins and those of the whole world). His sacrifice actually atones, redeems, and saves human nature. Ⓔ

Chapter 20

Apostolic Letters of Peter, James, John, and Jude

These seven letters are sometimes called the catholic Epistles, in the sense that the original meaning of the word "catholic" is "universal." Also known as the apostolic letters, they are not addressed to particular persons (like Titus or Philemon) or to particular places (like Corinth or Ephesus), but to the universal church in general. This chapter will look at the Epistles of 1 and 2 Peter; James; 1, 2, and 3 John; and Jude.

James

Although the exact date of James' letter is unknown, many scholars believe it was written by James the apostle around A.D. 50—making it the oldest book in the New Testament. The letter is written to the "twelve tribes scattered among the nations" (James 1:1). It is very practical, as opposed to the very theological nature of Hebrews. James begins with a word of extreme encouragement. Testing produces perseverance, he tells his readers, and gives this gem of wisdom: "Everyone should be quick to listen, slow to speak and slow to become angry" (James 1:19).

FACT

Some Protestant Christians consider James to be a blood brother or half-brother to Jesus. Other Christians (e.g., Catholic and Orthodox) contend that the Greek word used in the Gospels for "brother" is *adelphos*, which can also mean "relative" or "cousin." Genesis 14:16 refers to Lot as the "brother" (*adelphos* in the Septuagint) of Abram, yet Genesis 11:27 says that Lot is the son of Haran (brother of Abram), which makes Lot a nephew to Abram.

Denouncement of Favoritism

James begins with a denunciation of favoritism. He condemns the practice of giving preferential seating and treatment to those dressed in expensive clothing, while ignoring or mistreating the person in poor attire. "Has not God chosen those who are poor in the eyes of the world to be rich in faith and to inherit the kingdom he promised those who love him? But you have insulted the poor. Is it not the rich who are exploiting you? Are they not the ones who are dragging you into court?" (James 2:5–6).

Faith and Works

Paul and James appear to contradict one another on the doctrine of faith and good works. Paul said, "for it is by grace you have been saved, through faith . . . not by works, so that no one can boast" (Ephesians 2:8–9). James, on the other hand, said, "You see that a person is justified by what he does and not by faith alone" (James 2:24—The KJV reads "by works a man is justified"). Since both sacred authors were inspired and all of Scripture is inerrant, then there must be a resolution. Theologians maintain that both Paul and James are right but merely coming at the issue from different perspectives.

Paul never used the phrase "faith alone" (*sola fide*) but he did say, "It is by grace you have been saved." It is grace "through faith." James, on the other hand, said, "Faith by itself, if it is not accompanied by action [deeds or works], is dead" (James 2:17). Both can be correct if it is understood that grace is the catalyst. Grace is a supernatural gift from God. It is freely given and it cannot be earned nor merited. No amount of good works deserves the free gift of grace. At the same time, however, grace makes the soul prepared to receive and accept faith, a virtue.

ESSENTIAL

Saint Augustine combated the heresy of Pelagianism in the fifth century A.D. This teaching centered on the notion that human nature can do good without the help of God and that men and women can merit/earn their place in heaven. Augustine denounced this as heresy and formulated his doctrine on grace.

Wicked Tongues

"The tongue is a small part of the body, but it makes great boasts" (James 3:5). "With the tongue we praise our Lord and Father, and with it we curse men, who have been made in God's likeness. Out of the same mouth come praise and cursing. My brothers, this should not be" (James 3:9–10). James, therefore, points out that the human tongue is designed to speak the truth and to give praise to God, but evil people choose to use it to speak lies, insults, and obscenities. Just as a forest can be set ablaze by one small spark, a person's reputation or life can be ruined by one small lie, rumor, or piece of gossip.

He offers an insight into the two kinds of wisdom: worldly and heavenly. The former promotes envy, greed, pride, and so forth, whereas the latter, peace, love, mercy, and compassion. "What causes fights and quarrels among you? Don't they come from your desires that battle within you? You want something but don't get it. You kill and covet, but you cannot have what you want. You quarrel and fight. You do not have, because you do not ask God. When you ask, you do not receive, because you ask with wrong motives, that you may spend what you get on your pleasures" (James 4:1–3).

James also promotes patience. "Be patient, then, brothers, until the Lord's coming. See how the farmer waits for the land to yield its valuable crop and how patient he is for the autumn and spring rains. You too, be patient and stand firm, because the Lord's coming is near. Don't grumble against each other, brothers, or you will be judged. The Judge is standing at the door!" (James 5:7–9). He wants the believers to be tolerant of each other since it is not an individual journey of faith but one of a family of believers.

ALERT!

According to Tertullian, John was the only apostle not to die a martyr's death. He supposedly died of old age (about 100 years old) on the island of Patmos. It was said that attempts to kill him (such as boiling him in hot oil) failed, and he was left unscathed.

Anoint the Sick

"Is any one of you sick? He should call the elders [priests] of the church to pray over him and anoint him with oil in the name of the Lord. And the prayer offered in faith will make the sick person well; the Lord will raise him up. If he has sinned, he will be forgiven" (James 5:14–15). Some Christian churches (Catholic and Orthodox, e.g) used this passage as a basis for the sacrament (ordinance) of annointing of the sick, sometimes called "extreme unction." Even those faith communities who do not have that sacrament still have prayers and laying on of hands for healing of the sick.

The compassion for the sick is a hallmark of the Christians, and during the Middle Ages many hospitals were created not by the secular government, but by the church and religious communities to practice the work of mercy. Parenthetically, it was the close proximity of the priest to the sick he annointed that contributed to the loss of two-thirds of the clergy and one-third of Europe during the Black Plague of the fourteenth century A.D.

1 Peter

The Bishops of Rome, also known as the Popes, consider themselves to be the successors of Saint Peter. Recent times have produced a plethora of pastoral letters from Popes Pius XII, John XXIII, Paul VI, and most of all John Paul II. Peter, himself, wrote two pastoral letters to the universal church, and although he did not write as much or as well as Saint Paul, they are still considered inspired and part of the Bible. He talks about personal holiness and the Christian virtue of enduring suffering for the sake of the Gospel. He talks about being good citizens and neighbors despite persecution. He does not advocate political activism, revolution, or civil unrest as some were doing at that time. Peter opens with praise for God and a sense of hope:

"Praise be to the God and Father of our Lord Jesus Christ! In his great mercy he has given us new birth into a living hope through the Resurrection of Jesus Christ from the dead, and into an inheritance that can never perish, spoil or fade—kept in heaven for you, who through faith are shielded by God's power until the coming of the salvation that is ready to be revealed in the last time. In this you greatly rejoice, though now for a little while you may have had to suffer grief in all kinds of trials. These have come so that your faith—of greater worth than gold, which perishes even though refined by fire—may be proved genuine and may result in praise, glory and honor when Jesus Christ is revealed. Though you have not seen him, you love him; and even though you do not see him now, you believe in him and are filled with an inexpressible and glorious joy, for you are receiving the goal of your faith, the salvation of your souls."

(1 Peter 1:3–9)

Life of Holiness

Peter writes, "As obedient children, do not conform to the evil desires you had when you lived in ignorance. But just as he who called you is holy, so be holy in all you do; for it is written: 'Be holy, because I am holy'" (1 Peter 1:14–15). "You are a chosen people, a royal priesthood, a holy nation, a people belonging to God, that you may declare the praises of him who called you out of darkness into his wonderful light" (1 Peter 2:9). Peter encourages the Christian faithful to be good examples to their pagan neighbors by living holy lives. Not only will they be doing what God asks of them, they may also inspire others to aspire to holiness themselves.

1 Peter 5:8–9 is often used by many spiritual writers. "Your enemy the devil prowls around like a roaring lion looking for someone to devour. Resist him, standing firm in the faith." The idea is that the devil is our spiritual enemy, he can and ought to be resisted, and that he seeks to devour those weak in faith.

Humility

Another theme in 1 Peter is the humble acceptance of authority. "Submit yourselves for the Lord's sake to every authority instituted among men: whether to the king, as the supreme authority, or to governors, who are sent by him to punish those who do wrong and to commend those who do right" (1 Peter 2:13–14). Peter makes the analogy between Christ—who endured all kinds of insults, injuries, and subjected Himself, despite His divinity, to the authority of earthly rulers—and the life of a Christian, who must also endure hardship and humbly submit to others.

2 Peter

This letter shows Peter's concern for the threat of false teachers. Whereas in the first Epistle the danger was from the outside (external persecution), the second Epistle sees the peril from within the church (internal heterodoxy). "There were also false prophets among the people, just as there will be false teachers among you. They will secretly introduce destructive heresies, even denying the sovereign Lord who bought them—bringing swift destruction on themselves" (2 Peter 2:1).

FACT

Peter warns that the false prophets and their heretical teachings will not escape punishment. Just as the fallen angels were cast into hell for their sin of pride and just as the inhabitants of Sodom and Gomorrah felt the weight of Divine Justice, so, too, will those who espouse erroneous doctrines and lead others astray. "They will be paid back with harm for the harm they have done" (2 Peter 2:13).

Day of the Lord

Since the Day of the Lord—the end of the world and the Second Coming of Christ—is not known and will come like a thief in the night, Peter wants the faithful to live every day in expectation of the end times. He does not advocate a terror-stricken paranoia nor does he promote retreating to the hills and abandoning work and school. What he intends is a perspective change. "You ought to live holy and godly lives as you look forward to the day of God and speed its coming" (2 Peter 3:11–12).

1 John

The first half of the early church involved a struggle between the Hellenist (Greek-speaking) converts to Christianity and the Jewish (Hebrew-speaking) converts. The battle royal was over whether or not Gentiles had to first become Jewish before becoming Christian. The second half involved the war among the false teachers who were spreading heresy and error among the faithful. One of the original twelve apostles, John is believed to be the author of the fourth Gospel and the last book of the

Bible (Revelation or Apocalypse); he is the most theological of all the sacred authors. He wrote most of his works from A.D. 90–100.

Children of the Light

John uses the same imagery from his Gospel account of light and darkness representative of good and evil. "God is light; in him there is no darkness at all. If we claim to have fellowship with him yet walk in the darkness, we lie and do not live by the truth. But if we walk in the light, as he is in the light, we have fellowship with one another, and the blood of Jesus, his Son, purifies us from all sin" (1 John 1:5–7). He also speaks of his audience as dear "children" to symbolize their new and innocent faith.

The looming danger, however, is the antichrists. Who is an antichrist? "It is the man who denies that Jesus is the Christ" (1 John 2:22). Here, he is using the term generically whereas in Revelation (Apocalypse), the Antichrist (also known as the Beast) is a more personal individual who combats Jesus at the end of the world, although Revelation doesn't use the specific term "Antichrist." This reference in the Epistle, on the other hand, is a way of categorizing those who have abandoned their faith.

Love of God

John writes eloquently on divine love. "Dear friends, let us love one another, for love comes from God. Everyone who loves has been born of God and knows God. Whoever does not love does not know God, because God is love" (1 John 4:7–8). According to John, love means being willing to sacrifice even life itself for the sake of the other. He writes, "This is love: not that we loved God, but that he loved us and sent his Son as an atoning sacrifice for our sins" (1 John 4:10).

2 John

John identifies himself in this Epistle as a *presbyteros*, or elder, but not in the sense of the three-fold levels of ordained ministry (bishop, priest, and deacon) since he was an apostle. The term probably is in reference to his senior status as the last living apostle and an old man. He also uses the phrase *eklekte kyria* ("chosen lady"): "To the chosen lady and her children, whom I love in the truth" (2 John 1). This could be a female believer he brought into the faith or it could represent a church community since the church is considered the bride of Christ.

He warns again about those antichrists, who pervert the faith. "Many deceivers, who do not acknowledge Jesus Christ as coming in the flesh, have gone out into the world. Any such person is the deceiver and the antichrist" (2 John 7). The Gnostics proliferated a heresy that denied the humanity of Christ, that He only pretended to have a human nature; hence John reiterates the Christian doctrine of Jesus being "true God and true Man."

The Docetists were a heretical Gnostic sect of the early church, who maintained that the Second Person of the Trinity only pretended to have a human nature. They believed His humanity, from body to soul, was an illusion. Their name comes from *dokesis* meaning "appearance."

3 John

This letter is addressed to Gaius and concerns some professional rivalry and jealousy. Diotrephes is the local religious leader, either a presbyter (priest or pastor) or possibly a bishop. John refers to him as one "who loves to be first" (3 John 1:9). The conflict involved travelling missionary preachers, whom Diotrephes would not welcome. The real rub was that he was not recognizing the credentials of John who sent these missionaries. John gives this good advice: "Dear friend, do not imitate what is evil but what is good. Anyone who does what is good is from God. Anyone who does what is evil has not seen God" (3 John 1:11).

The Apocryphal book known as the Assumption of Moses tells of an incident where the devil argues with the archangel Michael over the dead body of Moses. Satan claims he owns it since Moses had murdered an Egyptian before he became the Deliverer. Michael simply rebukes the devil in the name of the Lord. The idea is not to stoop to the vicious arguing some of the heretics had adopted.

Jude

Jude describes himself as the brother of James. This letter concerns the same issue of false teachers and heretical doctrines. While he uses references to some apocryphal/pseudepigraphical writings, it is not to endorse them as candidates for the canon of Scripture, inasmuch as it is merely a didactic tool. Even if not accepted as inspired, Jude and his audience knew these writings and used them to make a point.

"Though you already know all this, I want to remind you that the Lord delivered his people out of Egypt, but later destroyed those who did not believe. And the angels who did not keep their positions of authority but abandoned their own home—these he has kept in darkness, bound with everlasting chains for judgment on the great Day. In a similar way, Sodom and Gomorrah and the surrounding towns gave themselves up to sexual immorality and perversion. They serve as an example of those who suffer the punishment of eternal fire."

(Jude 5–7)

Chapter 21

Book of Revelation (Apocalypse)

The Book of Revelation is like the Book of Daniel in the Old Testament—it is considered apocalyptic literature, and the Greek name for this work is The Apocalypse. Prophecy is definitely a part of Revelation, but so is the latent message to the early church not to give up—don't quit and keep persevering. This chapter will examine this last book of the Bible with all its colorful imagery, metaphors, and symbolism.

Greetings and Salutations
(Revelation 1:1–20)

Although the Book of Revelation speaks about things to come and describes events about the end of the world and the Second Coming of Christ, there is no way to discover the time and date of "doomsday." Jesus stated, "You know not the day nor the hour" (Matthew 24:36). Despite the colorful imagery, metaphors, and mystical symbolism, one shouldn't read this book hoping to find some "secret." John wrote this book to give encouragement to the Christians who were being persecuted by the Roman Empire, following the burning of Rome.

Letters to the Seven Churches
(Revelation 2:1–3:22)

John begins by making a profound statement: "The revelation of Jesus Christ." He wants to teach his readers that all revelation ultimately comes from Jesus Christ since He is the fullness of revelation of God the Father here on earth. John's Gospel account began with "in the beginning was the Word, and the Word was with God and the Word was God . . . and the Word became flesh and dwelt among us" (John 1:1,14). Hence, Jesus, the Word made flesh, is the revelation of the Father in His very person.

All revelation for John comes through Christ and centers on Christ. Jesus is much more than the written or spoken Word, He is the Living Word of God. John centers everything—time, space, and the entire cosmos—on Christ. "I am the Alpha and the Omega (the beginning and the end)" (Revelation 1:8).

Vision of Christ

John has a magnificent vision of Christ appearing between seven gold lampstands wearing a long robe and gold sash. His hair was white as wool, His eyes like flames of fire, and His feet like bronze. He held seven stars in His right hand and from His mouth came a two-edged sword. Certainly, nothing like the images of Jesus depicted in sacred art and not resembling the Jesus John remembers from the days of being one of His apostles—so different an image that John falls to his knees. He is told to not be afraid, get up, and get ready to take notes.

Some scholars question the authorship of Revelation (Apocalypse) by citing a few Fathers of the Church, such as Denis of Alexandria, Eusebius of Caesarea, Cyril of Jerusalem, Gregory Nanzien, and John Chrysostom. Nevertheless, many other scholars and notable Fathers, such as Jerome, Justin Martyr, Irenaeus, Tertullian, Hippolytus, Clement of Alexandria, and Origen, maintained the Johannine authorship to be authentic and accurate. The style of Greek used in the last book of the Bible is also extremely similar to the one used in the Gospel account according to John.

Seven Churches

John is instructed to send messages to seven churches in Asia Minor: Ephesus, Smyrna, Pergamum, Thyatira, Sardis, Philadelphia, and Laodicea. These are not the only churches in the area but the symbolic value of the number seven is what needs mention. Seven is considered a perfect number in the Bible. God blessed the seventh day as a day of rest after working on Creation for six days; after seven days, in other words, on the eighth day, the male child is circumcised. John is given the role of a prophet, which can entail making prophecies about the future but primarily—as seen in the prophets of the Old Testament—it is a job of relaying messages from God to people here on earth. Hence, he is told to send messages to these seven churches:

1. *Ephesus:* Jesus warns the church community in Ephesus that despite their trials with false teachers, they are in danger of losing or at least forgetting their first love, Christ Himself.
2. *Smyrna:* Jesus commends the church community in Smyrna, for though poor and persecuted, they are rich in faith. He also assures those who are loyal to Him unto death will win the crown of glory.
3. *Pergamum:* Jesus compliments the church community in Pergamum

for their fidelity even amidst persecution but He warns that some of them are getting into idolatry and immorality and they had better stop.

4. *Thyatira:* Jesus praises the church community in Thyatira for their love, faith, service, and patient endurance. However, the church is chastised for tolerating a prophetess named Jezebel, who was seducing believers into ritual fornication and other abominations.

5. *Sardis:* Jesus tells the church community in Sardis that while their body (the external appearance) appears alive and healthy, their soul (the interior, spiritual life) is dead. He urges them to obey and repent.

6. *Philadelphia:* Jesus gives high marks for the church community in Philadelphia. He commends and encourages them to persevere despite the efforts of some fanatical Jewish adversaries.

7. *Laodicea:* Jesus has nothing good to say about the church community in Laodicea. While other churches may have had some troubles, the Laodiceans were just plain apathetic. Jesus warns them of the tepid nature of their faith, which is so pathetic, they will be vomited out of His mouth as someone would spit out a glass of lukewarm milk.

A Peek into Paradise (Revelation 4:1–5:14)

In this section, John is transported to heaven and is taken before the heavenly court of the Almighty. His description is vivid and what he describes is reminiscent of a worship service—a heavenly liturgy. There is a main throne on which God the Father sits. Surrounding Him are twenty-four minor thrones upon which twenty-four elders sit. These are possibly the twelve patriarchs of the Old Testament and the twelve apostles of the New Testament. Everyone in the court is giving praise and worship to God.

FACT

In his description of paradise, John is probably making the connection for his audience of the weekly worship the Christian believers attended and participated in on Sundays (the day of the Lord's Resurrection). That, which they do once a week on earth, will be done every day in a perfect way in heaven.

Four Living Creatures

In Chapter 4, verse 7, John mentions the four living creatures, each with a different face or head. The first is like a lion, the second like an ox, the third like a man, and the fourth like an eagle. These four were first seen in Ezekiel 1:10. Scholars believe they represent the four evangelists as each image symbolizes the way Jesus is portrayed in the beginning of each Gospel account. The regal lion represents Mark who begins his account on the reign of God. The sacrificial ox represents Luke who begins his account with Zachariah, the father of John the Baptist, who was priest of the Temple. The human face represents Matthew who begins with the human genealogy and origins of Jesus. The soaring eagle represents John who begins with the heavenly pre-existence of the divine nature of Christ.

Saint Ambrose was the first one to make the connection of the four creatures and the four evangelists. Sacred art throughout the Middle Ages and the Renaissance have used these characters depicted as a lion, ox, man, and eagle with wings and a halo. You will often find them on pulpits in the church.

Scroll and Lamb

Next, John sees the Almighty holding a scroll with writing on the front and back. The scroll was protected by seven seals. An angel asks who is worthy to open the scroll and break open its seals but no one comes forward. John says this makes him sad to the point of tears. Finally, a slain lamb comes forward (symbolizing Christ, called the "lamb of God" by John the Baptist in John 1:29) and one by one opens the seven seals.

The Seven Seals (Revelation 6:1–8:5)

This section begins with the legendary seven seals, which mark the end of the world. Important documents, especially imperial ones, had seals made from clay or hardened wax upon which an impression of the monarch or emperor's insignia was made. Only when the authorized person opened all the seals could the contents be disclosed and implemented. John makes it clear that only the slain lamb could open the seals and it is because He paid the supreme price of offering up His own life.

Four Horsemen

When broken, the first four seals unleash the infamous four horsemen of the Apocalypse. The first seal releases a rider on a white horse with a bow who is given a crown. He allegedly represents war. The second seal releases a rider on a red horse with a giant sword. This horseman is supposed to represent bloodshed. The third seal releases a rider on a black horse carrying a scale. That horseman symbolizes famine. The fourth seal releases a rider on a pale green horse who represents death. He is given power of a quarter of the earth and right behind him was hell.

FACT

Some scholars propose that the first horseman on a white horse is actually the victorious and triumphant Christ as is the case in Revelation 19:11. Most scholars, however, believe the first horseman is merely war itself since it fits more with the character of the other three riders. Another candidate would be the Antichrist himself, who is supposed to usher in the mayhem of doomsday.

The Last Three Seals

After the four horsemen are released at the breaking of the first four seals, the last three are then opened. The fifth seal reveals all the souls of the martyrs who were slain for the faith. They ask how long before their deaths are avenged and they are assured that justice is not far behind. The sixth seal unleashes the Day of Wrath. This terrible day brings earthquakes, the sun goes dark, the moon turns blood red, the stars fall from the sky, and islands and mountains disappear.

After the sixth seal and before the seventh, four angels are stationed at the four corners of the earth. One of these angels places a mark on the foreheads of 144,000 souls (12,000 from each of the twelve tribes of Israel). This will protect them as the lamb's blood on the doorpost protected the Israelites from the last plague of Egypt the night of Passover.

E ALERT!

Some claim only 144,000 will be saved based on the passage in Revelation 7:4. However, that same paragraph mentions a great multitude which no one could count, clothed with white robes (Revelation 7:9), and they enter the heavenly court as much as the 144,000.

The seventh and the final seal ushers a half hour of silence. Then seven angels blow seven trumpets. This silence could be the pause given for the prayers of men and women on earth to rise to heaven, some biblical experts suggest. It could just be a pregnant moment of silence like the eye of the hurricane or the calm before the storm.

The Seven Trumpets (Revelation 8:6–11:19)

This section begins with the seven trumpets, which have followed the opening of the seven seals. An angel carrying a golden censor burns lots of incense at this point. Incense burning in the temple, synagogue, and church traditionally symbolizes prayers rising up to heaven as stated in Psalm 141. Incense was also one of the gifts left by the Magi to the Christ-child (Matthew 2:11). The seven trumpets are blown after the angel hurls the incense and burning coals down upon the earth.

The first trumpet heralds hail and fire mixed with blood consuming one-third of the earth. The second trumpet heralds a mountain ablaze being thrown into the sea. One-third of the water turns into blood, one-third of marine life perishes, and one-third of the ships are lost. The third trumpet heralds a fiery star falling from the sky and polluting one-third of the world's water, which will cause many to die. The fourth trumpet heralds the sun, moon, and one-third of the stars going dark.

The fifth trumpet heralds the arrival of someone falling from the sky who unleashes smoke and locusts, which, with stings like that of scorpions, torment only humans. The sixth trumpet heralds 200 million creatures and monsters who will kill one-third of humanity. The seventh and last trumpet heralds the impending return of Christ.

Good Versus Evil (Revelation 12:1–14:20)

This section concerns the great battle of the powers of darkness and the children of the light—in other words, between good and evil. The dragon represents the devil and evil, and the lamb is Christ who is the Lamb of God. This is the final conflict and the outcome is certain—good wins and evil loses. The archangel Michael is mentioned and a cosmic battle between the good angels and the fallen angels (called demons or devils) ensues. Michael will be the standard bearer who vanquishes the great dragon from heaven and casts him down to earth.

ESSENTIAL

Some believe the pregnant "woman clothed with the sun" of Revelation 12:1 could be the nation of Israel, while others claim it is the Virgin Mary, the mother of Jesus. Interestingly, the image of Our Lady of Guadalupe, which is on an alleged sixteenth-century peasant's tilma (Juan Diego) in Mexico City, depicts Mary as with child, wearing a crown of twelve stars with the moon under her feet.

"A great and wondrous sign appeared in heaven: a woman clothed with the sun, with the moon under her feet and a crown of twelve stars on her head. She was pregnant and cried out in pain as she was about to give birth" (Revelation 12:1–2). On earth, the dragon, who is Satan, sets his target on the woman with child. He is joined by the Beast of the Earth and the Beast of the Sea. The woman escapes and gives birth to a son, who will conquer the dragon and the beasts.

Revelation (Apocalypse) mentions the mark of the beast, and many people have debated on what that represents. Some claimed the zebra/bar code used in pricing products was the mark, others claimed it was the social security number, still others claim it will be a micro-tattoo everyone will have in the future to identify themselves in place of passports. Most scholars simply admit that no one knows what the mark is or was or will be. "This calls for wisdom. If anyone has insight, let him calculate the number of the beast, for it is man's number. His number is 666" (Revelation 13:18).

The Seven Plagues (Revelation 15:1–16:21)

Chapter 15 begins with the seven bowls of justice, which contain seven plagues that seven angels will pour upon the earth. The first plague consists of sores, like those that accompanied the boils in the Egyptian plague (Exodus 9:10). The second plague is the turning of the sea into blood, also like the ancient curse (Exodus 7:19–20). The third plague is like the second except it affects the rivers and lakes. The fourth plague is the heat of the sun becoming so scorching hot that people burn and die.

The fifth plague is total darkness upon the whole earth, again like one of the ten plagues of Egypt (Exodus 10:21). The sixth plague from the sixth bowl is the drying up of the Euphrates River, allowing passage of the kings of the east with their armies to cross. The seventh and final plague unleashed by the seventh angel is lightning and earthquakes and enormous hailstones (like Exodus 9:24).

FACT

Revelation 16:16 is the only place in the Bible where Armageddon is mentioned, the notorious place of the final conflict between Christ and the Beast. The word is a Greek transliteration of the Hebrew *har megiddo* (the mount of Megiddo in the valley of Jezreel and Esdraelon), a place of several historical battles in the Old Testament. Other than that, Armageddon does not exist on any known map.

The Whore of Babylon and the Beast (Revelation 17:1–19:10)

This section zeroes in on two of the most villainous characters of the Apocalypse, the Whore of Babylon and the Beast (sometimes called the Antichrist). Babylon was the center of the infamous Babylonian empire, which enslaved and scattered many Jews in the Old Testament. The word "Babylon" and the "Whore of Babylon" can also represent pagan Rome or the secular world, for that matter. "Whore" or "Prostitute" can have more than just sexual connotation. The prophets accused Israel of prostituting the faith, or John could just be talking about pagan Rome or about any believers who water down their principles and allow worldly desires to infect their religious values.

"I saw a woman sitting on a scarlet beast that was covered with blasphemous names and had seven heads and ten horns. The woman was dressed in purple and scarlet, and was glittering with gold, precious stones, and pearls. She held a golden cup in her hand, filled with abominable things and the filth of her adulteries. This title was written on her forehead: Mystery Babylon The Great The Mother of Prostitutes and of the Abominations of the Earth" (Revelation 17:3–5).

In the thirteenth century A.D., Thomas Aquinas defined evil as the "privation of good"; in other words, the absence of something which should be there. Modern ideologies often portray good and evil as equal "forces" in the universe.

The Beast is someone distinct and separate from the devil or Satan, who is given such titles as the "Prince of Darkness," "the Accuser," "the Evil One," "the Adversary", and so forth. Whether or not the Beast is somehow the son of Satan in a biological sense is speculation. Spiritually, however, he is the offspring of Satan, possibly the progeny of the serpent in Genesis 3:15. In any event, the Beast, as described in the Book of Revelation, will lead many astray through lies, false doctrine, sexual immorality, violence, greed, and other sinful acts.

The Second Coming (Revelation 19:11–22:5)

This section concerns the second arrival of Jesus Christ, otherwise known as the Second Coming. This precedes the General Judgment of the world before its end. "Hallelujah! Salvation and glory and power belong to our God, for true and just are his judgments. He has condemned the great prostitute who corrupted the earth by her adulteries. He has avenged on her the blood of his servants" (Revelation 19:1–2). The returning Christ, the Lamb of God, conquers the Beast, the Whore of Babylon, the devil, and all their allies.

"I saw heaven standing open and there before me was a white horse, whose rider is called Faithful and True. With justice he judges and makes war. His eyes are like blazing fire, and on his head are many crowns. He has a name written on him that no one knows but he himself. He is dressed in a robe dipped in blood, and his name is the Word of God" (Revelation 19:11–13). This rider on a white horse, unlike the one in Revelation 6:2, the first of the four horsemen (who is thought to be "war"), is understood to be the triumphant Christ instead. The beast (devil) and false prophet (Antichrist) are vanquished.

E ALERT!

Many associate the beast with the number 666, which has sparked much controversy. Hebrew and Greek letters have numerical equivalence; Roman Emperor Nero's name, for example, adds up to 666, the first archenemy of the church.

King of Kings

According to John the Apostle, Christ achieves victory not in winning a battle or war in the traditional understanding of warfare, but rather through his tongue. As stated above, His name is "the Word of God," and the word is spoken even before it is written. John's image of a double-edged sword as a tongue is most likely his way of saying that it is by the power of the TRUTH (the word) that Christ conquers the Author of All Lies (the devil, the Beast).

As was seen in Genesis 1, the Word is creative. God merely speaks, "let there be light" and then light exists. Jesus merely says, "Be healed," and the person immediately and miraculously is cured. Revelation and the Bible as a whole concentrate on the notion that the Word, spoken (Sacred Tradition) and written (Sacred Scripture or the Bible), is divine. Most of all, the Word is alive, as the Word became flesh (John 1:14), hence the Word is a person, the second person of the Holy Trinity.

Thousand Years

This is the most mysterious part of the Apocalypse. There are several schools of thought among Protestant Christians regarding Millennialism. Three predominant views are: Premillennialists, who believe there will be 1,000 years of peace with Christ after His Second Coming *before* the end of the world; Amillennialists, who believe the number is symbolic, meaning that Jesus will reign in the hearts of believers for a long time before the world ends; Postmillennialists, who believe that the Second Coming of Christ occurs after 1,000 years of peace and tranquility on earth.

There is also debate on when the Tribulation occurs: before, during, or after the Second Coming, and likewise for the time of the Millennium. The Book of Revelation introduces the idea of a "general judgment," and it differs from the "particular judgment," which happens at the moment of death of the individual. Christians believe that when a person dies, their immortal soul leaves the body and then is judged by God. Whether the soul goes to heaven or hell is decided then. The "general judgment" is on the entire world and all will be disclosed; in other words, the particular judgments will be revealed to manifest God's justice and mercy.

Epilogue (Revelation 22:6–21)

The Apocalypse ends with chapter 22, which prophesizes the reward for the just and the glory, which will ensue after the end of times. "He will wipe every tear from their eyes. There will be no more death or mourning or crying or pain, for the old order of things has passed away. No longer will there be any curse. The throne of God and of the Lamb will be in the city, and his servants will serve him. They will see his face, and his name will be on their foreheads. There will be no more night. They will not need the light of a lamp or the light of the sun, for the Lord God will give them light. And they will reign for ever and ever" (Revelation 22:3–5).

John's vision ends with a glimpse into the heavenly Jerusalem. Unlike the earthly city of the once unified kingdom, the heavenly city is heaven itself. John counts on his audience having some knowledge of the former splendor, beauty, and importance of the current capital of Israel. As lovely and wonderful as it was in its heyday, the earthly Jerusalem was only a symbol of what the heavenly Jerusalem is like.

FACT

Saint Augustine wrote a work entitled the "City of God" about two cities where he uses the terms "the Heavenly Jerusalem" for heaven and "the earthly Babylon" for this world. Believers, he says, are citizens of the heavenly Jerusalem while temporarily living in the earthly Babylon.

River of Life

John concludes with two important images. The first is the River of Life, which is associated with Genesis 2:10. Eden had four rivers running through it; the heavenly Jerusalem has one. The prophet Ezekiel saw a purifying river flowing from the Temple. Jesus was baptized in the River Jordan, and the river motif is traditionally identified with divine grace. John ends Revelation with "Whoever is thirsty, let him come; and whoever wishes, let him take the free gift of the water of life" (Revelation 22:17). This is perhaps an allusion to the dialogue Jesus had with the

Samaritan woman at the well in John 4: "whoever drinks the water I give him will never thirst. Indeed, the water I give him will become in him a spring of water welling up to eternal life" (John 4:14).

Tree of Life

Another image is that of a Tree of Life, about which much has been written outside the Bible. Folklore has it that some of the wood from the Tree of Life in Eden became part of the Temple of Jerusalem, and finally ended up as part of the cross on which Jesus was crucified. None of this is verified and it does not appear in the Scripture. However, the symbolism is phenomenal. The first man and woman are thrown out of Eden, due to their disobedience, and as a consequence are prevented from tasting of the Tree of Life, which would have given them immortality. Jesus, the Son of God, is nailed to the cross, and His obedience to the will of the Father and His sacrificial death on that cross can be also seen as a Tree of Life.

Judaism and Christianity do not see evil as being the equal dichotomy to good as would the Persian Zoroastrianism or dualistic Manicheanism of ancient times. The devil is not God's evil counterpart, and neither is the Beast the evil counterpart of Jesus Christ.

Conclusion

The Apocalypse ends with a stern admonition: "I warn everyone who hears the words of the prophecy of this book: "If anyone adds anything to them, God will add to him the plagues described in this book. And if anyone takes words away from this book of prophecy, God will take away from him his share in the tree of life and in the holy city, which are described in this book" (Revelation 22:18). This certainly reflects John's prior experience of having false teachers add, subtract, and modify Scripture for their own agendas.

The book is prolific with symbolism, metaphor, and imagery. Some is undoubtedly a result of the intense persecution being felt at the time John wrote the Apocalypse. The other factor is the prophecies of things to come. Signs, omens, and portents will be given that the end is near so that the faithful may be prepared to some degree.

The early church had to deal with some extremes, one of which was a strong belief that the end of the world and the Second Coming of Christ were so immanent that there was no need to go to work, pay taxes, marry, or have children. John wrote to correct that. There were others who took for granted that they would always have enough time and, therefore, procrastinated in repenting from evil ways or bad habits. Yet, there wasn't a paranoid obsession with doomsday.

There are some Christians who maintain that secrets to the nature and details of the end times can be found in Revelation. Maybe. Yet, when and how the world ends has nothing to do with one's eternal salvation. Many believe that faith in Christ and obedience to the Will of God throughout one's life is the determining factor of whether one ends up in heaven or hell and this is verified throughout the Bible. The end of the world, the Second Coming, General Judgment, and the Resurrection of the Dead are things yet to happen, but their occurrence does not affect particular judgment.

Where to Go from Here?

Whether you read the Bible from cover to cover, for the first time, or in just an occasional and prayerful moment, just keep in mind those principles mentioned before. Find an accurate text you can comprehend so you can first ascertain what the sacred author actually said. Then examine the context of the words, phrases, sentences, and paragraphs to help discover the sense being used and the intent of the author. Also, read a few good commentaries, which either reflect the theology of your espoused faith and religion, or which best reflect your personal perspective on faith. Share the word with others in a Bible study and benefit from other's insights as they will from yours.

The reason the Bible has endured so many centuries, cultures, civilizations, and languages/translations is because it is timeless and has no physical address. Written in time by inspired human authors, many believe it is also the Word of God revealing the truths He wanted all humankind of every time and place to know. While a product of time and space, it transcends both, yet is also influenced by them. See the Bible as more than just a religious book—see it as a collection of inspired books given as a precious gift of truth from God. Ⓔ

Appendices

Appendix A

Bible Reading Resources

Appendix B

Read the Bible
in a Year Plan

Appendix C

English Bible Versions

Bible Reading Resources

Bibles

American Standard Version (New York: Thomas Nelson, 1901)

Bibliorum Sacrorum Nova Vulgata (Vatican City: Libreria Editrice Vaticana, 1998)

Contemporary English Version (New York: American Bible Society, 1995)

Douay-Rheims Bible (Rockford, IL: TAN Books, 1995)

Good News Bible: The Bible in Today's English Version (New York: American Bible Society, 1976)

The Harper Collins Study Bible, with the Apocryphal/Deuterocanonical Books (edited by Wayne A. Meeks and the Society of Biblical Literature, New York: Harper Collins Publisher, 1993)

The Jerusalem Bible (New York: Doubleday, 1966)

King James Version: Holy Bible with Apocrypha, with Alternate Readings and Renderings (New York: American Bible Society, 1975)

The Living Bible, Paraphrased (Wheaton, IL: Tyndale House 1971)

New American Bible (Nashville: Thomas Nelson, 1980)

New American Standard Version (New York: Thomas Nelson, 1977)

New English Bible (New York: Oxford University Press, 1971)

New International Version (New York: International Bible Society, 1978)

New Jerusalem Bible (New York: Doubleday, 1985)

New Revised Standard Version: The New Oxford Annotated Bible with the Apocrypha: An Ecumenical Study Bible (edited by Bruce M. Metzger and Roland E. Murphy, New York: Oxford University Press, 1994)

Revised English Bible with the Apocrypha (Cambridge, England: Cambridge University Press, 1996)

Revised Standard Version (New York: National Council of Churches of Christ in the USA, 1952)

Revised Standard Version, Catholic edition (Birmingham, England: Catholic Biblical Association of Great Britain, 1997)

The Torah: A New Translation of the Holy Scriptures According to the Masoretic Text (Philadelphia: Jewish Publication Society, 1963)

The Treasury of Scripture Knowledge: Five Hundred Thousand Scripture References and Parallel Passages (Oak Harbor, WA: Logos Research Systems, Inc., 1995)

Today's English Version (New York: American Bible Society, 1976 & 1992)

Bible Commentaries

Collegeville Bible Handbook (Collegeville, MN: Liturgical Press, 1997)

HarperCollins Bible Commentary, Revised Edition (New York: Harper Collins, 2000)

The New Jerome Biblical Commentary (Englewood Cliff, NJ: Prentice-Hall, 1990)

Matthew Henry's Commentary on the Whole Bible (Peabody, MA: Hendrickson Publishers, Inc., 1991)

The Oxford Bible Commentary (New York: Oxford University Press, 2001)

Appendix B

Read the Bible in a Year Plan

Day	Reading 1	Reading 2	Reading 3
1	Genesis (Gn) 1–2	Psalms (Ps) 1–2	Matthew (Mt) 1–2
2	Gn 3–4	Ps 3–5	Mt 3–4
3	Gn 5–6	Ps 6–8	Mt 5
4	Gn 7–8	Ps 9–10	Mt 6
5	Gn 9–10	Ps 11–13	Mt 7
6	Gn 11–12	Ps 14–16	Mt 8
7	Gn 13–14	Ps 17	Mt 9
8	Gn 15–16	Ps 18	Mt 10
9	Gn 17–18	Ps 19–20	Mt 11
10	Gn 19	Ps 21–22	Mt 12
11	Gn 20–21	Ps 23–25	Mt 13
12	Gn 22–23	Ps 26–28	Mt 14
13	Gn 24	Ps 29–30	Mt 15
14	Gn 25–26	Ps 31	Mt 16
15	Gn 27	Ps 32	Mt 17
16	Gn 28–29	Ps 33	Mt 18
17	Gn 30	Ps 34	Mt 19
18	Gn 31	Ps 35	Mt 20
19	Gn 32–33	Ps 36	Mt 21
20	Gn 34–35	Ps 37	Mt 22
21	Gn 36	Ps 38	Mt 23
22	Gn 37	Ps 39–40	Mt 24
23	Gn 38	Ps 41–43	Mt 25
24	Gn 39–40	Ps 44	Mt 26
25	Gn 41	Ps 45	Mt 27
26	Gn 42–43	Ps 46–48	Mt 28
27	Gn 44–45	Ps 49	Mark (Mk) 1
28	Gn 46–47	Ps 50	Mk 2
29	Gn 48–50	Ps 51–52	Mk 3
30	Exodus (Ex) 1–2	Ps 53–55	Mk 4
31	Ex 3–4	Ps 56–57	Mk 5

Day	Reading 1	Reading 2	Reading 3
32	Ex 5–6	Ps 58–59	Mk 6
33	Ex 7–8	Ps 60–61	Mk 7
34	Ex 9	Ps 62–63	Mk 8
35	Ex 10	Ps 64–65	Mk 9
36	Ex 11–12	Ps 66–67	Mk 10
37	Ex 13–14	Ps 68	Mk 11
38	Ex 15	Ps 69	Mk 12
39	Ex 16	Ps 70–71	Mk 13
40	Ex 17–18	Ps 72	Mk 14
41	Ex 19–20	Ps 73	Mk 15–16
42	Ex 21	Ps 74	Luke (Lk) 1
43	Ex 22	Ps 75–76	Lk 2
44	Ex 23	Ps 77	Lk 3
45	Ex 24–25	Ps 78	Lk 4
46	Ex 26	Ps 79–80	Lk 5
47	Ex 27	Ps 81–82	Lk 6
48	Ex 28	Ps 83–84	Lk 7
49	Ex 29	Ps 85–86	Lk 8
50	Ex 30	Ps 87–88	Lk 9
51	Ex 31–32	Ps 89	Lk 10
52	Ex 33–34	Ps 90–91	Lk 11
53	Ex 35	Ps 92–93	Lk 12
54	Ex 36	Ps 94–95	Lk 13–14
55	Ex 37	Ps 96–99	Lk 15
56	Ex 38	Ps 100–101	Lk 16
57	Ex 39–40	Ps 102	Lk 17
58	Leviticus (Lv) 1–2	Ps 103	Lk 18
59	Lv 3–4	Ps 104	Lk 19
60	Lv 5–6	Ps 105	Lk 20
61	Lv 7	Ps 106	Lk 21
62	Lv 8	Ps 107	Lk 22
63	Lv 9–10	Ps 108–109	Lk 23
64	Lv 11	Ps 110–112	Lk 24
65	Lv 12–13	Ps 113–114	John (Jn) 1

Day	Reading 1	Reading 2	Reading 3
66	Lv 14	Ps 115–116	Jn 2–3
67	Lv 15	Ps 117–118	Jn 4
68	Lv 16	Ps 119 v1–40	Jn 5
69	Lv 17–18	Ps 119 v41–80	Jn 6
70	Lv 19	Ps 119 v81–128	Jn 7
71	Lv 20	Ps 119 v129–176	Jn 8
72	Lv 21	Ps 120–124	Jn 9–10
73	Lv 22	Ps 125–127	Jn 11
74	Lv 23	Ps 128–130	Jn 12
75	Lv 24	Ps 131–134	Jn 13–14
76	Lv 25	Ps 135–136	Jn 15–16
77	Lv 26	Ps 137–139	Jn 17–18
78	Lv 27	Ps 140–142	Jn 19
79	Numbers (Nm) 1	Ps 143–144	Jn 20–21
80	Nm 2	Ps 145–147	Acts (Act) 1
81	Nm 3	Ps 148–150	Act 2
82	Nm 4	Proverbs (Prv) 1	Act 3–4
83	Nm 5	Prv 2	Act 5–6
84	Nm 6	Prv 3	Act 7
85	Nm 7	Prv 4	Act 8
86	Nm 8–9	Prv 5	Act 9
87	Nm 10	Prv 6	Act 10
88	Nm 11	Prv 7	Act 11–12
89	Nm 12–13	Prv 8–9	Act 13
90	Nm 14	Prv 10	Act 14–15
91	Nm 15	Prv 11	Act 16–17
92	Nm 16	Prv 12	Act 18–19
93	Nm 17–18	Prv 13	Act 20
94	Nm 19	Prv 14	Act 21–22
95	Nm 20–21	Prv 15	Act 23–24
96	Nm 22–23	Prv 16	Act 25–26
97	Nm 24–25	Prv 17	Act 27
98	Nm 26	Prv 18	Act 28
99	Nm 27	Prv 19	Romans (Rom) 1–2

Day	Reading 1	Reading 2	Reading 3
100	Nm 28	Prv 20	Rom 3–4
101	Nm 29–30	Prv 21	Rom 5–6
102	Nm 31	Prv 22	Rom 7–8
103	Nm 32	Prv 23	Rom 9
104	Nm 33	Prv 24	Rom 10–11
105	Nm 34	Prv 25	Rom 12
106	Nm 35	Prv 26	Rom 13–14
107	Nm 36	Prv 27	Rom 15–16
108	Deuteronomy (Dt) 1	Prv 28	1 Corinthians (Cor) 1–2
109	Dt 2	Prv 29	1 Cor 3
110	Dt 3	Prv 30	1 Cor 4–5
111	Dt 4	Prv 31	1 Cor 6
112	Dt 5	Ecclesiastes (Ecc) 1	1 Cor 7
113	Dt 6–7	Ecc 2	1 Cor 8–9
114	Dt 8–9	Ecc 3	1 Cor 10
115	Dt 10–11	Ecc 4	1 Cor 11
116	Dt 12	Ecc 5	1 Cor 12–13
117	Dt 13–14	Ecc 6	1 Cor 14
118	Dt 15	Ecc 7	1 Cor 15
119	Dt 16	Ecc 8	1 Cor 16
120	Dt 17	Ecc 9	2 Corinthians (Cor)1–2
121	Dt 18	Ecc 10	2 Cor 3–4
122	Dt 19	Ecc 11	2 Cor 5–7
123	Dt 20	Ecc 12	2 Cor 8–9
124	Dt 21	Song of Songs (Song) 1	2 Cor 10–11
125	Dt 22	Song 2	2 Cor 12–13
126	Dt 23	Song 3	Galatians (Gal) 1–2
127	Dt 24	Song 4	Gal 3–4
128	Dt 25	Song 5	Gal 5–6
129	Dt 26	Song 6	Ephesians (Eph) 1–2
130	Dt 27	Song 7	Eph 3–4
131	Dt 28	Song 8	Eph 5–6
132	Dt 29	Isaiah (Is) 1	Philippians (Phil) 1–2
133	Dt 30	Is 2	Phil 3–4

Day	Reading 1	Reading 2	Reading 3
134	Dt 31	Is 3–4	Colossians (Col) 1
135	Dt 32	Is 5	Col 2
136	Dt 33–34	Is 6	Col 3–4
137	Joshua (Jos) 1	Is 7	1 Thessalonians (Thes) 1–2
138	Jos 2	Is 8	1 Thes 3–4
139	Jos 3–4	Is 9	1 Thes 5
140	Jos 5–6	Is 10	2 Thessalonians (Thes) 1–2
141	Jos 7	Is 11	2 Thes 3
142	Jos 8	Is 12	1 Timothy (Tim) 1–3
143	Jos 9	Is 13	1 Tim 4–5
144	Jos 10	Is 14	1 Tim 6
145	Jos 11	Is 15	2 Timothy (Tim) 1
146	Jos 12	Is 16	2 Tim 2
147	Jos 13	Is 17–18	2 Tim 3–4
148	Jos 14	Is 19	Titus 1–3
149	Jos 15	Is 20–21	Philemon
150	Jos 16	Is 22	Hebrews (Heb) 1–2
151	Jos 17	Is 23	Heb 3–5
152	Jos 18	Is 24	Heb 6–7
153	Jos 19	Is 25	Heb 8–9
154	Jos 20–21	Is 26–27	Heb 10
155	Jos 22	Is 28	Heb 11
156	Jos 23–24	Is 29	Heb 12
157	Judges (Jgs) 1	Is 30	Heb 13
158	Jgs 2–3	Is 31	James (Jas) 1
159	Jgs 4–5	Is 32	Jas 2
160	Jgs 6	Is 33	Jas 3–4
161	Jgs 7–8	Is 34	Jas 5
162	Jgs 9	Is 35	1 Peter (Pet) 1
163	Jgs 10–11	Is 36	1 Pet 2
164	Jgs 12–13	Is 37	1 Pet 3–5
165	Jgs 14–15	Is 38	2 Peter (Pet) 1–2
166	Jgs 16	Is 39	2 Pet 3
167	Jgs 17–18	Is 40	1 John (Jn) 1–2

Day	Reading 1	Reading 2	Reading 3
168	Jgs 19	Is 41	1 Jn 3–4
169	Jgs 20	Is 42	1 Jn 5
170	Jgs 21	Is 43	2 & 3 John
171	Ruth 1–2	Is 44	Jude
172	Ruth 3–4	Is 45	Revelation (Rev) 1–2
173	1 Samuel (Sam) 1	Is 46–47	Rev 3–4
174	1 Sam 2	Is 48	Rev 5–6
175	1 Sam 3	Is 49	Rev 7–9
176	1 Sam 4	Is 50	Rev 10–11
177	1 Sam 5–6	Is 51	Rev 12–13
178	1 Sam 7–8	Is 52	Rev 14
179	1 Sam 9	Is 53	Rev 15–16
180	1 Sam 10	Is 54	Rev 17–18
181	1 Sam 11–12	Is 55	Rev 19–20
182	1 Sam 13	Is 56–57	Rev 21–22
183	1 Sam 14	Is 58	Matthew (Mt) 1–2
184	1 Sam 15	Is 59	Mt 3–4
185	1 Sam 16	Is 60	Mt 5
186	1 Sam 17	Is 61	Mt 6
187	1 Sam 18	Is 62	Mt 7
188	1 Sam 19	Is 63	Mt 8
189	1 Sam 20	Is 64	Mt 9
190	1 Sam 21–22	Is 65	Mt 10
191	1 Sam 23	Is 66	Mt 11
192	1 Sam 24	Jeremiah (Jer) 1	Mt 12
193	1 Sam 25	Jer 2	Mt 13
194	1 Sam 26–27	Jer 3	Mt 14
195	1 Sam 28	Jer 4	Mt 15
196	1 Sam 29–30	Jer 5	Mt 16
197	1 Sam 31	Jer 6	Mt 17
198	2 Samuel 1	Jer 7	Mt 18
199	2 Sam 2	Jer 8	Mt 19
200	2 Sam 3	Jer 9	Mt 20
201	2 Sam 4–5	Jer 10	Mt 21

Day	Reading 1	Reading 2	Reading 3
202	2 Sam 6	Jer 11	Mt 22
203	2 Sam 7	Jer 12	Mt 23
204	2 Sam 8–9	Jer 13	Mt 24
205	2 Sam 10	Jer 14	Mt 25
206	2 Sam 11	Jer 15	Mt 26
207	2 Sam 12	Jer 16	Mt 27
208	2 Sam 13	Jer 17	Mt 28
209	2 Sam 14	Jer 18	Mark (Mk) 1
210	2 Sam 15	Jer 19	Mk 2
211	2 Sam 16	Jer 20	Mk 3
212	2 Sam 17	Jer 21	Mk 4
213	2 Sam 18	Jer 22	Mk 5
214	2 Sam 19	Jer 23	Mk 6
215	2 Sam 20–21	Jer 24	Mk 7
216	2 Sam 22	Jer 25	Mk 8
217	2 Sam 23	Jer 26	Mk 9
218	2 Sam 24	Jer 27	Mk 10
219	1 Kings (Kgs) 1	Jer 28	Mk 11
220	1 Kgs 2	Jer 29	Mk 12
221	1 Kgs 3	Jer 30	Mk 13
222	1 Kgs 4–5	Jer 31	Mk 14
223	1 Kgs 6	Jer 32	Mk 15
224	1 Kgs 7	Jer 33	Mk 16
225	1 Kgs 8	Jer 34	Luke (Lk) 1
226	1 Kgs 9	Jer 35	Lk 2
227	1 Kgs 10	Jer 36	Lk 3
228	1 Kgs 11	Jer 37	Lk 4
229	1 Kgs 12	Jer 38	Lk 5
230	1 Kgs 13	Jer 39	Lk 6
231	1 Kgs 14	Jer 40	Lk 7
232	1 Kgs 15	Jer 41	Lk 8
233	1 Kgs 16	Jer 42	Lk 9
234	1 Kgs 17	Jer 43	Lk 10
235	1 Kgs 18	Jer 44	Lk 11

Day	Reading 1	Reading 2	Reading 3
236	1 Kgs 19	Jer 45–46	Lk 12
237	1 Kgs 20	Jer 47	Lk 13–14
238	1 Kgs 21	Jer 48	Lk 15
239	1 Kgs 22	Jer 49	Lk 16
240	2 Kings (Kgs) 1–2	Jer 50	Lk 17
241	2 Kgs 3	Jer 51	Lk 18
242	2 Kgs 4	Jer 52	Lk 19
243	2 Kgs 5	Lamentations (Lam) 1	Lk 20
244	2 Kgs 6	Lam 2	Lk 21
245	2 Kgs 7	Lam 3	Lk 22
246	2 Kgs 8	Lam 4	Lk 23
247	2 Kgs 9	Lam 5	Lk 24
248	2 Kgs 10	Ezekiel (Ez) 1	John (Jn) 1
249	2 Kgs 11–12	Ez 2	Jn 2–3
250	2 Kgs 13	Ez 3	Jn 4
251	2 Kgs 14	Ez 4	Jn 5
252	2 Kgs 15	Ez 5	Jn 6
253	2 Kgs 16	Ez 6	Jn 7
254	2 Kgs 17	Ez 7	Jn 8
255	2 Kgs 18	Ez 8	Jn 9–10
256	2 Kgs 19	Ez 9	Jn 11
257	2 Kgs 20	Ez 10	Jn 12
258	2 Kgs 21	Ez 11	Jn 13–14
259	2 Kgs 22–23	Ez 12	Jn 15–16
260	2 Kgs 24–25	Ez 13	Jn 17–18
261	1 Chronicles (Chr) 1	Ez 14	Jn 19
262	1 Chr 2	Ez 15	Jn 20–21
263	1 Chr 3	Ez 16	Acts (Act) 1
264	1 Chr 4	Ez 17	Act 2
265	1 Chr 5	Ez 18	Act 3–4
266	1 Chr 6	Ez 19	Act 5–6
267	1 Chr 7	Ez 20	Act 7
268	1 Chr 8	Ez 21	Act 8
269	1 Chr 9	Ez 22	Act 9

Day	Reading 1	Reading 2	Reading 3
270	1 Chr 10	Ez 23	Act 10
271	1 Chr 11	Ez 24	Act 11–12
272	1 Chr 12	Ez 25	Act 13
273	1 Chr 13–14	Ez 26	Act 14–15
274	1 Chr 15	Ez 27	Act 16–17
275	1 Chr 16	Ez 28	Act 18–19
276	1 Chr 17	Ez 29	Act 20
277	1 Chr 18–19	Ez 30	Act 21–22
278	1 Chr 20–21	Ez 31	Act 23–24
279	1 Chr 22	Ez 32	Act 25–26
280	1 Chr 23	Ez 33	Act 27
281	1 Chr 24–25	Ez 34	Act 28
282	1 Chr 26	Ez 35	Romans (Rom) 1–2
283	1 Chr 27	Ez 36	Rom 3–4
284	1 Chr 28	Ez 37	Rom 5–6
285	1 Chr 29	Ez 38	Rom 7–8
286	2 Chronicles (Chr) 1–2	Ez 39	Rom 9
287	2 Chr 3–4	Ez 40	Rom 10–11
288	2 Chr 5–6	Ez 41	Rom 12
289	2 Chr 7	Ez 42	Rom 13–14
290	2 Chr 8	Ez 43	Rom 15–16
291	2 Chr 9	Ez 44	1 Corinthians (Cor) 1–2
292	2 Chr 10–11	Ez 45	1 Cor 3
293	2 Chr 12–13	Ez 46	1 Cor 4–5
294	2 Chr 14–15	Ez 47	1 Cor 6
295	2 Chr 16–17	Ez 48	1 Cor 7
296	2 Chr 18–19	Daniel (Dan) 1	1 Cor 8–9
297	2 Chr 20	Dan 2	1 Cor 10
298	2 Chr 21–22	Dan 3	1 Cor 11
299	2 Chr 23	Dan 4	1 Cor 12–13
300	2 Chr 24	Dan 5	1 Cor 14
301	2 Chr 25	Dan 6	1 Cor 15
302	2 Chr 26–27	Dan 7	1 Cor 16
303	2 Chr 28	Dan 8	2 Corinthians (Cor) 1–2

Day	Reading 1	Reading 2	Reading 3
304	2 Chr 29	Dan 9	2 Cor 3–4
305	2 Chr 30	Dan 10	2 Cor 5–7
306	2 Chr 31	Dan 11	2 Cor 8–9
307	2 Chr 32	Dan 12	2 Cor 10–11
308	2 Chr 33	Hosea (Hos) 1	2 Cor 12–13
309	2 Chr 34	Hos 2	Galatians (Gal) 1–2
310	2 Chr 35	Hos 3	Gal 3–4
311	2 Chr 36	Hos 4	Gal 5–6
312	Ezra (Ezr) 1–2	Hos 5	Ephesians (Eph) 1–2
313	Ezr 3–4	Hos 6	Eph 3–4
314	Ezr 5–6	Hos 7	Eph 5–6
315	Ezr 7	Hos 8	Philippians (Phil) 1–2
316	Ezr 8	Hos 9	Phil 3–4
317	Ezr 9	Hos 10	Colossians (Col) 1
318	Ezr 10	Hos 11	Col 2
319	Nehemiah (Neh) 1–2	Hos 12	Col 3–4
320	Neh 3	Hos 13	1 Thessalonians (Thes) 1–2
321	Neh 4	Hos 14	1 Thes 3–4
322	Neh 5–6	Joel 1	1 Thes 5
323	Neh 7	Joel 2	2 Thessalonians (Thes) 1–2
324	Neh 8	Joel 3	2 Thes 3
325	Neh 9	Amos 1	1 Timothy (Tim) 1–3
326	Neh 10	Amos 2	1 Tim 4–5
327	Neh 11	Amos 3	1 Tim 6
328	Neh 12	Amos 4	2 Timothy (Tim) 1
329	Neh 13	Amos 5	2 Tim 2
330	Est 1	Amos 6	2 Tim 3–4
331	Est 2	Amos 7	Titus 1–3
332	Est 3–4	Amos 8	Philemon
333	Est 5–6	Amos 9	Hebrews (Heb) 1–2
334	Est 7–8	Obadiah	Heb 3–5
335	Est 9–10	Jonah 1	Heb 6–7
336	Job 1–2	Jonah 2–3	Heb 8–9
337	Job 3–4	Jonah 4	Heb 10

Day	Reading 1	Reading 2	Reading 3
338	Job 5	Micah 1	Heb 11
339	Job 6–7	Micah 2	Heb 12
340	Job 8	Micah 3–4	Heb 13
341	Job 9	Micah 5	James (Jas)1
342	Job 10	Micah 6	Jas 2
343	Job 11	Micah 7	Jas 3–4
344	Job 12	Nahum (Nah) 1–2	Jas 5
345	Job 13	Nah 3	1 Peter (Pet) 1
346	Job 14	Habakkuk (Hab) 1	1 Pet 2
347	Job 15	Hab 2	1 Pet 3–5
348	Job 16–17	Hab 3	2 Pet 1–2
349	Job 18–19	Zephaniah (Zeph) 1	2 Pet 3
350	Job 20	Zeph 2	1 John (Jn) 1–2
351	Job 21	Zeph 3	1 Jn 3–4
352	Job 22	Haggai 1–2	1 Jn 5
353	Job 23–24	Zechariah (Zech) 1	2 and 3 John
354	Job 25–27	Zech 2–3	Jude
355	Job 28	Zech 4–5	Revelation (Rev) 1–2
356	Job 29–30	Zech 6–7	Rev 3–4
357	Job 31–32	Zech 8	Rev 5–6
358	Job 33	Zech 9	Rev 7–9
359	Job 34	Zech 10	Rev 10–11
360	Job 35–36	Zech 11	Rev 12–13
361	Job 37	Zech 12	Rev 14
362	Job 38	Zech 13–14	Rev 15–16
363	Job 39	Malachi (Mal) 1	Rev 17–18
364	Job 40	Mal 2	Rev 19–20
365	Job 41–42	Mal 3–4	Rev 21–22

Catholic Bible Reading Plan (One Year)		
Day	**Reading 1**	**Reading 2**	**Reading 3**
1	Genesis (Gn) 1–3	Psalm (Ps) 1	Matthew (Mt) 1:1–17
2	Gn 4–8	Ps 2	Mt 1:18–25
3	Gn 9–11:26	Ps 3	Mt 2:1–12
4	Gn 11:27–16:16	Ps 4	Mt 2:13–23
5	Gn 17:1–22:24	Ps 5	Mt 3:1–17
6	Gn 23:1–25:18	Ps 6	Mt 4:1–25
7	Gn 25:19–30:43	Ps 7	Mt 5:1–12
8	Gn 31:1–36:43	Ps 8	Mt 5:13–26
9	Gn 37:1–41:57	Ps 9	Mt 5:27–37
10	Gn 42:1–45:28	Ps 10	Mt 5:38–48
11	Gn 46:1–50:26	Ps 11	Mt 6:1–18
12	Exodus (Ex) 1:1–6:13	Ps 12	Mt 6:19–34
13	Ex 6:14–12:36	Ps 13	Mt 7:1–29
14	Ex 12:37–18:27	Ps 14	Mt 8:1–27
15	Ex 19:1–24:18	Ps 15	Mt 8:28–34
16	Ex 25:1–29:46	Ps 16	Mt 9:1–17
17	Ex 30:1–34:35	Ps 17	Mt 9:18–38
18	Ex 35:1–40:38	Ps 18	Mt 10:1–15
19	Leviticus (Lv) 1:1–5:26	Ps 19	Mt 10:16–33
20	Lv 6:1–10:20	Ps 20	Mt 10:34–11:1
21	Lv 11:1–13:59	Ps 21	Mt 11:2–19
22	Lv 14:1–16:34	Ps 22	Mt 11:20–30
23	Lv 17:1–20:27	Ps 23	Mt 12:1–15
24	Lv 21:1–24:23	Ps 24	Mt 12:16–37
25	Lv 25:1–27:34	Ps 25	Mt 12:38–50
26	Numbers (Nm) 1:1–5:31	Ps 26	Mt 13:1–30
27	Nm 6:1–10:10	Ps 27	Mt 13:31–53
28	Nm 10:11–14:45	Ps 28	Mt 13:54–14:21
29	Nm 15:1–18:32	Ps 29	Mt 14:22–36
30	Nm 19:1–22:1	Ps 30	Mt 15:1–20
31	Nm 22:2–25:18	Ps 31	Mt 15:21–39
32	Nm 26:1–30:17	Ps 32	Mt 16:1–12
33	Nm 31:1–36:13	Ps 33	Mt 16:13–28

Day	Reading 1	Reading 2	Reading 3
34	Deuteronomy (Dt) 1:1–4:43	Ps 34	Mt 17:1–27
35	Dt 4:44–11:32	Ps 35	Mt 18:1–18
36	Dt 12:1–17:20	Ps 36	Mt 18:19–19:2
37	Dt 18:1–23:26	Ps 37	Mt 19:3–15
38	Dt 24:1–26:19	Ps 38	Mt 19:16–30
39	Dt 27:1–31:29	Ps 39	Mt 20:1–16
40	Dt 31:30–34:12	Ps 40	Mt 20:17–34
41	Jeremiah (Jer) 1:1–4:31	Ps 41	Mt 21:1–17
42	Jer 5:1–8:23	Ps 42	Mt 21:18–32
43	Jer 9:1–12:17	Ps 43	Mt 21:33–46
44	Jer 13:1–16:21	Ps 44	Mt 22:1–14
45	Jer 17:1–20:18	Ps 45	Mt 22:15–33
46	Jer 21:1–24:10	Ps 46	Mt 22:34–46
47	Jer 25:1–29:23	Ps 47	Mt 23:1–39
48	Jer 29:24–33:26	Ps 48	Mt 24:1–28
49	Jer 34:1–37:21	Ps 49	Mt 24:29–51
50	Jer 38:1–45:5	Ps 50	Mt 25:1–30
51	Jer 46:1–49:39	Ps 51	Mt 25:31–26:2
52	Jer 50:1–52:34	Ps 52	Mt 26:3–25
53	Lamentations	Ps 53	Mt 26:26–56
54	Baruch	Ps 54	Mt 26:57–75
55	Ezekiel (Ez) 1:1–6:14	Ps 55	Mt 27:1–26
56	Ez 7:1–12:28	Ps 56	Mt 27:27–66
57	Ez 13:1–17:24	Ps 57	Mt 28:1–20
58	Ez 18:1–21:37	Ps 58	Mark (Mk) 1:1–13
59	Ez 22:1–24:27	Ps 59	Mk 1:14–31
60	Ez 25:1–29:16	Ps 60	Mk 1:32–45
61	Ez 29:17–32:32	Ps 61	Mk 2:1–17
62	Ez 33:1–37:28	Ps 62	Mk 2:18–28
63	Ez 38:1–42:20	Ps 63	Mk 3:1–19
64	Ez 43:1–45:25	Ps 64	Mk 3:20–35
65	Ez 46:1–48:35	Ps 65	Mk 4:1–25
66	Hosea (Hos) 1:1–4:19	Ps 66	Mk 4:26–41
67	Hos 5:1–9:9	Ps 67	Mk 5:1–20

Day	Reading 1	Reading 2	Reading 3
68	Hos 9:10–14:10	Ps 68	Mk 5:21–43
69	Joel	Ps 69	Mk 6:1–29
70	Amos 1:1–5:6, 5:7–8:9	Ps 70	Mk 6:30–56
71	Amos 8:10–9:15	Ps 71	Mk 7:1–23
72	Obadiah; Jonah	Ps 72	Mk 7:24–37
73	Micah (Mi) 1:1–3:12	Ps 73	Mk 8:1–26
74	Mi 4:1–7:20	Ps 74	Mk 8:27–38
75	Nahum; Habakkuk	Ps 75	Mk 9:1–32
76	Zephaniah; Haggai	Ps 76	Mk 9:33–10:1
77	Zechariah (Zech) 1:1–5:11	Ps 77	Mk 10:2–31
78	Zech 6:1–11:3	Ps 78	Mk 10:32–52
79	Zech 11:4–14:21	Ps 79	Mk 11:1–14
80	Malachi	Ps 80	Mk 11:15–33
81	Job 1:1–2:13	Ps 81	Mk 12:1–27
82	Job 3:1–26	Ps 82	Mk 12:28–44
83	Job 4:1–5:27	Ps 83	Mk 13:1–23
84	Job 6:1–7:21	Ps 84	Mk 13:24–37
85	Job 8:1–22	Ps 85	Mk 14:1–21
86	Job 9:1–10:22	Ps 86	Mk 14:22–52
87	Job 11:1–20	Ps 87	Mk 14:53–72
88	Job 12:1–14:22	Ps 88	Mk 15:1–15
89	Job 15:1–35	Ps 89	Mk 15:16–47
90	Job 16:1–17:16	Ps 90	Mk 16:1–20
91	Job 18:1–21	Ps 91	John (Jn) 1:1–18
92	Job 19:1–29	Ps 92	Jn 1:19–51
93	Job 20:1–29	Ps 93	Jn 2:1–12
94	Job 21:1–34	Ps 94	Jn 2:13–25
95	Job 22:1–30	Ps 95	Jn 3:1–21
96	Job 23:1–24:25	Ps 96	Jn 3:22–36
97	Job 25:1–27:21	Ps 97	Jn 4:1–42
98	Job 28:1–28	Ps 98	Jn 4:43–54
99	Job 29:1–31:37	Ps 99	Jn 5:1–30
100	Job 32:1–33:33	Ps 100	Jn 5:31–47

Day	Reading 1	Reading 2	Reading 3
101	Job 34:1–37	Ps 101; 102	Jn 6:1–24
102	Job 35:1–16	Proverbs (Prv) 1:1–7	Jn 6:25–59
103	Job 36:1–37:24	Prv 1:8–19	Jn 6:60–71
104	Job 38:1–39:30	Prv 1:20–33	Jn 7:1–13
105	Job 40:1–42:17	Prv 2:1–8	Jn 7:14–36
106	Ecclesiastes (Eccl) 1:1–11	Prv 2:9–22	Jn 7:37–52
107	Eccl 2:1–3:22	Prv 3:1–18	Jn 7:53–8:11
108	Eccl 4:1–5:19	Prv 3:19–35	Jn 8:12–30
109	Eccl 6:1–9	Prv 4:1–9	Jn 8:31–59
110	Eccl 6:10–7:29	Prv 4:10–27	Jn 9:1–41
111	Eccl 8:1–17	Prv 5	Jn 10:1–21
112	Eccl 9:1–10:15	Prv 6:1–19	Jn 10:22–42
113	Eccl 10:16–12:1	Prv 6:20–35	Jn 11:1–54
114	Song of Songs (Song) 1:1–2:17	Prv 7	Jn 11:55–12:36
115	Song 3:1–11	Prv 8	Jn 12:37–50
116	Song 4:1–5:16	Prv 9	Jn 13:1–17
117	Song 6:1–12	Prv 10:1–3	Jn 13:18–38
118	Song 7:1–8:4	Prv 10:4–6	Jn 14:1–31
119	Song 8:5–14	Prv 10:7–9	Jn 15:1–8
120	Acts 1:1–2:47	Prv 10:10–12	Jn 15:9–17
121	Acts 3:1–5:42	Prv 10:13–16	Jn 15:18–16:4a
122	Acts 6:1–8:3	Prv 10:17–21	Jn 16:4b–16
123	Acts 8:4–9:43	Prv 10:22–24	Jn 16:17–33
124	Acts 10:1–12:24	Prv 10:25–28	Jn 17:1–26
125	Acts 12:25–15:35	Prv 10:29–32	Jn 18:1–27
126	Acts 15:36–17:34	Prv 11:1–3	Jn 18:28–40
127	Acts 18:1–19:40	Prv 11:4–6	Jn 19:1–30
128	Acts 20:1–21:14	Prv 11:7–9	Jn 19:31–42
129	Acts 21:15–22:30	Prv 11:10–12	Jn 20:1–18
130	Acts 23:1–24:27	Prv 11:13–15	Jn 20:19–31
131	Acts 25:1–26:32	Prv 11:16–18	Jn 21:1–14
132	Acts 27:1–28:31	Prv 11:19–21	Jn 21:15–25
133	Wisdom (Wis) 1:1–2:24	Prv 11:22–24	Luke (Lk) 1:1–45

Day	Reading 1	Reading 2	Reading 3
134	Wis 3:1–6:21	Prv 11:25–27	Lk 1:46–80
135	Wis 6:22–8:21	Prv 11:28–31	Lk 2:1–21
136	Wis 9:1–11:1	Prv 12:1–4	Lk 2:22–52
137	Wis 11:2–12:27	Prv 12:5–10	Lk 3:1–22
138	Wis 13:1–15:17	Prv 12:11–13	Lk 3:23–38
139	Wis 15:18–19:22	Prv 12:14–16	Lk 4:1–13
140	Sirach (Sir) 1:1–2:18	Prv 12:17–19	Lk 4:14–44
141	Sir 3:1–6:4	Prv 12:20–22	Lk 5:1–26
142	Sir 6:5–8:19	Prv 12:23–28	Lk 5:27–39
143	Sir 9:1–12:18	Prv 13:1–3	Lk 6:1–26
144	Sir 13:1–15:20	Prv 13:4–6	Lk 6:27–49
145	Sir 16:1–17:27	Prv 13:7–10	Lk 7:1–28
146	Sir 18:1–21:28	Prv 13:11–13	Lk 7:29–50
147	Sir 22:1–24:31	Prv 13:14–16	Lk 8:1–25
148	Sir 25:1–27:21	Prv 13:17–19	Lk 8:26–56
149	Sir 27:22–29:28	Prv 13:20–22	Lk 9:1–27
150	Sir 30:1–32:13	Prv 13:23–25	Lk 9:28–50
151	Sir 32:14–35:24	Prv 14:1–3	Lk 9:51–62
152	Sir 36:1–37:30	Prv 14:4–6	Lk 10:1–24
153	Sir 38:1–39:35	Prv 14:7–9	Lk 10:25–42
154	Sir 40:1–42:8	Prv 14:10–12	Lk 11:1–28
155	Sir 42:9–43:35	Prv 14:13–16	Lk 11:29–54
156	Sir 44:1–45:26	Prv 14:17–19	Lk 12:1–34
157	Sir 46:1–47:24	Prv 14:20–22	Lk 12:35–59
158	Sir 47:25–50:24	Prv 14:23–26	Lk 13:1–17
159	Sir 50:25–51:24	Prv 14:27–29	Lk 13:18–35
160	1 Peter (Pet) 1:1–2:25	Prv 14:30–32	Lk 14:1–35
161	1 Pt 3:1–5:14	Prv 14:33–35	Lk 15:1–10
162	2 Pt	Prv 15:1–3	Lk 15:11–32
163	Joshua (Jos) 1:1–2:24	Prv 15:4–6	Lk 16:1–15
164	Jos 3:1–4:24	Prv 15:7–9	Lk 16:16–31
165	Jos 5:1–6:27	Prv 15:10–12	Lk 17:1–19
166	Jos 7:1–8:35	Prv 15:13–15	Lk 17:20–37
167	Jos 9:1–10:43	Prv 15:16–18	Lk 18:1–14

Day	Reading 1	Reading 2	Reading 3
168	Jos 11:1–12:24	Prv 15:19–21	Lk 18:15–43
169	Jos 13:1–14:15	Prv 15:22–24	Lk 19:1–27
170	Jos 15:1–17:18	Prv 15:25–27	Lk 19:28–48
171	Jos 18:1–19:51	Prv 15:28–30	Lk 20:1–19
172	Jos 20:1–21:45	Prv 15:31–33	Lk 20:20–47
173	Jos 22:1–34	Prv 16:1–3	Lk 21:1–19
174	Jos 23:1–24:33	Prv 16:4–6	Lk 21:20–38
175	Judges (Jgs) 1:1–3:6	Prv 16:7–11	Lk 22:1–38
176	Jgs 3:7–4:24	Prv 16:12–15	Lk 22:39–71
177	Jgs 5:1–31	Prv 16:16–17	Lk 23:1–31
178	Jgs 6:1–7:28	Prv 16:18–21	Lk 23:32–43
179	Jgs 8:1–10:18	Prv 16:22–24	Lk 23:44–56
180	Jgs 11:1–12:15	Prv 16:25–27	Lk 24:1–35
181	Jgs 13:1–14:20	Prv 16:28–30	Lk 24:36–53
182	Jgs 15:1–16:31	Prv 16:31–33	Matthew (Mt) 1:1–17
183	Jgs 17:1–18:31	Prv 17:1–3	Mt 1:18–25
184	Jgs 19:1–21:25	Prv 17:4–7	Mt 2:1–12
185	Ruth	Prv 17:8–10	Mt 2:13–23
186	1 Samuel (Sm) 1:1–2:36	Prv 17:11–13	Mt 3:1–17
187	1 Sm 3:1–4:22	Prv 17:14–16	Mt 4:1–17
188	1 Sm 5:1–7:17	Prv 17:17–19	Mt 4:18–25
189	1 Sm 8:1–10:27	Prv 17:20–23	Mt 5:1–12
190	1 Sm 11:1–12:25	Prv 17:24–28	Mt 5:13–26
191	1 Sm 13:1–14:48	Prv 18:1–2	Mt 5:27–37
192	1 Sm 14:49–16:23	Prv 18:3–5	Mt 5:38–48
193	1 Sm 17:1–58	Prv 18:6–8	Mt 6:1–10
194	1 Sm 18:1–19:24	Prv 18:9–11	Mt 6:11–24
195	1 Sm 20:1–42	Prv 18:12–14	Mt 6:25–34
196	1 Sm 21:1–22:23	Prv 18:15–17	Mt 7:1–29
197	1 Sm 23:1–24:23	Prv 18:18–20	Mt 8:1–27
198	1 Sm 25:1–43	Prv 18:21–24	Mt 8:28–34
199	1 Sm 26:1–25	Prv 19:1–3	Mt 9:1–17
200	1 Sm 27:1–28:25	Prv 19:4–6	Mt 9:18–38
201	1 Sm 29:1–31:13	Prv 19:7–9	Mt 10:1–15

Day	Reading 1	Reading 2	Reading 3
202	2 Sm 1:1–2:7	Prv 19:10–12	Mt 10:16–33
203	2 Sm 2:8–3:21	Prv 19:13–15	Mt 10:34–11:1
204	2 Sm 4:1–5:25	Prv 19:16–18	Mt 11:2–19
205	2 Sm 6:1–7:29	Prv 19:19–21	Mt 11:20–30
206	2 Sm 8:1–9:13	Prv 19:22–25	Mt 12:1–15
207	2 Sm 10:1–11:27	Prv 19:26–29	Mt 12:16–37
208	2 Sm 12:1–13:38	Prv 20:1–3	Mt 12:38–50
209	2 Sm 13:39–15:37	Prv 20:4–6	Mt 13:1–30
210	2 Sm 16:1–17:29	Prv 20:7–9	Mt 13:31–53
211	2 Sm 18:1–19:44	Prv 20:10–12	Mt 13:54–14:21
212	2 Sm 20:1–26	Prv 20:13–15	Mt 14:22–36
213	2 Sm 21:1–23:7	Prv 20:16–18	Mt 15:1–20
214	2 Sm 23:8–24:25	Prv 20:19–21	Mt 15:21–39
215	1 Kings (Kgs) 1:1–53	Prv 20:22–24	Mt 16:1–12
216	1 Kgs 2:1–3:28	Prv 20:25–27	Mt 16:13–28
217	1 Kgs 4:1–5:32	Prv 20:28–30	Mt 17:1–27
218	1 Kgs 6:1–7:51	Prv 21:1–3	Mt 18:1–18
219	1 Kgs 8:1–9:28	Prv 21:4–6	Mt 18:19–19:2
220	1 Kgs 10:1–11:43	Prv 21:7–9	Mt 19:3–15
221	1 Kgs 12:1–14:31	Prv 21:10–12	Mt 19:16–30
222	1 Kgs 15:1–16:34	Prv 21:13–14	Mt 20:1–16
223	1 Kgs 17:1–18:46	Prv 21:15–17	Mt 20:17–34
224	1 Kgs 19:1–20:43	Prv 21:18–20	Mt 21:1–17
225	1 Kgs 21:1–29	Prv 21:21–23	Mt 21:18–32
226	1 Kgs 22:1–54	Prv 21:24–26	Mt 21:33–46
227	2 Kgs 1:1–2:25	Prv 21:27–29	Mt 22:1–14
228	2 Kgs 3:1–4:44	Prv 21:30–31	Mt 22:15–33
229	2 Kgs 5:1–7:2	Prv 22:1–2	Mt 22:34–46
230	2 Kgs 7:3–8:29	Prv 22:3–5	Mt 23:1–39
231	2 Kgs 9:1–10:36	Prv 22:6–8	Mt 24:1–28
232	2 Kgs 11:1–12:22	Prv 22:9–11	Mt 24:29–51
233	2 Kgs 13:1–14:29	Prv 22:12–14	Mt 25:1–30
234	2 Kgs 15:1–16:20	Prv 22:15–16	Mt 25:31–26:2
235	2 Kgs 17:1–41	Prv 22:17–21	Mt 26:3–25

Day	Reading 1	Reading 2	Reading 3
236	2 Kgs 18:1–19:37	Prv 22:22–23	Mt 26:26–56
237	2 Kgs 20:1–21:26	Prv 22:24–25	Mt 26:57–75
238	2 Kgs 22:1–23:35	Prv 22:26–29	Mt 27:1–26
239	2 Kgs 23:1–25:30	Prv 23:1–5	Mt 27:27–66
240	1 Chronicles (Chr) 1:1–2:55	Prv 23:6–8	Mt 28:1–20
241	1 Chr 3:1–4:43	Prv 23:9–11	Mark (Mk) 1:1–13
242	1 Chr 5:1–6:66	Prv 23:12–14	Mk 1:14–31
243	1 Chr 7:1–8:40	Prv 23:15–16	Mk 1:32–45
244	1 Chr 9:1–34	Prv 23:17–18	Mk 2:1–17
245	1 Chr 9:35–12:41	Prv 23:19–21	Mk 3:1–19
246	1 Chr 13:1–15:29	Prv 23:22–25	Mk 3:20–35
247	1 Chr 16:1–17:27	Prv 23:26–28	Mk 4:1–25
248	1 Chr 18:1–20:8	Prv 23:29–35	Mk 4:26–41
249	1 Chr 21:1–22:19	Prv 24:1–2	Mk 5:1–20
250	1 Chr 23:1–24:31	Prv 24:3–4	Mk 5:21–43
251	1 Chr 25:1–26:32	Prv 24:5–7	Mk 6:1–29
252	1 Chr 27:1–29:30	Prv 24:8–9	Mk 6:30–56
253	2 Chr 1:1–2:17	Prv 24:10–12	Mk 7:1–23
254	2 Chr 3:1–4:22	Prv 24:13–14	Mk 7:24–37
255	2 Chr 5:1–7:22	Prv 24:15–16	Mk 8:1–26
256	2 Chr 8:1–9:31	Prv 24:17–18	Mk 8:27–38
257	2 Chr 10:1–11:23	Prv 24:19–20	Mk 9:1–32
258	2 Chr 12:1–13:23	Prv 24:21–22	Mk 9:33–10:1
259	2 Chr 14:1–15:19	Prv 24:23–26	Mk 10:2–31
260	2 Chr 16:1–17:19	Prv 24:27–29	Mk 10:32–52
261	2 Chr 18:1–19:11	Prv 24:30–34	Mk 11:1–14
262	2 Chr 20:1–21:20	Prv 25:1–3	Mk 11:15–33
263	2 Chr 22:1–23:21	Prv 25:4–5	Mk 12:1–27
264	2 Chr 24:1–25:28	Prv 25:6–7	Mk 12:28–44
265	2 Chr 26:1–27:9	Prv 25:8–10	Mk 13:1–23
266	2 Chr 28:1–29:36	Prv 25:11–14	Mk 13:24–37
267	2 Chr 30:1–31:21	Prv 25:15–17	Mk 14:1–21
268	2 Chr 32:1–32:25	Prv 25:18–20	Mk 14:22–52
269	2 Chr 34:1–36:1	Prv 25:21–24	Mk 14:53–72

Day	Reading 1	Reading 2	Reading 3
270	2 Chr 36:2–23	Prv 25:25–28	Mk 15:1–15
271	Ezra (Ezr) 1:1–2:70	Prv 26:1–2	Mk 15:16–47
272	Ezr 3:1–5:17	Prv 26:3–7	Mk 16:1–20
273	Ezr 6:1–22	Prv 26:8–12	John (Jn) 1:1–18
274	Ezr 7:1–8:36	Prv 26:13–16	Jn 1:19–51
275	Ezr 9:1–10:44	Prv 26:17–19	Jn 2:1–12
276	Nehemiah (Neh) 1:1–3:38	Prv 26:20–22	Jn 2:13–25
277	Neh 4:1–5:19	Prv 26:23–25	Jn 3:1–21
278	Neh 6:1–7:72	Prv 26:26–28	Jn 3:22–36
279	Neh 8:1–9:37	Prv 27:1–3	Jn 4:1–42
280	Neh 10:1–11:36	Prv 27:4–6	Jn 4:43–54
281	Neh 12:1–13:31	Prv 27:7–9	Jn 5:1–30
282	Tobit (Tb) 1:1–3:17	Prv 27:10–12	Jn 5:31–47
283	Tb 4:1–6:17	Prv 27:13–14	Jn 6:1–24
284	Tb 7:1–9:6	Prv 27:15–16	Jn 6:25–59
285	Tb 10:1–11:19	Prv 27:17–19	Jn 6:60–71
286	Tb 12:1–14:15	Prv 27:20–22	Jn 7:1–13
287	Judith (Jdt) 1:1–4:15	Prv 27:23–27	Jn 7:14–36
288	Jdt 5:1–7:32	Prv 28:1–3	Jn 7:37–52
289	Jdt 8:1–14:10	Prv 28:4–6	Jn 7:53–8:11
290	Jdt 14:10–16:25	Prv 28:7–9	Jn 8:12–30
291	Esther (Est) 1:1–2:23	Prv 28:10–13	Jn 8:31–59
292	Est 3:1–5:14	Prv 28:14–16	Jn 9:1–41
293	Est 6:1–10:3	Prv 28:17–19	Jn 10:1–21
294	1 Maccabees (Mc) 1:1–2:70	Prv 28:20–22	Jn 10:22–42
295	1 Mc 3:1–5:68	Prv 28:23–25	Jn 11:1–54
296	1 Mc 6:1–9:22	Prv 28:26–28	Jn 11:55–12:19
297	1 Mc 9:23–11:19	Prv 29:1–3	Jn 12:20–36
298	1 Mc 11:20–12:53	Prv 29:4–6	Jn 12:37–50
299	1 Mc 13:1–16:24	Prv 29:7–9	Jn 13:1–17
300	2 Mc 1:1–3:40	Prv 29:10–12	Jn 13:18–38
301	2 Mc 4:1–6:31	Prv 29:13–15	Jn 14:1–31
302	2 Mc 7:1–10:8	Prv 29:16–18	Jn 15:1–8
303	2 Mc 10:9–12:46	Prv 29:19–21	Jn 15:9–17

Day	Reading 1	Reading 2	Reading 3
304	2 Mc 13:1–15:39	Prv 29:22–24	Jn 15:18–16:4a
305	Daniel (Dn) 1:1–3:97	Prv 29:25–27	Jn 16:4b–16
306	Dn 3:98–6:29	Prv 30:1–6	Jn 16:17–33
307	Dn 7:1–9:27	Prv 30:7–9	Jn 17:1–26
308	Dn 10:1–12:13	Prv 30:10–14	Jn 18:1–27
309	Dn 13:1–14:42	Prv 30:15–17	Jn 18:28–40
310	Revelation (Rev) 1:1–3:22	Prv 30:18–20	Jn 19:1–30
311	Rev 4:1–7:17	Prv 30:21–23	Jn 19:31–42
312	Rev 8:1–11:19	Prv 30:24–28	Jn 20:1–18
313	Rev 12:1–15:8	Prv 30:29–33	Jn 20:19–31
314	Rev 16:1–19:10	Prv 31:1–9	Jn 21:1–14
315	Rev 19:11–22:21	Prv 31:10–31	Jn 21:15–25
316	1 Corinthians (Cor) 1:1–4:21	Psalm (Ps) 103	Luke (Lk) 1:1–45
317	1 Cor 5:1–11:1	Ps 104	Lk 1:46–80
318	1 Cor 11:2–16:24	Ps 105	Lk 2:1–21
319	2 Cor 1:1–7:1	Ps 106	Lk 2:22–52
320	2 Cor 7:2–13:13	Ps 107	Lk 3:1–22
321	Galatians	Ps 108	Lk 3:23–38
322	Ephesians	Ps 109	Lk 4:1–13
323	Philippians; Colossians	Ps 110	Lk 4:14–44
324	1 Thessalonians	Ps 111	Lk 5:1–26
325	2 Thessalonians	Ps 112	Lk 5:27–39
326	1 Timothy	Ps 113	Lk 6:1–26
327	2 Timothy	Ps 114	Lk 6:27–49
328	Titus; Philemon	Ps 115	Lk 7:1–28
329	Hebrews (Heb) 1:1–2:18	Ps 116	Lk 7:29–50
330	Heb 3:1–5:10	Ps 117	Lk 8:1–25
331	Heb 5:11–7:28	Ps 118	Lk 8:26–56
332	Heb 8:1–10:39	Ps 119	Lk 9:1–27
333	Heb 11:1–13:25	Ps 120	Lk 9:28–50
334	James; Jude	Ps 121	Lk 9:51–62
335	Isaiah (Is) 1:1–4:1	Ps 122	Lk 10:1–24
336	Is 4:2–5:30	Ps 123	Lk 10:25–42
337	Is 6:1–8:20	Ps 124	Lk 11:1–28

Day	Reading 1	Reading 2	Reading 3
338	Is 8:21–12:6	Ps 125	Lk 11:29–54
339	Is 13:1–16:14	Ps 126	Lk 12:1–34
340	Is 17:1–19:25	Ps 127	Lk 12:35–59
341	Is 20:1–21:17	Ps 128	Lk 13:1–17
342	Is 22:1–23:18	Ps 129	Lk 13:18–35
343	Is 24:1–25:12	Ps 130	Lk 14:1–35
344	Is 26:1–27:13	Ps 131	Lk 15:1–10
345	Is 28:1–30:33	Ps 132	Lk 15:11–32
346	Is 31:1–33:24	Ps 133	Lk 16:1–15
347	Is 34:1–35:10	Ps 134	Lk 16:16–31
348	Is 36:1–39:8	Ps 135	Lk 17:1–19
349	Is 40:1–42:25	Ps 136	Lk 17:20–37
350	Is 43:1–45:24	Ps 137	Lk 18:1–14
351	Is 46:1–48:22	Ps 138	Lk 18:15–43
352	Is 49:1–51:23	Ps 139	Lk 19:1–27
353	Is 52:1–53:12	Ps 140	Lk 19:28–48
354	Is 54:1–55:13	Ps 141	Lk 20:1–19
355	Is 56:1–57:21	Ps 142	Lk 20:20–47
356	Is 58:1–60:22	Ps 143	Lk 21:1–19
357	Is 61:1–64:11	Ps 144	Lk 21:20–38
358	Is 65:1–66:24	Ps 145	Lk 22:1–38
359	1 John (Jn) 1:1–3:3	Ps 146	Lk 22:39–71
360	1 Jn 3:4–5:21	Ps 147; 148	Lk 23:1–31
361	2 Jn–3 Jn	Ps 149; 150	Lk 23:32–43
362	Romans (Rm) 1:1–5:21	Ps 1	Lk 23:44–56
363	Rm 6:1–8:39	Ps 2	Lk 24:1–35
364	Rm 9:1–11:36	Ps 3	Lk 24:36–53
365	Rm 12:1–16:27	Ps 4	John 1:1–18

English Bible Versions

Bible Version	Abbreviation
The Complete Bible: An American Translation	AAT
The Afro Bible Translation	ABT
The Alternate Translation Bible	ATB
American Sign Language Translation	ASL
American Standard Version	ASV
The Amplified Bible	AB or AMP
Analytical–Literal Translation	ALT
Authorized Version same as KJV	AV
Bible in WorldWide English	BWE
Christian Community Bible	CCB
The Common Edition: New Testament	CE
Complete Jewish Bible	CJB
Concordant Version	CV
Contemporary English Version	CEV
Darby	Dar or DARBY
Douay–Rheims	DR or DRB
Extreme New Testament	ENT
Easy-to-Read Version	ERV
English Standard Version	ESV
God's Living Word	GLW
God's Word	GW
Good News Bible	GNB
Holman Christian Standard Bible	HCSB
International Children's Bible	ICB
International Standard Bible	ISB
The International Standard Version	ISV
New Testament in Modern English	JBP
Jewish New Testament	JNT
King James Version	KJV
Defined King James Bible	DKJB
King James Version II	KJII
King James for the 21st Century	KJ21
King James 2000	KJ2000
The Literal Translation of the Holy Bible	LITV
Living Bible	LB
Modern American English Vernacular	MAEV

Modern King James Version	MKJV
Modern Language Bible	MLB
Modern Literal Version	MLV
New American Bible	NAB
New American Standard Bible	NASB
New Century Version	NCV
New English Bible	NEB
New English Translation	NET
New International Version	NIV
New Jerusalem Bible	NJB
New King James Version	NKJV
New Life Version	NLV
New Living Translation	NLT
New Revised Standard Bible	NRSV
New World Translation	NWT
The Original Bible Project	OBP
The Original New Testament	ONT
Orthodox Study Bible	OSB
Postmodern Bible—Amos	PMB
Revised Authorized Version	RAV
The Revised English Bible	REB
Revised King James New Testament	RKJV
Revised Standard Version	RSV
Revised Version	RV
The Schocken Bible	Sch
The Simple English Bible	SEB
The Message	TM
The Third Millenium Bible	TMB
Today's English Version	TEV
Today's New International Version	TNIV
Tyndale	Tyn
Updated King James Version	UKJV
Webster Bible	WB
Wesley's New Testament	WNT
Weymouth	Wey
World English Bible	WEB
Worldwide English NT	WE
Wycliffe	Wyc
Young Literal Translation of the Bible	YLT

Index

Aaron, 96–97
Abandoned books, 57–65
    author endorsements, 60
    Gnostic influence, 60–62
    supernatural obsession, 61
    See also Apocrypha
Abraham (Abram), 43, 44–45, 92, 152,
    153–54, 181
Acts of the Apostles, 53, 148–49, 203–14
    Barnabas and Paul, 210–11, 212
    council of Jerusalem, 211–12
    deacon ordination, 206
    early church history, 204–5
    Gentile mission, 209–12
    healing arrest, 206
    Jerusalem mission, 205–7
    Judea mission, 207–8
    mission preparation, 204–5
    Paul's mission, 212–14
    Pentecost, 205
    replacing Judas, 204–5
    Samaria mission, 207–8
    Saul becomes Paul, 208
    Silas and Paul, 212–13
    simony, 207
    third missionary journey, 214
    unknown God, 213–14
Adam and Eve, 36, 41–42, 91, 217
A.D. (Anno Domini), 143
Adultery, 165, 171
Alexandrian canon, 51, 55
Allegorical meanings. *See* Symbolic meanings
Alternative names, 2
Ambiguous passages, 85
Ambrose, Saint, 245
American Standard version, 16
Amillennialism, 252
Amos, 134
Anagogical sense, 6
Ananias, 208
Andrew (apostle), 157, 161

Angel stories, 64
Annunciation, 179
Anointing, 173, 234–35
Antediluvian period, 41
Antichrist(s), 238, 239, 246, 250, 251
Apocalyptic apocrypha, 63
Apocalyptic Messiah, 140–41
Apocalyptic writing, 83–84, 129, 132
Apocrypha, 16, 54, 58–59
    angel stories, 64
    apocalyptic apocrypha, 63
    didactic apocrypha, 64
    Gnostic influence, 60–62
    historical apocrypha, 64
    historical origins, 59–60
    incongruities, 61–62
    New Testament, 65
    Old Testament, 63–65
    Protestant versions omitting, 73–74
    reasons abandoned, 63
    supernatural obsession, 61
    See also specific books; Deuterocanonical
      books
Apostles, 148–49
    instructions to, 161–62
    Luke account of, 183, 185
    Matthew account of, 157, 161–62, 163–65
    replacing Judas, 204–5
    See also specific apostles; Acts of the
      Apostles
Apostolic letters, 231–40
    James, 232–35
    Jude, 240
    1 John, 237–38
    1 Peter, 235–36
    3 John, 239
    2 John, 238–39
    2 Peter, 236–37
Aquinas, Thomas, 250
Aramaic, 50, 68
Armageddon, 249

Assumption of Mary, 65
Assumption of Moses, 240
Assyrian empire, 15
Augustine, Saint
    battling Pelagianism, 233
    Biblical error sources, 35, 85
    heavenly vs. earthly cities, 253
    Jesus birth date, 144
    numbering Commandments, 96
    Original Sin connection, 217
    translations of, 50, 69
Authors, 9–12
    compilation of, 10, 11–12
    development stages, 10–12
    documenting oral tradition, 9, 10–12,
      24–25
    endorsements, 60
    extinct originals of, 25–26
    false, 60
    God inspiring, 10, 78, 79
    interpretation and, 78–79
    redactors (editors), 11–12
    sacred writers, 7
    understanding. *See* Interpretation(s)
    See also specific authors; Divine
      Revelation; Inspiration
Autographs, 70

Babylon, 9, 15
Barnabas, 210–11, 212
Bartholomew, 161, 183
Baruch, 128
Battle of Jericho, 100
B.C., 143
Beasts, 248–49, 250, 251, 252
Bede, Venerable, 69
Bible
    alternative names, 2
    chapter/verse numbers, 10
    text inclusion measures, 12
    timelessness of, 255–56